The Chartered Institute of Marketing

D0335436

Chartered Postgraduate D

STUDY TEXT

Analysis and Decision

For exams up to and including December 2010

First edition August 2009

ISBN 9780 7517 6817 6

e-learning ISBN 9780 7517 7690 4

British Library Cataloguing-in-Publication Data
A catalogue record for this book
is available from the British Library

Published by

BPP Learning Media Ltd
Aldine House, Aldine Place
London W12 8AA

www.bpp.com/learningmedia

Printed in the United Kingdom

We are grateful to the Chartered Institute of Marketing for
permission to reproduce in this text the syllabus, tutor's
guidance notes and past examination questions. We are also
grateful to Superbrands and The Centre for Brand Analysis for
their support of our online feature 'A Word From...'

Author: Kate Machattie
CIM Publishing Manager: Dr Kellie Vincent
Template design: Yolanda Moore
Photography: Terence O'Loughlin

Your learning materials, published by BPP Learning Media Ltd,
are printed on paper sourced from sustainable, managed
forests.

Contents

Introduction

- Aim of the Study Text • Studying for CIM qualifications
- The Chartered Postgraduate Diploma Syllabus • Assessing this Unit
- The CIM's Magic Formula • A guide to the features of the Study Text
- A note on Pronouns • Additional resources • Your personal study plan v

Chapters

Review form & free prize draw

1 Aim of the Study Text

This book has been deliberately referred to as a 'Study Text' rather than *text book* , because it is designed to help you though your specific CIM Chartered Postgraduate Diploma in Marketing studies. It covers Unit 2 Analysis and Decision.

So, why is it similar to but not actually a text book? Well, the CIM have identified key texts that you should become familiar with. The purpose of this workbook is not to replace these texts but to pick out the important parts that you will definitely need to know in order to pass, simplify these elements and, to suggest a few areas within the texts that will provide good additional reading but that are not absolutely essential. We will also suggest a few other sources and useful press and CIM publications which are worth reading.

We know some of you will prefer to read text books from cover to cover whilst others amongst you will prefer to pick out relevant parts or dip in and out of the various topics. This text will help you to ensure that if you are a 'cover to cover' type, then you will not miss the emphasis of the syllabus. If you are a 'dip in and out' type, then we will make sure that you find the parts which are essential for you to know. Unlike a standard *text book* which will have been written to be used across a range of alter native qualifications, this *study text* has been specifically for your CIM course, therefore if a topic appears in this book then it is part of the syllabus and therefore will be a subject the examiners could potentially test you.

Throughout the study text you will find real examples of marketing in practice as well as key concepts highlighted. The book also aims to encourage you to not only learn the theory but also provides cues and helps you to plan your own project work. You should use the activities to help you to build a portfolio of your own organisation.

2 Studying for CIM qualifications

There are a few key points to remember as you study for your CIM qualification:

(a) You are studying for a **professional** qualification. This means that you are required to use professional language and adopt a business approach in your work.

(b) You are expected to show that you have 'read widely'. Make sure that you read the quality press (and don't skip the business pages), read Marketing, The Marketer, Research and Marketing Week avidly.

(c) Become aware of the marketing initiatives you come across on a daily basis, for example, when you go shopping look around and think about why the store layout is as it is, consider the messages, channel choice and timings of ads when you are watching TV. It is surprising how much you will learn just by taking an interest in the marketing world around you.

(d) Get to know the way CIM write their exam papers and assignments. They use a specific approach which is referred to as The Magic Formula to ensure a consistent approach when designing assessment materials. Make sure you are fully aware of this as it will help you interpret what the examiner is looking for (a full description of the Magic Formula appears later and is heavily featured within the chapters).

(e) Learn how to use Harvard referencing. This is explained in detail in our Chartered Postgraduate Assessment Workbook.

(f) Ensure that you read very carefully all assessment details sent to you from the CIM. They are very strict with regard to deadlines eg. completing the correct paperwork to accompany any assignment or project and making sure you have your CIM membership card with you at the exam. Failing to meet any assessment entry deadlines or completing written work on time will mean that you will have to wait for the next round of assessment dates and will need to pay the relevant assessment fees again.

3 The Chartered Postgraduate Diploma Syllabus

The Chartered Postgraduate Diploma in Marketing is aimed at Brand Manager, Strategic Marketing, Marketing Manager, Business Development Manager, middle to senior Marketing Managers. If you are a graduate, you will be expected to have covered a minimum of half your credits in marketing subjects. You are therefore expected at this level of the qualification to demonstrate the ability to manage marketing resources and contribute to business decisions from a marketing perspective or senior marketing management and pass Entry test to level 7.

The aim of the qualification is to provide the knowledge and skills for you to develop an 'ability to do' in relation to marketing planning. CIM qualifications concentrate on applied marketing within real work-places.

The complete Chartered Postgraduate qualification is split into two stages. Stage 1 compromises four units. Stage 2 is a work based project to enable students to gain Chartered Marketer status immediately.

The Stage 1 qualification is made from four units:

- Unit 1 Emerging Themes
- Unit 2 Analysis and Decision
- Unit 3 Marketing Leadership and Planning
- Unit 4 Project Managing Corporate Reputation

The syllabus as provided by the CIM can be found below with reference to our coverage within this study text.

Unit characteristics

This unit consists of three parts: **Strategic audit**, **Strategic options**, and **Making strategic marketing decisions**. The overall purpose of the unit is to prepare students to undertake a strategic audit of an organisation, assess its capability and capacity to deliver the organisation's business and marketing strategy in a challenging, dynamic and diverse global market place, and to recommend a strategic option, or decision, based on a full critical evaluation of the various options available.

To achieve this aim, students will be expected to carry out the following:

- First they will undertake a sophisticated strategic audit which will help to prioritise the key issues, opportunities and risks facing an organisation in meeting its future objectives. This will be based on a clear and detailed assessment of an organisation and its performance, and the issues and challenges it faces in creating and delivering best value.

- They will use their strategic audit of an organisation to generate strategic options and critically evaluate those options in respect of the key issues faced by the organisation.

- Finally, after exploring the wide range of strategic options available to an organisation to meet its corporate and business strategy, students will need to recommend an option based on, and justified by, a critical evaluation of its suitability in the specific situation.

In doing the above, students should be able to undertake both qualitative and quantitative analysis of the relevant options and be able to make strategic marketing decisions based upon such analysis, justifying decisions and providing reasoned arguments for their recommendations. They will be expected to apply a range of financial and risk models to support their assessments and demonstrate an understanding of how the decisions will support the achievement of the organisation's vision, mission and strategic business and marketing objectives.

Overarching learning outcomes

By the end of this unit students should be able to:

- Undertake a strategic marketing audit, assessing an organisation's competencies, competitive advantage, market performance, customers, competitors, product and service portfolios, positioning, value proposition and market impact

- Assess the impact of external factors on an organisation and its strategic intent and direction

- Utilise the strategic marketing audit to critically evaluate a range of strategic marketing options available to an organisation, including innovation, mergers, acquisitions, partnering, alliances, environmental sustainability and CSR, in order to deliver best value growth and expansion opportunities for the organisation

- Utilise a range of financial and other measurement tools to assess the financial and non-financial benefits of recommended strategic marketing decisions

- Utilise a range of risk assessment tools to critically assess the risk of strategic market decisions and their impact upon an organisation, including financial, corporate and reputational risk.

Part 1 – The strategic audit

SECTION 1 – The strategic marketing audit (weighting 35%)

		Covered in chapter(s)
1.1.1	Utilise a range of techniques, processes and market information to assess the external marketing environment including: • The competitive environment • Customers • Channels (local, international and global) • Market structures	1
1.1.2	Utilise market-based information to critically evaluate an organisation's strategic position within the market place, including consideration of specific positioning issues: • Competitive positioning • Competitive advantage • Value creation • Competitor analysis	1
1.1.3	Utilise a range of tools to critically evaluate an organisation's ability to understand its current customer base and their buying behaviour, in order to be able to develop customer insight and meet their preferences: • Value proposition • Segmental analysis and consumer profiling • Strategic account analysis • Consumer profiling	2
1.1.4	Assess the potential for strategic uncertainty in the external market and the extent to which it involves trends or events, and show how it will impact upon an organisation: • Scenario construction • Market sensing • Forecasting techniques to assess the potential and probability that trends or events will occur • Forecasting techniques utilised to assess timeline for trends and events arising and their impact • Assessing market stability and attractiveness	1

SECTION 2 – The Strategic marketing audit: internal (weighting 35%)

		Covered in chapter(s)
1.2.1	Utilise a range of models and techniques to undertake a strategic audit of the internal environment:	3
	• Resource and competency audit (physical, human and intangibles)	
	• Portfolio analysis	
	• Value chain and resource utilisation	
	• Innovation audit	
	• Cost efficiency	
	• Product life-cycle	
	• Organisation's vision, mission and values	
	• Degree of customer and market orientation	
	• Comparative and best practice analysis	
	• Core competencies	
	• Organisational culture	
	• Financial performance	
1.2.2	Critically evaluate the resource-based view of an organisation and the value of this approach in developing resource and capability to deliver an organisation's vision and mission:	4
	• Resources, capabilities and competencies	
	• The elements of resource-based competitive advantage	
	• Knowledge as a resource	
1.2.3	Critically evaluate the fit between an organisation's culture and its current strategy, and assess its ability to be flexible and agile in a changing marketing environment:	4
	• Environmental influences on organisational culture	
	• Mintzberg's organisational structures	
	• Handy's cultural styles	
1.2.4	Utilise a range of internal information and assessment tools to evaluate an organisation's strengths and weaknesses in order to assess its readiness for development, including an assessment of:	4
	• Competencies, assets and culture	
	• Value chain and value proposition	
	• The state of the organisation's financial and non-financial assets	

SECTION 3 – Developing the organisation's strategic intent and direction (weighting 30%)

		Covered in chapter(s)
1.3.1	Critically evaluate an organisation's current strategic intent, based upon its vision, mission, values and stakeholder expectations: • Organisational purpose, mission and values • Defining organisational focus • Stakeholders analysis • Relationship portfolios • Organisational configuration • CSR and ethics	5
1.3.2	Critically analyse the role of strategic intent in shaping an organisation's strategy development: • Strategic intent and strategic vision • Strategic intent and leadership • Intent and flexibility • Strategic opportunism versus strategic drift	5

Part 2 – Strategic options

SECTION 1 – Assessing strategic marketing decisions (weighting 20%)

		Covered in chapter(s)
2.1.1	Critically evaluate the determinants of strategic options and choices: • Past and current strategies • Organisational capabilities and constraints (financial and non-financial) • Financial capabilities and constraints • Organisational strengths and weaknesses • Product-market opportunities • Sources of competitive advantage (Porter) • Warfare analogies in strategy (Kotler)	6
2.1.2	Critically evaluate how strategic options can be developed to reflect an organisation's: • Value proposition • Assets and competencies • Business function strategies • Functional strategies and programmes • Competitive advantage • Sustainability	6

SECTION 2 – Strategic options available to a growing organisation (weighting 80%)

	Covered in chapter(s)
2.2.1 Critically evaluate the nature of innovation and new product development (NPD) in marketing and the related factors impacting upon marketing decisions, including ongoing innovation management within an organisation: • Importance of innovation • Models of innovation • Managing innovation	7
2.2.2 Critically evaluate the appropriateness of developing an international marketing strategy for an organisation investing in international markets: • Access to low cost materials and labour • Economies of scale • Avoiding or bypassing trade barriers • Access to national/regional incentives eg DFID/Government funding, gateways to strategic markets	8
2.2.3 Critically evaluate a range of issues that impact on an organisation when entering new countries and markets and consider how they may be managed to achieve the organisation's objectives: • Extent of global coverage • Sequence of countries and timing of entry • Value proposition for global markets • Standardisation versus customisation	8
2.2.4 Assess the relevance to an organisation of mergers, acquisitions and strategic alliances in growing, expanding and maximising business potential: • Motives for strategic alliances • Types of strategic alliance • Value chain analysis of the competitive potential in alliances, mergers and acquisitions	7
2.2.5 Critically evaluate a range of growth strategies for an organisation: • Incremental growth • Significant growth • The concept of big ideas	7
2.2.6 Critically evaluate the concept of relationship marketing (CRM) as a means of achieving growth and profitability within an organisation: • Long term orientation versus transactional marketing • Partnering • Keeping of promises and developing mutual trust • Share of customer's wallet versus market share • Customisation • Customer loyalty	7
2.2.7 Critically evaluate the development of an organisation's brand and its contribution towards increasing the organisation's value and brand equity: • Brand associations • Brand identity and image • Brand proposition and promise • Branding strategies	7

2.2.8	Critically assess the impact of changing an organisation's strategic position within the market place in order to:	6

- Reflect the business strategy
- Resonate with customers
- Differentiate from competitors
- Express the values and culture of an organisation in a relevant way
- Express an organisation's corporate social responsibility (CSR), corporate reputation, sustainability and ethics.

Part 3 – Making strategic marketing decisions

SECTION 1 – Making and justifying strategic marketing decisions (weighting 20%)

	Covered in chapter(s)
3.1.1 Critically assess strategic alternatives against pre-determined criteria for an organisation, including:	1, 4, 9

- Scenario planning – stability versus uncertainty
- Potential for Return on Investment (ROI)
- Opportunity to achieve competitive advantage
- Feasibility, viability and resource
- Capacity and capability to deliver

	Covered in chapter(s)
3.1.2 Assess an organisation's readiness for developing a global strategy including:	8

- Strategic importance of the market
- Position of competitors internationally
- Cost effectiveness
- Barriers to trade

SECTION 2 – Financial assessment of marketing opportunities (weighting 30%)

	Covered in chapter(s)
3.2.1 Utilising a range of financial tools, assess the financial benefits and risks for an organisation when selecting from its strategic options:	9

- Ratios (INITIAL Financial Descriptors), eg Return on Investment (ROI)
- Investment Appraisal Techniques, eg Payback, Net Present Value (NPV), Discounted Cash Flows (DCF), Internal Rate of Return (IRR)
- Cost of capital and Weighted Average Cost of Capital (WACC)

	Covered in chapter(s)
3.2.2 Critically evaluate the source of funds appropriate to the strategic marketing choice and the long-term sustainability and impact of their utilisation:	9

- The concept of the cost of capital
- Capital Asset Pricing Model (CAPM)
- Weighted Average Cost of Capital (WACC)
- Optimal capital structure

	Covered in chapter(s)
3.2.3 Assess the impact of the strategic choice upon the shareholder value of organisations in different contexts: • The concept of shareholder value-added • Cash flow based valuation methods • Economic value methods • Financial value drivers • Timing, sustainability and risk factors in financial valuation	9
3.2.4 Assess the impact on the economic value of an organisation arising from specific decisions on expenditures/cash flows: • The concept of economic value added • Cash flow based valuation methods • Financial value drivers	9

SECTION 3 – Corporate and reputational risk of marketing decisions – (weighting 30%)

	Covered in chapter(s)
3.3.1 Utilising a range of risk analysis tools, assess the strategic risks facing an organisation in the selection of strategic alternatives leading to strategic choice: • Risk of strategic uncertainty • Risk of diverting from core business, vision and core competencies • Risk of changing technology and capability • Risk of reputation visibility and vulnerability • Financial risk, including shareholder value, investment, liability and loss	10
3.3.2 Assess the potential for organisational constraints to limit an organisation's success in using any given strategic choice: • Regulation • Structure and competencies • Capital and investment capability • Stakeholder/shareholder engagement and involvement • Competitor activity	10
3.3.3 Assess the risk to an organisation of hostile or declining markets and recommend mitigation strategies, including: • Milk, harvest, divest, liquidate, consolidate • Review margins and develop stronger cost structures • Reduce potential for proliferation of the product and/or brand • Manage share-shifting • Focus on customer	10
3.3.4 Recommend a range of mitigation strategies designed to reduce risks, so as to enhance an organisation's selection of a strategic option: • Scenario planning • Forecasting • Changing approach/direction • Avoidance strategies	10

SECTION 4 – Impact analysis of strategic marketing decisions– (weighting 20%)

	Covered in chapter(s)
3.4.1 Critically analyse the impact of the priority decisions on an organisation: • Strategic vision and direction • The organisation's value proposition • The key success factors • Assets and competencies • Positioning, segmentation and targeting • Distribution • Branding • Investment • Innovation • Manufacturing • Increased opportunities and threats	10

4 Assessing this Unit

The unit covered by this Study Text (Unit 10 *Analysis and Decision*) is assessed in a three-hour formal examination, with compulsory set tasks which are based upon pre-seen material. This pre-seen material takes the form of a company case study, which will be sent to you prior to the exam. As part of your exam preparation you will need to carry out a detailed analysis of the information contained in the case study.

In order to help you revise and prepare for the exam, we have also written a Chartered Postgraduate Diploma in Marketing Assessment Workbook, which is available either through your usual book retailer or our website: www.bpp.com/learningmedia.

5 The CIM's Magic Formula

The Magic Formula is a tool used by the CIM to help both examiners write exam and assignment questions and you to more easily interpret what you are being asked to write about. It is useful for helping you to check that you are using an appropriate balance between theory and practice for your particular level of qualification.

Contrary to the title, there is nothing mystical about the Magic Formula and simply by knowing it (or even mentioning it in an assessment) will not automatically secure a pass. What it does do however is to help you to check that you are presenting your answers in an appropriate format, including enough marketing theory and applying it to a real marketing context or issue. Students working through the range of CIM qualifications, are expected to evaluate to a greater extent and apply a more demanding range of marketing decisions as they progress from the lower to the higher levels. At the Chartered Postgraduate Diploma level, there will be an emphasis on evaluation whilst at the Introductory Certificate level the emphasis is on developing concepts.

Graphically, the Magic Formula for the Chartered Postgraduate Diploma in Marketing is shown below:

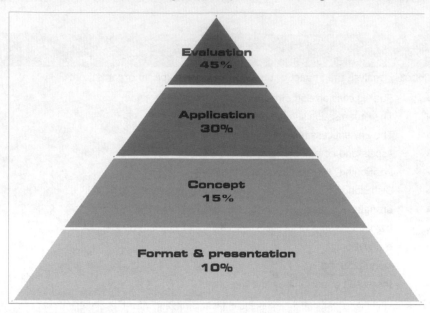

The Magic Formula for the Chartered Postgraduate Diploma in Marketing

You can see from pyramid that for the Professional Diploma marks are awarded in the following proportions:

- ### Format and presentation – 10%

  Remember, you are expected to present your work professionally which means that it should ALWAYS be typed and attention should be paid to making it look as visually appealing as possible even in an exam situation. It also means that the CIM will stipulate the format that you should present your work in. The assessment formats you will be given will be varied and can include things like reports to write, slides to prepare, emails, memos, formal letters, press releases, discussion documents, briefing papers, agendas, and newsletters.

- ### Concept – 15%

  Concept refers to your ability to state, recall and describe marketing theory. The definition of marketing is a core CIM syllabus topic. If we take this as an example, you would be expected to recognise, recall, and write this definition to a word perfect standard to gain the full marks for concept. Understanding marketing concepts is clearly the main area where marks will be given within your assessment.

- ### Application – 30%

  Application based marks are given for your ability to apply marketing theories to real life marketing situations. For example, you may be asked to discuss the definition of marketing, and how it is applied within your own organisation. Within this sort of question 30% of the marks would have been awarded within the 'concept' aspect of the Magic Formula. You will gain the rest of the marks through your ability to evaluate to what extent the concept is applied within your own organisation. Here you are not only using the definition but are applying it in order to consider the market orientation of the company.

- ### Evaluation – 45%

  Evaluation is the ability to asses the value or worth of something sometimes through careful consideration or related advantages and disadvantages or weighing up of alternatives. Results from your evaluation should enable you to discuss the importance of an issue using evidence to support your opinions.

  Using the example of you being asked whether or not your organisation adopts a marketing approach, if you were asked to 'evaluate' this, it would be expected that you would provide reasons and specific examples why you thought they might take this approach but to also consider issues why they may not be marketing orientated before coming to a final conclusion.

  You should have noticed that for the Professional Diploma, you are expected to consider the equal weightings of concept, application and evaluation in order to gain maximum marks in assessments.

6 A guide to the features of the Study Text

Each of the chapter features (see below) will help you to break down the content into manageable chunks and ensure that you are developing the skills required for a professional qualification.

Chapter feature	Relevance and how you should use it	Corresponding icon
Chapter topic list	Study the list. Each numbered topic denotes a numbered section in the chapter. Identified as a key concept within the syllabus	–
Introduction	Shows why topics need to be studied and is a route guide through the chapter.	–
Syllabus linked Learning Objectives	Outlines what you should learn within the chapter based on what is required within the syllabus	–
Format & Presentation	Outlines a key marketing presentation format with reference to the Magic Formula	
Concept	Key concept to learn with reference to the Magic Formula	
Application	An example of applied marketing with reference to the Magic Formula	
Evaluation	An example of evaluation with reference to the Magic Formula	
Activity	An application based activity for you to complete	
Key text links	Emphasises key parts to read in a range of other texts and other learning resources	
Marketing at work	A short case study to illustrate marketing practice	
Exam/ Assessment tip	Key advice based on the assessment or exam	
Quick quiz	Use this to check your learning	–
Objective check	Review what you have learnt	–

7 A note on Pronouns

On occasions in this Study Text, 'he' is used for 'he or she', 'him' for 'him or her' and so forth. Whilst we try to avoid this practice it is sometimes necessary for reasons of style. No prejudice or stereotyping accounting to sex is intended or assumed.

8 Additional resources

8.1 The CIM's supplementary reading list

We have already mentioned that the CIM requires you to demonstrate your ability to 'read widely'. The CIM issue an extensive reading list for each unit. For this unit they recommend supplementary reading. Within the study text we have highlighted within the wider reading links specific topics where these resources would help. The CIM's supplementary reading list for this unit is:

Aaker, D. and McLoughlin, D. (2007) Strategic market management. European edition. Chichester, John Wiley & Sons.

Drummond, G., Ensor, J. and Ashford, R. (2007) Strategic marketing: planning and control. 3rd edition. Oxford, Butterworth Heinemann

Mintzberg, H. (1995) Structure in fives: designing effective organisations. International edition. Englewood Cliffs, Prentice Hall

Mintzberg, H. (1994) The rise and fall of strategic planning. NY, Free Press.

Mintzberg.H. and Quinn, J. (2003) The strategy process. 4th global edition. US, Prentice Hall.

Johnson, G. and Scholes, K. (2008) Exploring corporate strategy. 8th edition. Harlow, Prentice Hall.

Lynch, R. (2005) Strategic management. 5th edition. Harlow, FT Prentice Hall.

Porter, M.E. (2004) Competitive advantage: creating and sustaining superior performance. NY, Free Press.

Doole, I. and Lowe, R. (2008) CIM Coursebook: Strategic marketing decisions. Oxford, Butterworth Heinemann.

Kerin, R.A. and Peterson, R.A. (2008) Strategic marketing problems – cases and comments. 11th edition.Harlow, Pearson.

Johansson, J. (2009) Global marketing: foreign entry, local marketing and global management. 5th edition.Maidenhead, McGraw-Hill.

Chaffey, D. et al (2008) Internet marketing; strategy, implementation and practice. 4th edition. Harlow, Prentice Hall.

Hooley, G. et al (2007) Marketing strategy and competitive positioning. 4th edition. Harlow Prentice Hall.

Bolton, B. and Thompson, J. (2004) Entrepreneurs, talent, temperament, technique. 2nd edition. Oxford, Butterworth Heinemann.

Doyle, P. (2008) Value-based marketing: marketing strategies for corporate growth and shareholder value. 2nd edition. Chichester, John Wiley & Sons.

Hamel, G. and Prahalad, C.K.(1996) Competing for the future. Harvard, Harvard Business Press.

Lumby, S. and Jones, C. (2003) Corporate finance: theory and practice. 7th edition. London, Thomson.

8.2 Assessment preparation materials from BPP Learning Media

To help you pass the entire Stage 1 of the Chartered Postgraduate Diploma in Marketing we have created a complete study package. **The Professional Diploma Assessment Workbook** covers all four units for the Postgraduate Diploma level. Practice question and answers, tips on tackling assignments and work-based projects are written to help you succeed in your assessments.

This case is assessed by 2 work-based projects.

Our A6 set of spiral bound **Passcards** are handy revision cards and are ideal to reinforce key topics for the pre-seen case study exam.

8.3 BPP Learning Media's Online Material

To complement this study text, our Assessment Workbook and Passcards we have also produced some online materials for both students and tutors. These materials have not been designed to remain static but we will be developing more and adding to the content over time. If you have purchased a product within our CIM range then you will be able to access the online materials for free at:

www.bpp.com/lm/cim

Typical content will include:

- Links to the most useful websites for marketers
- Syllabus links to key marketing developments and 'big news' stories
- Suggested exam answers to the most recent exams (available to those who purchase the Assessment Workbook)
- Pro forma's for key marketing documents such as Marketing Plans, Research Proposals etc
- Tutor only content including slides and case studies

We are also pleased to announce an exciting partnerships with Superbrands and The Centre for Brand Analysis to bring you a new online feature titled 'A Word From . . .'. This feature is covered online and from time to time will include more material gathered from the Superbrand Marketers.

9 Your personal study plan

Preparing a Study Plan (and sticking to it) is one of the key elements to learning success.

Think about the number of hours you should dedicate to your studies. Guided learning hours will include time spent in lesson, working on fully prepared distance learning materials, formal workshops and work set by your tutor. We also know that to be successful, students should spend *at least* the same amount of time spent working through guided learning conducting self study. This means that for the entire qualification with four units you should spend time working in a tutor guided manner and at least the same time completing recommended reading, working on assignments, and revising for exams. This study text will help you to organise this portion of self study time.

Now think about the exact amount of time you have (don't forget you will still need some leisure time!) and complete the following tables to help you keep to a schedule.

	Date	Duration in weeks
Course start		
Course finish		Total weeks of course:
Submission date	Assignment to commence on preparation	Total weeks to complete assignment:

Content chapter coverage plan

Chapter	To be completed by	Incorporated into project
1 The external marketing environment		
2 Understanding the customer base		
3 The internal marketing environment		
4 Developing organisational capability		
5 Developing strategy		
6 Assessing strategic marketing options		
7 Growth strategies		
8 International marketing strategy		
9 Financial assessment of marketing opportunities		
10 Corporate and reputational risk		

Chapter 1

The external marketing environment

Topic list

1   Assessing the external environment
2   Evaluating the current strategic position
3   Strategic uncertainty

Introduction

This part of the syllabus prepares you for undertaking a strategic audit of an organisation and the assessment of how far the organisation is able to deliver its strategic objectives and create value.

Each firm is positioned differently in each particular market and in the industry as a whole, and so will require its own market analysis (section 1). Each industry contains companies aiming to offer similar satisfaction to customers. However, each company has a unique profile compared to its competitors. Market analysis and customer analysis shows what companies and industries are competing for.

Identifying who your competitors are is easier said than done, as competition exists outside any particular industry. While competitors are important, only paying customers can determine which firms have competitive advantage with their particular strategic position (section 2).

A wide variety of techniques and tools are available (section 3) to deal with the uncertainty inherent in modern business markets.

Syllabus-linked learning objectives

By the end of the chapter you will be able to:

Learning objectives	Syllabus link
1 Utilise a range of techniques, processes and market information to assess the external marketing environment	1.1.1
2 Utilise market-based information to critically evaluate an organisation's strategic position within the market place, including consideration of specific positioning issues	1.1.2
3 Assess the potential for strategic uncertainty in the external market and the extent to which it involves trends or events, and show how it will impact upon an organisation	1.1.4
4 Critically assess strategic alternatives against pre-determined criteria for an organisation	3.1.1

1   Assessing the external environment

'An organisation has to understand the nature of the relationships within its industry, in order to allow the enterprise to develop strategies to gain advantage of the current relationships' Drummond et al (2008) p.26

The following table illustrates how a thorough market analysis will be made up of a range of factors.

Statistical data	2007	2008	2009 (forecast)
Company/SBU data			
Market name			
Unit sales			
£ sales			
Profitability			
Market data			
Market size			
Market share			
No. of main customers			
No. of dealers/distributors			
Concentration ratio			

Qualitative data			
Environmental factors			
Critical success factors			
Growing/stable/declining			
Key competitors and their strategies			
Future competitors			
Segmentation opportunities			
Ease of entry			

We can expand upon some elements of the above checklist.

(a) **Market size**. This refers to both actual and potential (forecast) size. A company cannot know whether its market share objectives are feasible unless it knows the market's overall size and the position of competitors. Forecasting areas of growth and decline is also important.

(b) **Customers**. The analysis needs to identify who the customers are, what they need, and their buying behaviour (where, when and how they purchase products or services). This will help to point out opportunities.

(c) **Distributors**. The company will need to evaluate its current arrangements for getting goods or services to the customer. Changes in distribution channels can open up new fields of opportunity (eg the Internet).

Often these factors overlap and PEST factors will affect many areas. For example, at the present time the UK government is considering how best to free the country's postal systems from monopoly. Parliamentary bills will eventually need to be passed. Here the major driving force could be said to be political, triggered by economic necessity, facilitated by law. The markets will cease to be a monopoly. They might fragment into public and private sectors.

1.1 Market structures and the competitive environment

 KEY CONCEPT   concept

A **market** is a group of actual and potential customers, who can make purchase decisions.

In order to trade in a market it is vital to have a detailed knowledge of the market structure and behaviour. Knowledge of the composition, profile and behaviour of the market is fundamental to marketing, whether domestic or internationally based. Typically, information is required on the following points.

(a) Who are the main **customers**? How, why, where, when and how much do they buy?

(b) What are the main **channels of distribution** used in such markets? Who are the main distributors, agents etc? Do reciprocal or other possibly limiting trading practices exist that could hamper market entry?

(c) What **product** attributes, specifications and developments are there in the market?

(d) Who are the main **suppliers** to the market? What are their relative positions, shares, strengths and weaknesses, strategies and performance?

(e) Are there significant **geographic variations** in customer requirements, distribution costs, product use, and promotional needs?

(f) What facilities are there for **promoting** the product into the market? What is the effectiveness of the various forms of promotion and media available?

(g) What is the **size** of the total market and potential target segments? How durable is the market? For example, is it likely to disappear in adverse economic or political conditions?

In discussing competition Porter (2004) distinguishes between factors that characterise the nature of competition:

(a) **In one industry compared with another** (eg in the chemicals industry compared with the clothing retail industry) and make one industry as a whole potentially more profitable than another (ie yielding a bigger return on investment).

(b) **Within a particular industry**. These relate to the competitive strategies that individual firms might select.

 EXAM TIP

application

Five competitive forces influence the state of competition in an industry, which collectively determine the profit (ie long-run return on capital) potential of the industry as a whole. **Learn them**.

(a) The threat of new entrants to the industry
(b) The threat of substitute products or services
(c) The bargaining power of customers
(d) The bargaining power of suppliers
(e) The rivalry among current competitors in the industry

 MARKETING AT WORK

application

Aaker & McLoughlin (2007) give examples of each of these factors.

Threat of new entrants

The level of threat depends upon the size and nature of the barriers to entry. Such barriers include required capital investment (eg mobile phone networks), economies of scale (large supermarkets), distribution channels and product differentiation (Apple computers).

Substitutes

Mobile phones have become substitutes for home land lines. Online music availability threatens more traditional music stores.

Customer power

When customers have more power (by size of purchase, or the presence of alternatives) they can force prices down. Tyre manufacturers have very powerful customers in the car manufacturing companies.

Supplier power

The oil industry is powerful enough to influence profits in its customer industries, because it is either too expensive, or currently impossible, to convert from oil to another energy supply.

Existing competitors

A major factor in the bursting of the 'dot.com' bubble was that there were simply too many companies. Offerings were often very similar in what was still a small, and therefore overcrowded, market.

1.2 Customers

It is a curious fact that most customers are not worth selling to! The loyal, long-term customer that pays full price and requires little special service attention is the ideal – but very few fall into this category. Nevertheless, it is appropriate to target this class of customer specifically rather than simply to aim for a large customer base. Desirable customers display four important characteristics.

- They are **strategic** in that their needs match the company's core capabilities
- They are **significant** in terms of their size or potential for growth
- They are **profitable**
- They are **loyal**

To satisfy customers we need to know how they behave, and why they take the purchasing decisions they do. A number of models and theories exist to explain the dynamics of the 'not always rational' customer's behaviour.

 ## MARKETING AT WORK

application

Capital One's competitive advantage comes not from the brand strength of American Express, or the economies of scale that Citibank enjoys, or from its links with affinity groups such as those that benefit MBNA Bank. Its strength is in gathering and using data. 'It is the best data mining shop anywhere in the US', is the assessment of Eric Clemons, professor of marketing at Wharton Business School at the University of Pennsylvania.

Its special skill is spotting the patterns that identify 'micro-segments' in the market for consumer credit. Last year, the company offered thousands of variations of credit card. It also conducted 64,000 marketing tests on small groups of customers to gauge how new varieties would be received.

The ability to segment the credit card market more finely than its competitors, and customise products accordingly, is what sets Capital One apart. Many companies talk about mass customisation. This Virginia based company really does it.

Financial Times, 14 May 2002

1.2.1 What influences customer behaviour?

Customers are subject to a wide range of influences, including their own needs and attitudes; and cultural and social conditioning.

Understanding customer behaviour assists effective marketing management. However, there are many influences on customer behaviour and so the outcome in terms of purchasing decisions can be very difficult to understand from a rational viewpoint. Emotional and rational influences intertwine and lead to purchase outcomes which can seem illogical even to the buyer.

Buyer behaviour models aim to help the marketing manager to understand the buying process, so as to select a marketing strategy which is most applicable to the specific situation. One of these is the Howard-Sheth model.

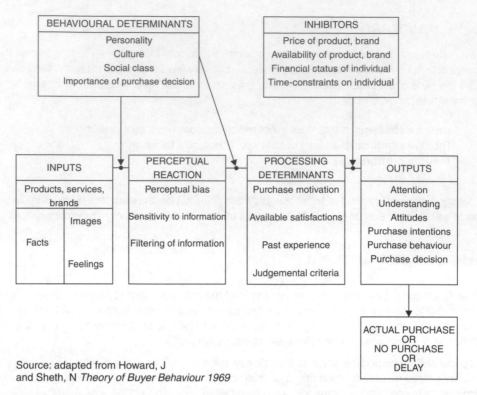

BEHAVIOURAL DETERMINANTS	INHIBITORS
Personality	Price of product, brand
Culture	Availability of product, brand
Social class	Financial status of individual
Importance of purchase decision	Time-constraints on individual

INPUTS	PERCEPTUAL REACTION	PROCESSING DETERMINANTS	OUTPUTS
Products, services, brands	Perceptual bias	Purchase motivation	Attention
			Understanding
Facts / Images / Feelings	Sensitivity to information	Available satisfactions	Attitudes
			Purchase intentions
	Filtering of information	Past experience	Purchase behaviour
			Purchase decision
		Judgemental criteria	

ACTUAL PURCHASE
OR
NO PURCHASE
OR
DELAY

Source: adapted from Howard, J
and Sheth, N *Theory of Buyer Behaviour 1969*

Elements in the Howard-Sheth model

(a)   **Inputs**. Information inputs about the alternative services available include both rational and emotional elements.

(b)   **Behavioural determinants**. These elements include the existing predispositions of the purchaser which have been influenced by culture, socio-economic group, family and personality factors, amongst others. This element will have a larger role for major or otherwise significant purchase decisions.

(c)   **Perceptual reaction**. Information from inputs is not accepted at face value but interpreted. For example, an individual is likely to value information more highly if it has been actively sought than if it has been passively received (from TV advertisements for example).

(d)   **Processing determinants**. These are the factors affecting how the information gathered is evaluated.

(e)   **Inhibitors**. There are external constraints on actual or potential purchase behaviour.

(f)   **Outputs**. The outcome of the complex process of interacting elements may be a purchase decision, a decision not to buy or a decision to delay buying.

 ACTIVITY 1

application

Eleanor Plantagenet works for Mast, Rick, Tree and Tee, an advertising agency which is beginning to fall on hard times. For example, Bill Mast (the MD) has had to make do with a cheaper company car. There are ominous rumours about making the agency 'leaner and fitter', 'optimising the agency's human resources' and 'delayering'. Eleanor assumes that all this means possible redundancy for people like her, although the managing director has denied all such rumours.

Mortgage payments account for 25% of Eleanor's post-tax monthly salary. Her husband is a freelance financial journalist. His earnings are erratic, but he has recently been commissioned to write a book for the non-specialist reader about the single European currency. They have two children. They invested an inheritance of £15,000 in the Carlowe Bowes saving scheme but the scheme was run by a fraudster, and they lost all their money. Both Eleanor and her husband are hard-working individuals with severe demands on their time. Eleanor earns significantly more than her husband.

One evening, Eleanor's husband tells her of a new financial services product offered by the International Bank of Canonbury. It offers redundancy insurance. This means that Eleanor will be paid £100 per month of unemployment (up to 12 months)

for every £5 invested per month, to a maximum monthly benefit of £1,000. No benefit will be paid if Eleanor becomes unemployed within six months of taking out the policy.

Identify the behavioural determinants, inhibitors, inputs, possible perceptual reactions processing determinants and outputs (as in the Howard-Sheth model) in the above situation.

'Understanding the customer base' is the subject of Chapter 2.

1.3 Channels

In order for a product to be distributed a number of basic functions usually need to be fulfilled.

- The **transport** function may be provided by the supplier, the distributor or may be sub-contracted to a specialist. For some products, such as perishable goods, transport planning is vital.

- For production planning purposes, an uninterrupted flow of production is often essential, so **stocks of finished goods** accumulate and need to be stored, incurring significant costs and risks. For consumer goods, holding stock at the point of sale is very costly; the overheads for city centre retail locations are prohibitive. A good stock control system is essential, designed to avoid stockouts while keeping stockholding costs low.

- As production has tended to become centralised in pursuit of economies of scale, the need to understand **local markets** has grown, particularly when international marketing takes place. The intricacies and idiosyncrasies of local markets constitute key marketing information.

- While major **promotional campaigns** for national products are likely to be carried out by the supplier, the translation of the campaign to local level is usually the responsibility of the local distributor, often as a joint venture.

- **Presentation and display** of the product at the local level is often a function of the local distributor. Specialist help from merchandisers can be bought in but decisions on layout and display need to be taken by local distributors, often following patterns produced centrally.

1.3.1 Points in the chain of distribution

(a) **Retailers**. These are traders operating outlets which sell directly to households. They may be classified in a number of ways.

    (i)   Type of goods sold (eg hardware, furniture)

    (ii)   Type of service (self-service, counter service)

    (iii)   Size

    (iv)   Location (rural, city-centre, suburban shopping mall, out-of-town shopping centre)

    (v)   Independent retailers (including the local corner shop, although independents are not always as small as this)

    (vi)   Multiple chains, some of which are associated with one class of product while others are 'variety' chains, holding a wide range of different stocks

    (vii)   Still others are voluntary groups of independents, usually grocers.

(b) **Wholesalers**. These are intermediaries who stock a range of products from competing manufacturers to sell on to other organisations such as retailers. Many wholesalers specialise in particular products. Most deal in consumer goods, but some specialise in industrial goods, such as steel stockholders and builders' merchants.

(c) **Distributors and dealers.** These are organisations which contract to buy a manufacturer's goods and sell them to customers. Their function is similar to that of wholesalers, but they usually offer a narrower product range, sometimes (as in the case of most car dealers) the products of a single manufacturer. In addition to selling on the manufacturer's product, distributors often promote the products and provide after-sales service.

(d) **Agents.** Agents differ from distributors in that distributors buy the manufacturer's goods and re-sell them at a profit, whereas agents do not purchase the manufacturer's goods, but earn a commission on whatever sales they make.

(e)   **Franchisees.** These are independent organisations which, in exchange for an initial fee and (usually) a share of sales revenue, are allowed to trade under the name of a parent organisation. Most fast food outlets are franchises.

(f)   **Multiple stores** (eg supermarkets) buy goods for retailing direct from the producer, many of them under their 'own label' brand name.

1.3.2 Types of distribution channel

Choosing distribution channels is important for any organisation, because once a set of channels has been established, subsequent changes are likely to be costly and slow to implement. Distribution channels fall into one of two categories: **direct** and **indirect** channels.

 KEY CONCEPTS

concept

Direct distribution means the product going directly from producer to consumer without the use of a specific intermediary. These methods are often described as active since they typically involve the supplier making the first approach to a potential customer. Direct distribution methods generally fall into two categories: those using media such as the press, leaflets and telephones to invite response and purchase by the consumer and those using a sales force to contact consumers face-to-face.

Indirect distribution is a system of distribution, common among manufactured goods, which makes use of intermediaries; wholesalers, retailers or perhaps both. In contrast to direct distribution, these methods are often thought of as being passive in the sense that they rely on consumers to make the first approach by entering the relevant retail outlet.

In building up efficient channels of distribution, a manufacturer must consider several factors.

(a)   How many intermediate stages should be used and how many dealers at each stage?

(b)   What support should the manufacturer give to the dealers? It may be necessary to provide an after-sales and repair service, and regular visits to retailers' stores. The manufacturer might need to consider advertising or sales promotion support, including merchandising.

(c)   To what extent does the manufacturer wish to dominate a channel of distribution? A market leader might wish to ensure that its market share is maintained, so that it could, for example, offer exclusive distribution contracts to major retailers.

(d)   To what extent does the manufacturer wish to integrate its marketing effort up to the point of sale with the consumer? Combined promotions with retailers, for example, would only be possible if the manufacturer dealt directly with the retailer (rather than through a wholesaler).

1.3.3 Factors in channel design decisions

Customers

The number of potential customers, their buying habits and their geographical locations are key influences. The use of mail order for those with limited mobility (rural location, illness) is an example of the influence of customers on channel design. Marketing industrial components to the car industry needs to take account of the geographic distribution of the car industry in the UK. The growth of Internet trading, both in consumer and business-to-business markets, has been built on the rapid spread of fast Internet access.

Product characteristics

Some product characteristics have an important effect on the design of the channel of distribution.

(a)   **Perishability**

Fresh fruit and newspapers must be distributed very quickly or they become worthless. Speed of delivery is therefore a key factor.

(b)   **Customisation**

Customised products tend to be distributed direct. When a wide range of options is available, sales may be made using demonstration units, with customised delivery to follow.

(c)   **After-sales service/technical advice**

Extent and cost must be carefully considered, staff training given and quality control systems set up. Training programmes are often provided for distributors by suppliers.

(d)   **Franchising**

Franchising has become a popular means of growth both for suppliers and for franchisees who carry the set-up costs and licence fees. The supplier gains additional outlets quickly and exerts more control than is usual in distribution.

Distributor characteristics

The capability of the distributor to take on the distributive functions' already discussed above' is obviously an important influence on the supplier's choice.

Competitors' channel choice

For many consumer goods, a supplier's brand will sit alongside its competitors' products and there is little the supplier can do about it. For other products, distributors may stock one name brand only (for example, in car distribution) and in return be given an exclusive area. In this case, new suppliers may face difficulties in breaking into a market if all the best distribution outlets have been taken up.

Supplier characteristics

A strong financial base gives the supplier the option of buying and operating their own distribution channel. Boots the Chemist is a prime example. The market position of the supplier is also important: distributors are keen to be associated with the market leader but the third, fourth or fifth brand in a market is likely to find more distribution problems.

2   Evaluating the current strategic position

'Strategic position, the face of the business strategy, specifies how the business aspires to be perceived ... relative to its competitors and market.' Aaker & McLoughlin (2007) p.25

A strategic position should be:

(a)   Strategic – reflecting the business strategy, and reflecting a long term effort to gain competitive advantage

(b)   Defined relative to competitors and the market – via a point of differentiation that the organisation can position itself on

(c)   Resonant with customers – appealing to customers and their perceptions of value

'There are as many strategic positioning avenues as there are products, markets and business strategies.' Aaker & McLoughlin (2007) p.233. They cite the following examples.

The quality player with the defined product	eg Victorinox Swiss Army knives
The **'value'** option	Ryanair, Aldi
The innovator	Apple
A narrow product focus	Ferrari
A target segment focus	Hamleys
Being global	HSBC

2.1 Competitive advantage

 KEY CONCEPT

concept

Competitive advantage: a business achieves competitive advantage when it earns higher than average profits.

Whatever overall objective is set for a firm: to survive, to create value, to make profit; the key to achieving it lies in the attainment of some form of competitive advantage. Business therefore revolves around the means by which competitive advantage may be attained and sustained. Competitive advantage distinguishes the successful business from the average enabling it to earn an above average level of profit.

There are two main kinds of approach to achieving competitive advantage, each encompassing several strands of strategic thinking.

(a)   **The positioning approach**

The positioning approach to strategy is closely related to the traditional concept of marketing orientation. It starts with an assessment of the commercial environment and positions the business so that it fits with environmental requirements.

(b)   **The resource-based approach**

The resource-based approach starts with the idea that competitive advantage comes from the possession of distinctive and unique resources.

 EXAM TIP   application

Understand the definition, and the importance, of competitive advantage. Whatever overall objective is set for a firm: to survive, to create value, to make profit; the key to achieving it lies in the attainment of some form of competitive advantage, and all strategic alternatives need to be assessed for their ability to deliver it. Business therefore revolves around the means by which competitive advantage may be attained and sustained. Make no mistake about it: competitive advantage distinguishes the successful business from the average, enabling it to earn an above average level of profit.

2.2 Competitive positioning and target markets

Having analysed the attractiveness of a segment, the firm will choose one or more **target markets**. Marketing policy may be **undifferentiated** (mass), **concentrated** or **differentiated**. The extreme form of differentiated marketing is **micromarketing**.

 KEY CONCEPT   concept

A **target market** is a market or segment selected for special attention by an organisation (possibly served with a distinct marketing mix).

2.2.1 Policy options

Having identified distinct market segments, it is necessary to choose which ones to target and how to go about it. Careful consideration must be given to the criteria by which segments will be chosen. **Profitability** is clearly an important consideration but so are **accessibility**, **resources** required and **potential for growth**. Targeting is a continuing process, since segments change and develop and so do competitors. The company is, to some extent, able to plan and control its own development and it must respond to changes in the market place.

The marketing management of a company may choose one of the following policy options.

Policy	Comment
Undifferentiated marketing	This policy is to produce a single product and hope to get as many customers as possible to buy it; segmentation is ignored entirely. This is sometimes called **mass marketing**.
Concentrated marketing	The company attempts to produce the ideal product for a single segment of the market (for example, Rolls Royce cars, Mothercare mother and baby shops).
Differentiated marketing	The company attempts to introduce several product versions, each aimed at a different market segment (for example, the manufacture of different styles of the same article of clothing).

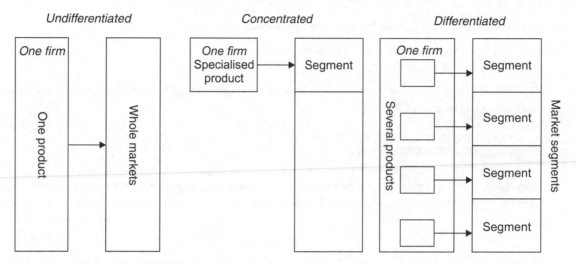

The major **disadvantage of differentiated marketing** is the additional costs of marketing and production (more product design and development costs, the loss of economies of scale in production and storage, additional promotion costs and administrative costs and so on). When the costs of differentiation of the market exceed the **benefits** from further segmentation and target marketing, a firm is said to have **over-differentiated**.

The major **disadvantage of concentrated marketing** is the business risk of relying on a single segment of a single market. On the other hand, specialisation in a particular market segment can give a firm a profitable, although perhaps temporary, competitive edge over rival firms.

The choice between undifferentiated, differentiated or concentrated marketing as a marketing strategy will depend on the following factors.

(a)   The extent to which the product and/or the market may be considered **homogeneous**. **Mass marketing** may be sufficient if the market is largely homogeneous (for example, for safety matches).

(b)   The **company's resources** must not be over extended by differentiated marketing. Small firms may succeed better by concentrating on only one segment.

(c)   The product must be sufficiently **advanced in its life cycle** to have attracted a substantial total market; otherwise segmentation and target marketing is unlikely to be profitable, because each segment would be too small in size.

2.2.2 Micromarketing

Segmentation, as part of target marketing, looks certain to play an even more crucial role in the marketing strategies of consumer organisations in the years ahead. The move from traditional mass marketing to **micromarketing** is rapidly gaining ground as marketers explore more cost-effective ways to recruit new customers. This has been brought about by a number of trends.

(a)   The ability to create large numbers of product variants without the need for corresponding increases in resources is causing markets to become overcrowded.

(b)   The growth in minority lifestyles is creating opportunities for niche brands aimed at consumers with very distinct purchasing habits.

(c)   The fragmentation of the media to service ever more specialist and local audiences is denying mass media the ability to assure market dominance for major brand advertisers.

(d)   The advance in information technology is enabling information about individual customers to be organised in ways that enable highly selective and personal communications.

Such trends have promoted the developments in benefit, lifestyle and geodemographic segmentation techniques outlined. Consumer market segmentation has developed so much in the last few years that the vision of multinational marketers accessing a PC to plan retail distribution and supporting promotional activity in cities as far apart as Naples, Nottingham and Nice is now a practical reality.

2.2.3 Mass customisation

Micromarketing is made possible by **mass customisation**, which features:

- The huge economies of scale of mass production
- The tailoring of products precisely to the customer's requirements

New manufacturing technology makes this possible. There is less need for a standard product if people's individual preferences can be catered for.

 MARKETING AT WORK   application

Since 1999, *Levi Jeans* in the US has offered a service whereby customers' measurements are fed through to an automated garment cutting process. By 2004, 27% of **LandsEnd.com's** online sales in categories like jeans and chinos were made to order.

2.3 Positioning

Positioning can be 'psychological' and 'real'. **Perceptual maps** enable users to identify positioning options. The foundation of a **positioning strategy** is to align what the company can do with what customers want. Repositioning is a risky and expensive response to poor performance.

2.3.1 Steps in positioning

Step 1   Identify differentiating factors in products or services in relation to competitors.

Step 2   Select the most important differences.

Step 3   Communicate the position to the target market.

The value of positioning is that it enables **tactical marketing mix decisions to be made**.

 KEY CONCEPT   concept

Positioning is the act of designing the company's offer and image so that it achieves a distinct and valued place in the target customer's mind.

In 2001, *The Economist* suggested that the car industry faced four challenges.

- A slump in demand (down perhaps by 20%) in the US and Europe, the two biggest markets
- Financial weakness
- Falling prices
- 21% overcapacity

In Europe, the biggest losers were GM, Ford, Toyota, Nissan and Honda.

- GM – 'quality problems and tired designs' exacerbated by having four bosses in three years
- Japanese firms' 'product weakness' aggravated by exchange rate difficulties

The three American manufacturers were vulnerable because their profits came from too narrow a model range. 'Car makers must dream up some exciting new vehicles to entice jaded and cautious consumers to open their wallets in a downturn.'

The Economist, 31 March 2001

Now, in 2009, the car industry is experiencing huge problems. Carmakers around the world are cutting production as inventories build up to unprecedented levels. Storage areas and docksides are packed with vast expanses of unsold cars as demand slumps. With many manufacturers on extended Christmas shutdown, the number of cars rolling off production lines in December 2008 fell 47.5% to just 53,823.

In the UK, Nissan announced plans to cut its Sunderland workforce by 1,200. Honda halted production at its Swindon plant in April and May, extending the two-month closure announced before Christmas to four months. Honda and Japanese rival Toyota are both cutting production in Japan and elsewhere. Land Rover has announced that 450 British jobs will go.

Meanwhile in the US, GM has filed for bankruptcy:

'Many factors have contributed to the timely death of **General Motors** but when the industrial postmortem is conducted, one cause will stand out: debt – too much of it, to be precise.

'... **GM** is a business no longer able to pay its creditors and therefore seeking court protection to shed some of its liabilities. But the company's customers are also drowning in too much debt. A generation of car buyers had grown used to funding big purchases on the never-never. When the banks and financing companies withdrew this artificial stimulus, many households decided they could wait and save up until they really needed a new car. The combination of plunging sales and soaring liabilities would have crippled even a well-run company.

'Of course, GM was far from well run. It has consistently made products that people didn't want to buy ... [but] ... protection of the court gives one of the world's most important companies a chance to reinvent itself. There will be howls of protest from bondholders and other creditors forced to share the pain but at last there is a chance to move beyond immediate survival and think about creating a transportation company strong enough to weather the next recession.'

www.guardian.co.uk, 1 June 2009 (accessed 18 June 2009)

2.3.2 Problems with positioning

How much do people remember about a product or brand?

(a)   Many products are, in fact, very similar, and the key issue is to make them distinct in the customer's mind.

(b)   People remember 'number 1', so the product should be positioned as 'number 1' in relation to a valued attribute.

(c)   Cosmetic changes can have the effect of repositioning the product in the customer's mind. To be effective, however, this psychological positioning has to be reinforced by real positioning.

As **positioning is psychological as well as real**, we can now identify **positioning errors**.

Mistake	Consequence
Underpositioning	The brand does not have a clear identity in the eyes of the customer
Overpositioning	Buyers may have too narrow an image of a brand
Confused positioning	Too many claims might be made for a brand
Doubtful positioning	The positioning may not be credible in the eyes of the buyer

2.3.3 Positioning strategy checklist

Positioning variable	Comment
Attributes	Size, for example
Benefit	What benefits we offer
Use/application	Ease of use; accessibility
User	The sort of person the product appeals to
Product category	Consciously differentiated from competition
Quality/price	One should support and validate the other, so that it makes sense to the customer and he understands what he is buying. For example, low quality at a high price is unlikely to sell.

  ACTIVITY 2

application

Identify examples of positioning strategies in the table above.

2.3.4 Perceptual maps

One simple perceptual map that can be used is to plot brands or competing products in terms of two key characteristics such as price and quality.

A perceptual map of market positioning can be used to **identify gaps in the market**. This example might suggest that there could be potential in the market for a low-price high-quality **'bargain brand'**. A company that carries out such an analysis might decide to conduct further research to find out whether there is scope in the market for a new product which would be targeted at a market position where there are few or no rivals.

2.3.5 Mapping positions

Kotler (2001) identified a 3 × 3 matrix of nine different competitive positioning strategies.

Product quality	Product price		
	High price	*Medium price*	*Low price*
High	Premium strategy	Penetration strategy	Superbargain strategy
Medium	Overpricing strategy	Average-quality strategy	Bargain strategy
Low	Hit-and-run strategy	Shoddy goods strategy	Cheap goods strategy

Once selected, the needs of the targeted segment can be identified and the marketing mix strategy developed to provide the benefits package needed to satisfy them. Positioning the product offering then becomes a matter of matching and communicating appropriate benefits.

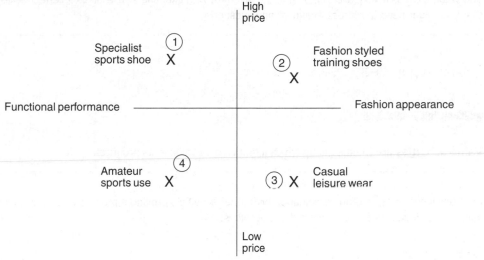

2.3.6 Repositioning

Strategic managers must be prepared to deal with under performance and failure. One possible response is repositioning of the market offering.

 KEY CONCEPT   concept

Repositioning is a competitive strategy aimed at changing position in order to increase market share.

However, this is a difficult and expensive process, since it requires the extensive remoulding of customer perceptions. The danger is that the outcome will be confusion in the mind of the customer and failure to impress the selected new segments.

Type of position	Comment
Real	Relates to actual product features and design
Psychological	Change the buyer's beliefs about the brand
Competitive	Alter beliefs about competing brands
Change emphasis	The emphasis in the advertising can change over time

2.4 Value creation

2.4.1 The value chain

The **value chain** models how an organisation creates value through managing value activities and the linkages between them. These can be deployed to give distinct customer benefits.

The **value chain** model of corporate activities, developed by Michael Porter (2004), offers a bird's eye view of the firm and what it does. Competitive advantage, says Porter, arises out of the way an organisation uses its inputs and transforms them into the outputs that customers pay for. The processes involved in this transformation are called **value activities**.

EXAM TIP   application

The value chain is a very useful model and a favourite with examiners. It is an excellent checklist of the things in a business that you might need to discuss in almost any question.

2.4.2 Activities

KEY CONCEPT   concept

Value activities are the means by which a firm creates value in its products.

Activities incur costs, and, in combination with other activities, provide a product or service that earns revenue. 'Firms create value for their buyers by performing these activities.'

Example

Let us explain this point by using the example of a **restaurant**. A restaurant's activities can be divided into buying food, cooking it, and serving it (to customers). There is no reason, in theory, why the customers should not do all these things themselves, at home. The customer, however, is not only prepared to **pay for someone else** to do all this but also **pays more than the cost of** the resources. The ultimate value a firm creates is measured by the amount customers are willing to pay for its products or services above the cost of carrying out value activities. A firm is profitable if the realised value to customers exceeds the collective cost of performing the activities.

(a)   Customers **purchase value**, which they measure by comparing a firm's products and services with similar offerings by competitors.

(b)   The business **creates value** by carrying out its activities either more efficiently than other businesses, or combining them in such a way as to provide a unique product or service.

ACTIVITY 3   application

Outline different ways in which the restaurant can create value.

Porter's (1991) diagram of the value chain looks like this.

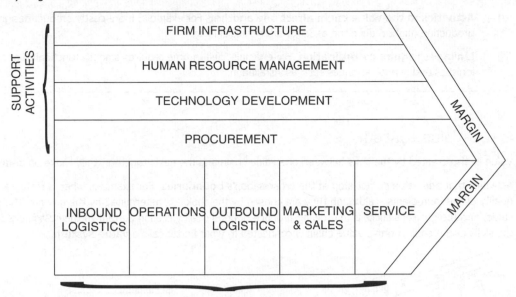

The **margin** is the excess the customer is prepared to **pay** over the **cost** to the firm of obtaining resource inputs and providing value activities.

Primary activities are directly related to production, sales, marketing, delivery and service.

Activity	Comment
Inbound logistics	Receiving, handling and storing inputs to the production system: warehousing, transport, stock control.
Operations	Convert resource inputs into a final product. Resource inputs are not only materials. People are a resource especially in service industries.
Outbound logistics	Storing the product and its distribution to customers: packaging, warehousing, testing.
Marketing and sales	Informing customers about the product, persuading them to buy it, and enabling them to do so: advertising, promotion.
After-sales service	Installing products, repairing them, upgrading them, providing spare parts and so forth.

Support activities provide purchased inputs, human resources, technology and infrastructural functions to support the primary activities.

Activity	Comment
Procurement	Acquire the resource inputs to the primary activities (eg purchase of materials, subcomponents equipment).
Technology development	Product design, improving processes and/or resource utilisation.
Human resource management	Recruiting, training, developing and rewarding people.
Management planning	Planning, finance, quality control: Porter believes they are crucially important to an organisation's strategic capability in all primary activities.

Linkages connect the activities of the value chain.

(a) **Activities in the value chain affect one another**. For example, more costly product design or better quality production might reduce the need for after-sales service.

(b) **Linkages require co-ordination**. For example, just-in-time requires smooth functioning of operations, outbound logistics and service activities such as installation.

2.4.3 Value system

Value is also created by the links between one value chain and the next: together, they make up a **value system**.

Activities that add value do not stop at the organisation's **boundaries**. For example, when a restaurant serves a meal, the quality of the ingredients – although they are chosen by the cook – is determined by the grower. The grower has added value, and the grower's success in growing produce of good quality is as important to the customer's ultimate satisfaction as the skills of the chef. A firm's value chain is connected to what Porter calls a **value system**.

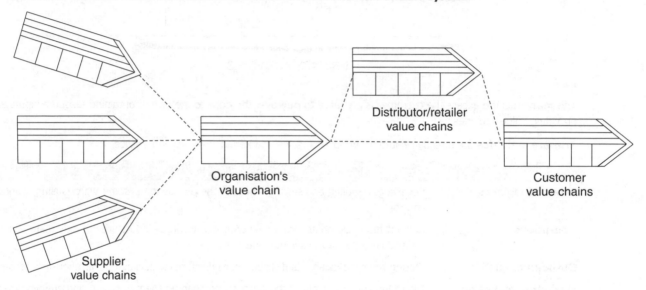

2.4.4 Using the value chain

A firm can secure competitive advantage by:

- Inventing new or better ways to do activities
- Combining activities in new or better ways
- Managing the linkages in its own value chain
- Managing the linkages in the value system

 ACTIVITY 4
application

Sana Sounds is a small record company. Representatives from Sana Sounds scour music clubs for new bands to promote. Once a band has signed a contract (with Sana Sounds) it makes a recording. The recording process is subcontracted to one of a number of recording studio firms which Sana Sounds uses regularly. (At the moment Sana Sounds is not large enough to invest in its own equipment and studios.) Sana Sounds also subcontracts the production of records and CDs to a number of manufacturing companies. Sana Sounds then distributes the disks to selected stores, and engages in any promotional activities required.

What would you say were the activities in Sana Sounds' value chain?

The examples below are based on two supermarket chains, one concentrating on low prices, the other differentiated on quality and service. See if you can tell which is which.

(a)

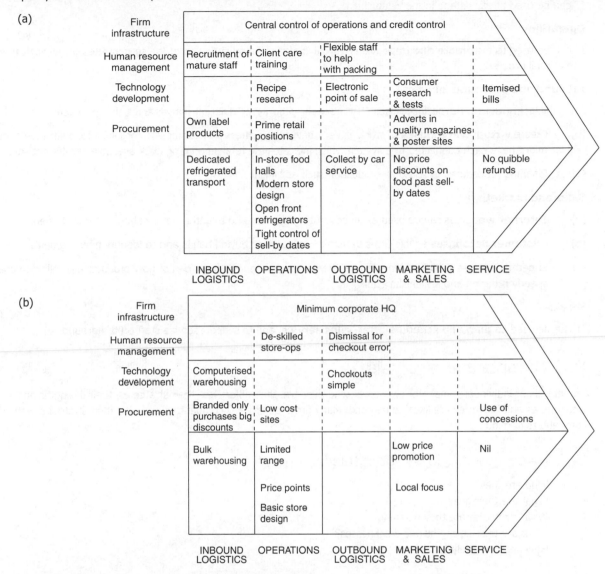

Firm infrastructure	Central control of operations and credit control				
Human resource management	Recruitment of mature staff	Client care training	Flexible staff to help with packing		
Technology development		Recipe research	Electronic point of sale	Consumer research & tests	Itemised bills
Procurement	Own label products	Prime retail positions		Adverts in quality magazines & poster sites	
	Dedicated refrigerated transport	In-store food halls Modern store design Open front refrigerators Tight control of sell-by dates	Collect by car service	No price discounts on food past sell-by dates	No quibble refunds
	INBOUND LOGISTICS	OPERATIONS	OUTBOUND LOGISTICS	MARKETING & SALES	SERVICE

(b)

Firm infrastructure	Minimum corporate HQ				
Human resource management		De-skilled store-ops	Dismissal for checkout error		
Technology development	Computerised warehousing		Checkouts simple		
Procurement	Branded only purchases big discounts	Low cost sites			Use of concessions
	Bulk warehousing	Limited range Price points Basic store design		Low price promotion Local focus	Nil
	INBOUND LOGISTICS	OPERATIONS	OUTBOUND LOGISTICS	MARKETING & SALES	SERVICE

The two supermarkets represented are based on the following.

(a)   The value chain in (a) is based on a firm which seeks to differentiate on quality and service. Hence the 'no quibble' refunds, the use of prime retail sites, and customer care training.

(b)   The value chain in (b) is similar to that of a 'discount' supermarket chain which differentiates on price, pursuing a cost leadership, or perhaps more accurately, a cost-focus strategy. This can be seen in the limited product range and its low-cost sites.

 MARKETING AT WORK   application

Caterpillar is the world's biggest manufacturer of diesel generators. Owing to problems in California's electricity supply market, demand has been growing.

* Technology development: Caterpillar is investing in innovative energy technology such as fuel cells, for the long term.
* Caterpillar is moving into after-sales service, to operate and service generators on-site.

Website address: www.cat.com

2.4.5 IT and the value chain

IT can be used at each stage in the value chain.

Operations

IT can be used to **automate and improve physical tasks** in the operating core. It also **provides information** about operational processes.

Inbound and outbound logistics

(a)   **Warehousing**. **Parcelforce** uses IT to track the progress of different parcels through the system.

(b)   Create **virtual warehouses** of stock actually held at **suppliers**. For example an organisation with several outlets might have each connected to a system which indicates the total amount of stock available at different sites.

(c)   Planning procedures to schedule production such as MRPII.

Sales and marketing

(a)   **Internet websites** can be used as an advertising medium and to gather information about customers.

(b)   **Customer databases** enable firms to monitor consumers' buying habits and to identify new segments.

(c)   Supermarkets use **EPOS** systems to give them a precise hour-by-hour idea of how products are selling to enable speedy ordering and replenishments.

Services

IT can be used **to plan and schedule after-sales service**, and to support service staff on the ground.

2.5 Competitor analysis

An analysis of individual competitors will cover who they are, their objectives, their strategies, their strengths and weaknesses and how they are likely to respond. Many firms identify key competitors and plan their strategies with competitors in mind.

2.5.1 Key questions for competitor analysis

*   Who are they?
*   What are their goals?
*   What strategies are they pursuing?
*   What are their strengths and weaknesses?
*   How are they likely to respond?

 MARKETING AT WORK   application

Southwest Airlines is one of the most profitable in the US, partly because it defined its competition carefully. Most airlines in the US have a 'hub' airport and 'spokes' from it. They compete with each other heavily on matters such as air miles and price. Southwest does not use this arrangement; instead it flies 'point to point' over short distances. It has defined its competitor as the motor car – a substitute product – and has designed its marketing mix so as to minimise the time the customer takes travelling. This has meant flying from smaller, less congested airports and speeded-up check-in times.

2.5.2 Who are our competitors?

Identifying current competitors is easy. Identifying potential competitors is harder as potential competitors might be:

*   Smaller companies attacking the market segment
*   Companies operating in other markets wishing to expand
*   Companies wishing to diversify

Finally, a firm can define who its competitors actually are. Coca-Cola, for example, competes against:

- Pepsi in the Cola market
- All other soft drinks
- Tea and coffee
- Tap water: Coca-Cola's chief executive has declared that 'the main competitor is tap water: any other share definition is too narrow'

2.5.3 What are competitors' goals?

(a) **Relevant goals and objectives**

    (i)   Goals and objectives of the parent company, if the competitor is part of a larger group.

    (ii)   The competitors' assessment of risk; a higher risk will require a higher return from a market.

    (iii)   The personal goals of key managers. For example, a new chief executive may be brought in to 'turn the company round'. The new chief executive may have made a public commitment to one set of goals and may have invested a lot of prestige in achieving these goals.

    (iv)   A company facing cash flow problems may do anything to maximise cash inflow.

    (v)   The competitors' history, position and the underlying assumptions of their management. For example, some firms consider themselves to be 'market leaders'.

    (vi)   How dependent the competitor is on the current business? A competitor with one main business will fight much harder to defend it than a competitor exposed to several sectors.

(b) **Types of goals**

    (i)   Profit
    (ii)   Market share
    (iii)   Cash flow
    (iv)   Technological leadership
    (v)   Service leadership

2.5.4 Competitors' strengths and weaknesses

It is relatively easy to assess a competitor's strengths and weaknesses. Here are some examples:

- Brand strengths, customer loyalty
- Market share
- Quality of management team
- Resources, financial and otherwise
- Intellectual property
- Distribution network
- Relative cost structure
- Distinctive competence

    - Technical assistance
    - Customer awareness
    - Sales staff
    - Product quality and availability

2.5.5 Analysing competitors' costs

Clearly the strategic response of competitors can vary significantly on the cost profile of the competitor. Relative costs are more important than absolute costs: It took Western firms too long to understand that Japanese firms had sustainable cost advantages, and hence were able to compete on price on a sustained basis.

Furthermore, even if the competitor is not competing on price, despite having a lower cost base, the competitor is:

- Under no pressure to raise prices, thus limiting the firm's ability to raise its own
- More profitable, and hence can invest more

2.5.6 Competitor reaction and response

Kotler identifies the following types of competitor response.

(a) **Laid-back**: competitor does not respond
(b) **Selective**: competitor only responds to certain types of attack
(c) **Tiger**: competitor reacts to any attack
(d) **Stochastic**: impossible to predict how competitor will react

ACTIVITY 5 — application

Why might a competitor be **'laid-back'**?

Jot down a list of items of information that might be obtained from an environmental analysis of competitors.

2.5.7 Good competitors

Monopolies are hard to come by, but some competitors are definitely easier to deal with than others. A good competitor makes life easy for its rivals by:

- Deterring new entrants (assuming you are not a new entrant)
- Sharing similar assumptions about the industry
- Preferring differentiation and focus to competing on price

3 Strategic uncertainty

'Strategic uncertainty, that which has strategic implications, is a key construct in external analysis. A typical external analysis will emerge with dozens of strategic uncertainties' Aaker & McLoughlin (2007) p.103

3.1 The effect of strategic uncertainty

According to Aaker & McLoughlin (2007) the overall impact of strategic uncertainty is related to:

- The extent to which it involves trends and events that will impact the business
- The importance of that business
- The number of involved businesses
- The likelihood of a trend or event occurring (ie its **'immediacy'**) – a low probability of occurrence is not necessarily worth acting upon

Categories of strategic uncertainty

Impact \ **Immediacy**	*Low*	*High*
High	Monitor, and consider contingencies	Analyse in detail and develop a strategy
Low	Monitor	Monitor and analyse

3.2 Scenario construction

Because the external environment can be so complex, it is easy to become overwhelmed by the many factors which are at work. Firms, therefore, try to model the future by constructing scenarios to assist them with setting their strategic direction, especially if there is uncertainty, or inherently unpredictable trends at work.

 EXAM TIP   application

Scenario planning is also referred to at 3.1 in the syllabus in the context of 'Making and justifying strategic marketing decisions'.   It can be a way of establishing criteria for the organisation, to be applied when assessing different strategic options, and an attempt to control some of the uncertainty inherent in strategic planning. Scenarios are valuable in that preparing and updating them forces the managers at the strategic apex to look carefully at the business environment, and to monitor developments within it.

There are two types of scenario analysis:

1   **Strategy developing scenarios** – used to evaluate existing strategies and stimulate new ones

2   **Decision driven scenarios** – a strategy is proposed first, then tested against scenarios that are developed

In either case, there are three general steps to be taken.

* Create the scenarios
* Relate them to existing/potential strategies
* Assess their probability

 KEY CONCEPT   concept

A **scenario** is 'an internally consistent view of what the future might turn out to be'.

Scenario analysis accepts that uncertainties are in effect 'certain' to occur, and uses these uncertainties to create descriptions of the future.

3.2.1 Macro scenarios

Macro scenarios use macroeconomic or political factors, creating alternative views of the future environment (taking into account factors such as global economic growth, political changes, interest rates). Macro scenarios developed because the activities of oil and resource companies (which are global and at one time were heavily influenced by political factors) needed techniques to deal with uncertainties.

Steps in scenario planning

Step 1   **Decide on the drivers for change**

* Environmental analysis helps determine key factors
* At least a ten-year time horizon is needed, to avoid simply extrapolating from the present
* Identify and select the important issues and degree of certainty

Step 2   **Bring drivers together into a viable framework**

* This relies almost on an intuitive ability to make patterns out of 'soft' data, so is the hardest
* Items identified can be brought together as mini-scenarios
* There might be many trends, but these can be grouped together

Step 3   **Produce seven to nine mini-scenarios**

Step 4   **Group mini-scenarios into two or three larger scenarios containing all topics**

- This generates most debate and is likely to highlight fundamental issues
- More than three scenarios will confuse people
- The scenarios should be complementary and equally likely
- The scenarios should be tested to ensure they hang together

Step 5   **Write the scenarios**

- The scenarios should be written-up in the form most suitable for managers
- Most scenarios are qualitative rather than quantitative in nature

Step 6   **Identify issues arising**

- Determine the most critical outcomes
- Role play can be used to test what the scenarios mean to key staff involved

3.2.2 Industry scenarios

Porter believes that the most appropriate use for scenario analysis is if it is restricted to an industry. An **industry scenario** is an internally consistent view of an industry's future structure. Different competitive strategies may be appropriate to different scenarios. The entire range, not the most likely 'future', is used to design a competitive strategy.

 MARKETING AT WORK   application

Aaker & McLoughlin (2007) give the example of a publishing company that may be worried about the impact of TV, lifestyle changes, educational trends, population shifts and printing technology – a wide range of uncertainties!

The process for constructing industry scenarios is as follows.

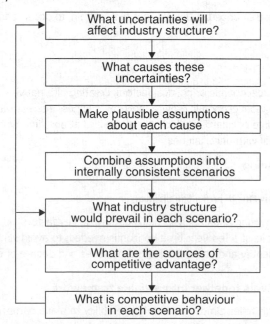

3.2.3 Using scenarios to formulate competitive strategy

(a)   **Assume the most probable**. This choice puts too much faith in the scenario process and guesswork. A less probable scenario may be one which has the worst consequences for the firm.

(b)   **Hope for the best**. A firm designs a strategy based on the scenario most attractive to the firm: wishful thinking.

(c)   **Hedge**. The firm chooses the strategy that produces satisfactory results under all scenarios. Hedging, however, is not optimal. The low risk is paid for by a low reward.

(d)   **Flexibility**. A firm taking this approach plays a 'wait and see' game. It is safer, but sacrifices first mover advantages.

(e)   **Influence**. A firm will try and influence the future, for example, by influencing demand for related products in order that its favoured scenario will be realised in events as they unfold, or even by attempting to influence government and regulatory bodies.

3.3 Market sensing

Some market signals are hard to pick up, even though they may be of long-term significance. Managers thus need to be skilled in market sensing.

 KEY CONCEPT   concept

Market sensing: 'how those ..... inside the company understand and react to the market place and the way it is changing'. It does not relate to the gathering and processing of information (market research) but how the information is interpreted and understood by decision-makers in the company.   (*Piercy*, 2008).

Market sensing does not relate to the gathering and processing of information (market research) but how the information is interpreted and understood by decision-makers in the company.

3.3.1 Process of market sensing

Step 1   Capture information by identifying the environment (eg five forces), the dimension (eg substitute products), the time frame and the market.

Step 2   'Brainstorm' the events in the environment that are currently developing and assess the probability of their occurrence and their likely effect.

Step 3   Categorise the event on the basis of probability and effect.

Utopia: likely, desirable
Dreams: unlikely, desirable
Danger: likely, undesirable
Future risks: unlikely, undesirable
Things to watch: medium likelihood, neutral effect

Probability of event

	High		Low
Utopia			Field of dreams
		Things to watch	
Danger			Future crises

Effect of event

Step 4   Answer the following questions

- Where are we planning for Utopia?
- Where are we planning for dangers?
- Where are we monitoring the factors in the MkIS?

It may be quite possible that managers have not made plans to deal with these eventualities or that the information systems do not report on these key issues.

Step 5   Link conclusions from the sensing approach explicitly to marketing plans.

Step 6   Encourage participation across functions and across levels. (Customer service staff have a very different perspective from the board of directors.)

Step 7   Where necessary, change information provision to provide a richer or more relevant picture of the world, while avoiding:

- Information overload
- Confusion as the existing model appears outdated
- Fear of making any decisions at all
- Creating conflict between groups who may have shared a sense of direction

3.4 Forecasting techniques

Conventionally, forecasting techniques can be used to predict demand in the short- to medium-term. However, such techniques depend on the reliability of past data. The uncertainties in using statistical forecasting to predict the future are considerable.

3.4.1 Types of forecast

KEY CONCEPTS

concept

Forecasting is 'the identification of factors and quantifications of their effect on an entity, as a basis for planning'.

A **projection** is 'an expected future trend pattern obtained by extrapolation. It is principally concerned with quantitative factors whereas a forecast includes judgements'.

Extrapolation is 'the technique of determining a projection by statistical means'.

Statistical forecasts take past data and endeavour to direct it to the future, by assuming that patterns or relationships which held in the past will continue to do so. Many statistical techniques aim to reduce the uncertainty managers face. In simple/static conditions the past is a relatively good guide to the future.

Judgemental forecasts are used principally for the long-term, covering several decades. However, because of the limitations of short-term forecasting they are used for the short-term too. Effectively, they are based on hunches or educated guesses. Sometimes, these prove surprisingly accurate. At other times they are wide of the mark.

3.4.2 Sales potential

Sales potential is an estimate of the part of the market that is within the possible reach of a product.

Factors governing sales potential

- The price of the product
- The amount of money spent on sales promotion
- How essential the product is to consumers
- Whether it is a durable commodity whose purchase is postponable
- The overall size of the possible market
- Competition

Whether sales potential is worth exploiting will depend on the cost which must be incurred to realise the potential.

Estimating market demand

Estimating market demand is not necessarily as straightforward as you might at first think. Imagine you are the marketing manager of a company producing sports footwear. What is your market demand? Is it the volume of shoes purchased in the UK, or Europe, or the whole world? Should you be considering tennis shoes as well as running shoes? Shoes for children or only adults? And should you be forecasting demand for next year or over the next five years? The permutations seem endless.

A demand function is simply an expression which shows how sales demand for a product is dependent on several factors. These demand variables can be grouped into two broad categories.

(a)   Controllable variables or strategic variables. These are factors over which the firm's management should have some degree of control, and which they can change if they wish.

        Controllable variables are essentially the marketing mix.

(b)   Uncontrollable variables. These are factors over which the firm's management has no control.

        (i)   Consumer variables depend on decisions by consumers, or the circumstances of consumers (for example, their wealth).

        (ii)   Competitor variables depend on decisions and actions by other firms, particularly competitors.

        (iii)   Other variables. These include decisions by other organisations (for example the government) or factors which are outside the control of anyone (for example weather conditions, or the total size of the population).

3.4.3 Time series analysis

Time series analysis data can be used to make forecasts as follows.

Step 1   Plot a trend line: use the line of best fit method or the moving averages method.

Step 2   Extrapolate the trend line. This means extending the trend line outside the range of known data and forecasting future results from historical data.

Step 3   Adjust forecast trends by the applicable average seasonal variation to obtain the actual forecast.

3.5 Market attractiveness

In making a decision as to which market(s) to enter the firm must start by establishing its objectives. Here are some examples.

(a)   What **proportion of total sales** will be in these markets?

(b)   What are the **longer-term objectives**?

(c)   Will it enter one, a few, or many markets? In most cases it is better to start by selling in markets with which there is some familiarity, and then expand into others gradually, as experience is gained. Reasons to **enter fewer markets at first** include the following.

   (i)   Market entry and market control costs are high
   (ii)   Product and market communications modification costs are high
   (iii)   There is a large market and potential growth in the initial markets chosen
   (iv)   Dominant competitors can establish high barriers to entry

(d)   What **types of market** should it enter (in terms of environmental factors, economic development, language used and cultural similarities)? Three major decision criteria are as follows.

   (i)   Market attractiveness
   (ii)   Competitive advantage
   (iii)   Risk

The matrix which follows can be used to bring together these three major criteria and assist managers in their decisions.

(a)   **Market attractiveness**. This concerns such indicators as GNP/head and forecast demand, and market accessibility.

(b)   **Competitive advantage**. This is principally dependent on prior experience in similar markets, language and cultural understanding.

(c)   **Risk**. This involves an analysis of political stability, the possibility of government intervention and similar external influences.

The best markets to enter are those located at the top left of the diagram. The worst are those in the bottom right corner. Obtaining the information needed to reach this decision requires detailed and often costly marketing research and analysis. Making these decisions is not easy, and a fairly elaborate screening process will be instituted.

Evaluating which markets to enter

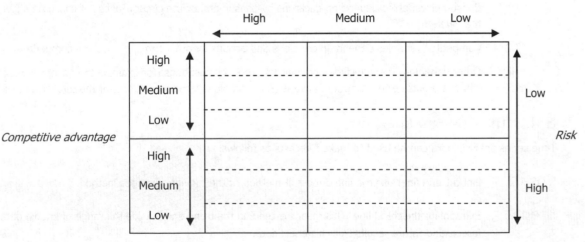

Source: Kotler

Learning objectives	Covered
1 Utilise a range of techniques, processes and market information to assess the external marketing environment	☑ Market structures and the competitive environment (1.1)
	☑ Customers (1.2)
	☑ Channels (1.3)
2 Utilise market-based information to critically evaluate an organisation's strategic position within the market place, including consideration of specific positioning issues	☑ Competitive advantage (2.1)
	☑ Competitive positioning and target markets (2.2)
	☑ Positioning (2.3)
	☑ Value creation (2.4)
	☑ Competitor analysis (2.5)
3 Assess the potential for strategic uncertainty in the external market and the extent to which it involves trends or events, and show how it will impact upon an organisation	☑ The effect of strategic uncertainty (3.1)
	☑ Scenario construction (3.2)
	☑ Market sensing (3.3)
	☑ Forecasting techniques (3.4)
	☑ Market attractiveness (3.5)
4 Critically assess strategic alternatives against pre-determined criteria for an organisation	☑ The techniques examined in section 3 present ways of establishing criteria that can be applied when assessing different strategic options, and overcoming strategic uncertainties. This chapter demonstrates the importance of a full understanding of developments in the business environment.

1 Give a definition of 'market'

2 What are the five competitive forces?

3 What are the elements of the Howard-Sheth model of buyer behaviour?

4 What is 'indirect' distribution?

5 List the characteristics of a strong strategic position

6 What is competitive advantage?

7 What are the features of mass customisation?

8 Define 'repositioning'?

9 What is 'margin'?

10 When undertaking competitor analysis, what are some of the key questions to be asked?

11 What is a 'stochastic' competitor response?

12 How should a firm respond to an uncertainty that is of high immediacy and of high impact?

13 Give the two types of scenario analysis

14 What is 'market sensing'?

15 What criteria are brought together when considering market attractiveness?

1   Behavioural determinants. Eleanor and her husband work in service industries. They are used to the concept of investing (even if unsuccessfully), and have financial interests to protect. The family is perhaps slightly unusual in that the female is the breadwinner, and her husband's income is unlikely to be large.

Inputs. Only one product is detailed. As a financial journalist, Eleanor's husband might know of more. He is likely to be interested in the small print, rather than images and feelings.

Inhibitors. If Eleanor feels she is likely to be made redundant within the next six months, she is unlikely to take out the policy as it would not be of much use to her.

Perceptual reaction. Having lost £15,000 in a previous investment, Eleanor and her husband are possibly very risk averse. They will be sensitive to information regarding the status and reputation of the service provider.

Processing determinants. There is a perceived risk that Eleanor will be made redundant, and she is looking for a product which will reduce the financial impact.

Outputs. They will want a benefit which will cover at least the mortgage and regular bills.

2   **Attributes**: Ads for PCs emphasise 'speed', what sort of chip they have.

Benefit: Holidays are advertised as offering relaxation or excitement.

Use/application: 'Easy to use' products (eg hair tints that can be 'washed' in)

User: Reflect user characteristics, to appeal to the target audience and confirm their choice. May use celebrity endorsement, such as David Beckham in Vodafone advertisements.

Product category: The Natural History Museum is fundamentally educational, but is moving towards a 'theme park' image for the schools market.

Quality/price: 'Value for money' advertisements.

3   Here are some ideas:

(a)   It can become more efficient, by automating the production of food, as in a fast food chain.

(b)   The chef can develop commercial relationships with growers, so he or she can obtain the best quality fresh produce.

(c)   The chef can specialise in a particular type of cuisine (eg Nepalese, Korean).

(d)   The restaurant can be sumptuously decorated for those customers who value atmosphere and a sense of occasion, in addition to a restaurant's purely gastronomic pleasures.

(e)   The restaurant can serve a particular type of customer (eg celebrities).

Each of these options is a way of organising the activities of buying, cooking and serving food in a way that customers or chosen customers will value.

4   Sana Sounds is involved in the record industry from start to finish. Although recording and CD manufacture are contracted out to external suppliers, this makes no difference to the fact that these activities are part of Sana Sounds' own value chain. Sana Sounds earns its money by managing the whole set of activities. If the company grows then perhaps it will acquire its own recording studios. A value chain of activities is not the same as an organisation's business functions.

5   A 'laid back' competitor may be:

- Unable to respond: lack of capability
- Unwilling to respond owing to differing assumptions about the segment
- Unconcerned about the threat, which it does not take seriously

In this example, it would not be worth spending an extra £5,000 on selling in order to realise an extra sales potential of £10,000, because the net effect would be a loss of £ (5,000 – 4,000) = £1,000.

1   A group of actual and potential customers, who can make purchase decisions.

2   (a)   The threat of new entrants to the industry
     (b)   The threat of substitute products or services
     (c)   The bargaining power of customers
     (d)   The bargaining power of suppliers
     (e)   The rivalry among current competitors in the industry

3   Inputs
     Behavioural determinants
     Perceptual reaction
     Processing determinants
     Inhibitors
     Outputs

4   A system of distribution which makes use of intermediaries; wholesalers, retailers or perhaps both. They rely on consumers to make the first approach by entering the relevant retail outlet.

5   A strong strategic position will be strategic, clearly defined and resonant with customers

6   A business achieves competitive advantage when it earns higher than average profits. Whatever overall objective is set for a firm: to survive, to create value, to make profit; the key to achieving it lies in the attainment of some form of competitive advantage

7   Economies of scale via mass production
     The tailoring of products precisely to the customer's requirements

8   A competitive strategy aimed at changing position in order to increase market share.

9   The margin is the excess the customer is prepared to pay over the cost to the firm of obtaining resource inputs and providing value activities.

10   Who are they?
     What are their goals?
     What strategies are they pursuing?
     What are their strengths and weaknesses?
     How are they likely to respond?

11   With a stochastic response, it is impossible to predict how the competitor will react

12   The situation should be analysed in detail, and a response developed

13   Strategy developing scenarios – used to evaluate existing strategies and stimulate new ones.
     Decision driven scenarios – a strategy is proposed first, then tested against scenarios that are developed.

14   Market sensing has been defined as 'how those ..... inside the company understand and react to the market place and the way it is changing'. It relates to how market information is interpreted and understood by decision-makers in the company.

15   Market attractiveness
     Competitive advantage
     Risk

Aaker, D. & McLoughlin, D. (2007) Strategic Market Management, John Wiley, Chichester.

Blythe, J. (2006), Principles and Practice of Marketing, Thomson Learning, London.

Blythe, J. (2005), Essentials of Marketing, (3rd edition), FT Prentice Hall, London.

Brassington, F & Pettitt, S, (2003), *Principles of Marketing*, (3rd edition), FT Prentice Hall, London.

Dibb, S. & Simkin, L. (2008) Marketing Planning, Cengage Learning, London.

Drummond, G. Ensor, J. & Ashford, R. (2008) Strategic Marketing Planning and Control, (3rd edition), Elsevier Ltd, Oxford.

Howard, J.A & Sheth, N.J. (1969) Theory of Buyer Behaviour, John Wiley and Sons, London.

Kotler, P. (2001), Principles of Marketing, FT Prentice Hall, London.

Kotler, P. & Armstrong, G. (2003), Principles of Marketing, 10th edition, Prentice Hall, New Jersey.

Piercy, N.F (2008) Market-Led Strategic Change – Transforming the Process of Going to Market, 4th edition, Butterworth-Heinemann, Oxford.

Porter, M.E. (1980), Competitive Strategy, Free Press, New York.

Porter, M.E (2004) Competitive Advantage, new edition, Free Press, New York.

Porter, M.E (2008) On Competition, (2nd edition), Harvard Business School Press, Boston.

Roberts, D. *'GM bankruptcy is a good thing'*, Guardian.co.uk, 1 June 2009, [accessed 18 June 2009].

Chapter 2
Understanding the customer base

Topic list

Introduction

Organisations with a large customer base, a wide range of products, a global market, and several discrete product/brand names may be tempted to treat customers as if they were all alike, all wanting much the same things, all applying similar criteria when judging the product, the service, or the organisation as a whole.

In practice, this is bound to be a misleading assumption. Customer A may want reliability of delivery on an hourly basis; Customer B may want an unusual range of financial options; Customer C may want the highest possible standards of after-sales support; Customer D is only interested in one product.

Research shows that there are differences in customers' expectations which can be exploited, if they are identified and recorded, by offering levels of service which match the needs of particular sectors, possibly withdrawing from some or increasing prices/charges to an economically-justified level.

Understanding the customer base is a critical part of the detailed assessment of an organisation and its performance, and the issues and challenges of providing value to these customers.

This chapter examines the range of tools that can be used to understand customers and their buying behaviour.

- Value proposition
- Segmental analysis
- Value creation
- Competitor analysis

Syllabus-linked learning objective

By the end of the chapter you will be able to:

Learning objective	Syllabus link
1 Utilise a range of tools to critically evaluate an organisation's ability to understand its current customer base and their buying behaviour, in order to be able to develop customer insight and meet their preferences	1.1.3

1   The value proposition

"A customer value proposition is the perceived functional, emotional, social, or self expressive benefit that is provided by the organisation's offering. One or more value propositions need to be relevant and meaningful to the customer, and reflected in the positioning of the product or service. To support a successful strategy, the propositions should be sustainable over time and differentiate the offering from its competition." Aaker & McLoughlin (2007) p.7

1.1 What is it?

KEY CONCEPT

concept

The **value proposition** has been defined as 'an offering's performance and price promise to potential buyers.' (www.cval.com), or alternatively:

'the sum total of benefits which a vendor promises that a customer will receive in return for the customer's associated payment (or other value-transfer)' (www.wikipedia.org)

The value proposition is therefore 'what the customer gets for his money'.

A customer can evaluate a company's value proposition on two levels:

(a)   **Relative performance**: what the customer gets, relative to what he or she would get from a competitor

(b)   **Price**: payments made to acquire the product or service

The company's marketing and sales efforts offer the value proposition, and its delivery and customer-service processes then fulfill it.

The term 'value proposition' is often used interchangeably with **differentiation**. It is one of the factors to consider when determining a marketing strategy. Marketing strategists can check how their value proposition works in the perception of customers, uslng market research for example.

A value proposition can assist in a firm's marketing strategy, and may guide a business to target a particular market segment. For example: "Firm Any Co. can provide benefits a, b, and c because of competences x, y, and z."

 ## MARKETING AT WORK   application

A company may have defined its value proposition as increasing its market share and growing revenue by:

- Superior customer service
- Product differentiation
- Operational efficiency

Aaker & McLoughlin (2007) give the example of Tod's, an Italian luxury shoe manufacturer that is defying the competition from low cost Chinese manufacturers with its emphasis on, and heavy investment in, high quality and innovation. Profits grew from 60 million to 90 million euros between 2001 and 2005. Presumably the Tod's brand conveys social, emotional and self expressive benefits for its customers, as well as purely functional ones.

1.2 The value proposition and competitive advantage

An effective sustainable competitive advantage such as product reliability should enhance the value proposition.

A lot of the benefit from delivering the value proposition is derived from perception. Business reputation for delivering on quality, price (or whatever the value proposition is) is strategically extremely important, as it can give the company valuable breathing space in the event of faltering actual performance, and is hard for competitors to break in to.

Conversely, a solid value proposition may not hold up in the wake of changing perceptions or tastes.

 ## MARKETING AT WORK   application

Consumer trust in retail financial services has been severely shaken in the current economic downturn. Many have seen their assets slashed, and are likely to remain cautious even when the recovery arrives.

Opportunities will emerge for innovative companies. Charles Schwub founded his hugely successful brokerage in the wake of the recession of the early 1970's, introducing a new value proposition that resonated with consumers. The current recession has induced a 'deficit of trust', and it is likely that new value propositions will emerge from it in a similar way.

FT.com Special Reports, 5 February 2009

2 Segmental analysis

"In a strategic context, segmentation means the identification of customer groups that respond differently from other groups to competitive offerings." Aaker & McLoughlin (2007) p.42

Different segments and different customers offer different levels of profit. As you know, one of the most important tools for market analysis is that of **segmentation**.

A company can approach this first by examining what market segments it currently markets in, and how big a contribution each segment is making to total turnover and profit. Finally, it should consider whether each market segment is in growth or decline.

A segmental analysis might look like this.

Market segment	Turnover £k	Proportion of total turnover %	Profit £k	Proportion of total profit %
A	500	14	50	9
B	1,000	29	200	36
C	1,500	43	150	27
D	500	14	150	27
	3,500		550	

Market segment	Turnover £k	Profit £k	Profit as a % of turnover %
A	500	50	10
B	1,000	200	20
C	1,500	150	10
D	500	150	30
	3,500	550	

You will note that each segment offers different profit opportunities.

2.1 Evaluating market segments

When evaluating market segments it is necessary to review two issues.

1   **Market attractiveness**, based upon

- Segment size
- Segment's rate of growth
- Segment's profitability
- Customer price sensitivity
- Stage of industry life cycle
- Predictability
- Demand patterns
- Potential for substitutes
- Five forces analysis
- PEST factors

2   **Ability to address segment needs**

Organisational capability is made up of specific assets and competencies.

 KEY CONCEPT   concept

Assets are organisational attributes, tangible or intangible, that can be utilised to gain advantages in the market.

2.2 How to calculate profits on a segmental basis

Identifying total turnover is easy. A segment is a collection of customers, and revenue streams from them are fairly easy to identify. Identifying costs is much harder. Here are some different types of cost.

(a) **Fixed or variable**

    (i)   **Fixed costs** will be incurred however many or however few items are produced or sold. Factory rent is an example. These are also called overheads.

    (ii)   **Variable costs** relate directly to the number of units produced. For example, a variable cost item in producing books is paper. These are also called direct costs.

(b) **Controllable or uncontrollable**

    (i)   **Controllable costs** are incurred at management discretion, such as an advertising campaign.

    (ii)   **Uncontrollable costs** are those which, in the short-run at least, management are committed to.

(c) **Avoidable or unavoidable**

    (i)   **Avoidable cost:** this cost is affected by a decision.

    (ii)   **Unavoidable cost:** this cost will not be affected by a decision.

For example, the cost of the managing director's salary will not be affected by a decision not to serve an individual customer.

Typical marketing costs

Cost	Comment
Direct selling expenses	Personal calls by salesperson
Indirect selling	Sales admin, supervision
Marketing research	Consultancies, primary data collection, analysis
Advertising	Media costs
Sales promotion	Consumer, trade etc
Transport	Carriage costs
Storage	Warehousing
Order processing	Checking, billing, bad debts

These can be allocated, in different ways, to products, customer groups, and sales territories. We are currently interested in segments. The steps involved in segmental analysis are as follows.

Step 1   Identify revenue derived from a segment

Step 2   Identify direct product costs (eg materials)

Step 3   Identify marketing costs

Step 4   Allocate avoidable costs to the segment (ie those costs which would be saved if the segment were not serviced)

3 Strategic account analysis

"With the creation of a database, marketers segment customers based upon customer profitability and other bases appropriate to their business. Thus marketers can match customers with appropriate levels of investment, with the most profitable customers in the future receiving one set of communications and other groups such as low profit and dormant customers receiving communications appropriate to their status." Aaker & McLoughlin (2007) p.200

3.1 What is a strategic account?

No doubt you are already aware that it is far more expensive to attract a new customer than to do business with an established one. There are several reasons for this.

(a)   Established customers do not qualify for inducements such as introductory offers and discounts.

(b)   There are communications and other marketing costs associated with obtaining new business.

There are other benefits to retaining satisfied customers.

(a)   Established customers do not require as much customer service assistance as new ones.

(b)   Established customers are more likely to generate new business through referrals.

(c)   Established customers tend to purchase more as their relationship with the brand or supplier lengthens.

These advantages mean that customer retention is an important factor in successful trading. Marketers need to be able to monitor such matters as the amount of business that comes from new customers, the number of referrals and the proportion of business that comes from established customers. Of those established customers, some will be defined as 'strategic accounts'.

 KEY CONCEPT   concept

A **key (strategic) account** is a customer in a B2B market identified by the selling company as being of strategic importance. It often displays the following characteristics (Blythe, 2006):

*   It accounts for a significant proportion of sales
*   There is co-operation between channel members rather than conflict
*   There are lengthy negotiations and frequent contact
*   There are often servicing aspects, as well as delivery of physical products

Many firms – especially in business-to-business markets – sell to a relatively small number of customers. Not all customers are as important as others, and the checklist below can help to identify the most important.

Strategic importance evaluation guide	High	Medium	Low
Fit between customer's needs and our capabilities, at present and potentially			
Ability to serve customer compared with our major competitors, at present and potentially			
'Health' of customer's industry, current and forecast			
'Health' of the customer, current and forecast			

Strategic importance evaluation guide	High	Medium	Low
Customer's growth prospects, current and forecast			
What can we learn from this customer?			
Can the customer help us to attract others?			
Relative significance: how important is the customer compared with other customers?			
What is the profitability of serving the customer?			

ACTIVITY 1

application

A firm might wish to identify which customer offer the most profit opportunity. Strategic account analysis calls for six main areas of investigation into customers, as listed below:

- Key customer identity
- Customer history
- Relationship of customer to product
- Relationship of customer to market
- Customer attitudes and behaviour
- Financial performance of the customer

Can you suggest specific topics of investigation under each of these headings?

3.2 Customer profitability

KEY CONCEPT

concept

Customer profitability analysis is an analysis of the total sales revenue generated from a customer or customer group, less all the costs that are incurred in servicing that customer group.

An understanding of the different profitability levels that exist within the customer base enables the company to concentrate its efforts on the customers most deserving of them.

MARKETING AT WORK

application

The Post Office is a good example to illustrate how profitability might work. A uniform price is paid for a first class stamp to send a letter irrespective of whether it is to be delivered to an address five miles away or five hundred (in the UK), despite the significant differences in transport costs. Of course, the advantages of a uniform price are that there are savings on the costs of administering a wide range of prices, and that people are encouraged to use the postal services.

It is possible to analyse customer profitability over a single period but more useful to look at a longer time frame. Such a multi-period approach fits in with the concept of **relationship marketing**, with its emphasis upon customer retention for the longer-term.

 ACTIVITY 2

application

Seth Ltd supplies shoes to Narayan Ltd and Kipling Ltd. Each pair of shoes has a list price of £50 each; as Kipling buys in bulk, Kipling receives a 10% trade discount for every order over 100 shoes. It costs £1,000 to deliver each order. In the year so far, Kipling has made five orders of 100 pairs of shoes each. Narayan Ltd receives a 15% discount irrespective of order size, because Narayan Ltd collects the shoes, thereby saving Seth Ltd any distribution costs. The cost of administering each order is £50. Narayan makes ten orders in the year, totalling 420 pairs of shoes. Which relationship is most profitable for Seth?

Customer profitability analysis (CPA) focuses upon profits generated by customers and suggests that profit does not automatically increase with sales revenue. CPA can benefit a company in the following ways:

- It enables a company to focus resources on the most profitable areas
- It identifies unexpected differences in profitability between customers
- It helps to quantify the financial impact of proposed changes
- It helps to highlight the cost of obtaining new customers and the benefit of retaining existing ones
- It helps to highlight whether product development or market development is to be preferred
- An appreciation of the costs of servicing clients assists in negotiations with customers

3.3 Cost allocation

It is necessary to focus on the right costs for comparison.

(a)   Costs common to all customers (eg sales director's basic salary) would not be avoided by failing to serve one of them.

(b)   Furthermore, you have to be careful that you choose the 'right' product cost. The 'cost' of a product as revealed by the accounting system might include an amount of marketing overhead, which may not be avoided by ceasing to serve a customer. Therefore only avoidable costs should be taken into account.

The following is a suggested format for a statement of customer or segment profitability. It could be applied equally in a B2B or B2C context.

			£'000
Sales revenue			X
Less direct product cost			(X)
			X
Customer or segment-specific variable costs	– distribution	X	
	– rebates and discounts	X	
	– promotion etc	X	
			(X)
Other costs	– sales force	X	
	– customer service	X	
	– management cost	X	
			(X)
			X
Financing cost	– credit period	X	
	– customer-specific inventory	X	
			(X)
Customer or segment profitability			X

Such a report can highlight the differences between the cost of servicing different individuals or firms. This information can be used for the following purposes.

(a)   Directing management effort to cutting customer or segment specific costs. Installing an EDI system can save the costs of paperwork, data input and so forth.

(b)   Identifying those customers who are expensive to service, thereby suggesting action to increase profitability.

(c)   Using this as part of a comparison with competitors' costs. A firm which services a customer more cheaply than a competitor can use this cost advantage to offer extra benefits to the customer.

(d)   CPA can indicate cases where profitability might be endangered, for example by servicing customers for whom a firm's core competence is not especially relevant.

CPA might provide answers to the following questions:

*   What **profit/contribution** is the organisation making on sales to the customer, after discounts and selling and delivery costs?

*   What would be the **financial consequences** of losing the customer?

*   Is the customer buying in order sizes that are **unprofitable** to supply?

*   What is the **return on investment** on the plant used?

*   What is the level of **inventory** required to supply these customers?

*   Are there any **specific costs** involved in supplying this customer, eg technical and test facilities, R&D facilities, special design staff?

*   What is the **ratio** of net contribution per customer to total investment?

3.4 The customer lifecycle

It has already been mentioned that, in line with the principles of relationship marketing, it is probably appropriate to think in terms of customer revenues and costs over more than one period. We can refine our financial analysis by working in terms of the present value of customer costs and revenues, and by incorporating the concept of the **customer life cycle**. This is less developed than the equivalent product and industry life-cycle models, but it can be useful to consider the following matters.

(a)   **Promotional expense** relating to a single customer is likely to be heavily front loaded.

(b)   It is likely that **sales** to a customer will start at a low level and increase to a higher level as the customer gains confidence, though this is not certain and will vary from industry to industry.

(c)   A customer who purchases a basic or commodity product initially may move on to **more differentiated products** later.

(d)   In consumer markets, career progression is likely to provide the individual customer with steadily increasing amounts of **disposable income**, with the family life cycle dictating the likely range of purchases as time passes.

4   Consumer profiling

Building **accurate and up-to-date profiles** of customers enables a company to:

*   Extend **help** to a company's target audience
*   **Stimulate further demand**
*   **Stay close** to them

Keeping an electronic database of customers and prospects (and of all communications and commercial contacts) helps to improve all future contacts.

4.1 Customer intelligence – why is it so important?

For years the rhetoric of marketing has been that of **warfare**: targets, campaigns, offensives. The approach has been one of trying to beat the 'enemy' into submission and 'win' new customers. Many organisations now realise that there is more to be gained from alternative strategies.

(a)   Investing in activities which seek to **retain existing customers**, based on the argument that it costs more to attract new customers

(b)   Encouraging existing customers to **spend more**

Retaining customers is the basis of such relationship marketing techniques. Customers are seen not only in terms of what they are buying today, but also in terms of their **potential for future purchases**.

Although it is clear that **added services** and **quality of service** are the key to retaining customers, this still begs questions: precisely what services to add, for instance?

To be effective at **retention marketing**, the organisation has to have a good database **profiling past, present and prospective customers**, with details of the nature of the relationship; it has to know about their attitudes, their perceptions of the organisation's products and service, and their expectations. Just as importantly, the organisation must know, from systematically-acquired **customer feedback**, precisely what it is doing wrong.

A well-developed customer database will use **postcodes** to overlay specialist **geodemographic data** from **ACORN** or other source , or include **lifestyle information** allowing detailed customer profiles to be developed.

  application

You can use ACORN yourself for free when you use the website www.upmystreet.co.uk This site uses geodemographic profiling from ACORN to give a neighbourhood profile. You can enter your postcode (or one where you are familiar with the area) and then go to 'read neighbourhood profile'. You may be initially shown a short version but click on 'real full profile'. The type of information you will find included will be:

* Education levels
* Social activities
* The type of TV watched and newspapers and magazines read
* Typical family composition
* Level of interest in current affairs and social issues
* Types of shops visited

  application

It is worth empahsising that this unit is about *strategy*, rather than the design of tactical marketing programmes. Understanding customer is a huge contributor to that stretegy. The list below, covers some of the issues:

* Customers: does the firm take customers seriously and work for customer satisfaction? How do you create a customer-focused organisation?

* How are markets defined and segmented around issues that matter to customers?

* How do we create a value proposition based on our mission and our ability to differentiate from competitors?

Learning objective	Covered
1 Utilise a range of tools to critically evaluate an organisation's ability to understand its current customer base and their buying behavior, in order to be able to develop customer insight and meet their preferences	☑ The value proposition (section 1)
	☑ Segmental analysis (section 2)
	☑ What is a strategic account? (3.1)
	☑ Customer profitability (3.2)
	☑ Cost allocation (3.3)
	☑ The customer lifecycle (3.4)
	☑ Consumer profiling (section 4)

1   Define 'value proposition'

2   How does the customer evaluate a company's value proposition?

3   Give an example of a value proposition

4   What is segmentation?

5   What are two issues to consider when evaluating market segments?

6   Give an example of a fixed cost, and explain why it is regarded as such

7   Present two organisational benefits from retaining satisfied customers

8   What is customer profitability analysis?

9   Why might a company want to build profiles of its customers?

10 "Customers are seen not only in terms of what they are buying ...., but also in terms of their .... purchases" (Fill in the blanks)

1

Area	Detail
Key customer identity	Name of each key customer
	Location
	Status in market
	Products they make and sell
	Size of firm (revenue, number of employees, capital employed)
Customer history	First purchase date
	Who makes the buying decision in the organisation?
	What is the average order size, by product?
	What is the regularity of the order, by product?
	What is the trend in the size of orders?
	What is the motive in purchasing?
	What does the customer know about the firm's and competitors' products?
	On what basis does the customer re-order?
	How is the useful life of the product judged?
	Were there any lost or cancelled orders? For what reason?
Relationship of customer to product	What does the customer use the product for?
	Do the products form part of the customer's own service/product?
Relationship of customer to potential market	What is the size of the customer in relation to the total end-market?
	Is the customer likely to expand, or not? Diversify or integrate?
Customer attitudes and behaviour	What interpersonal factors exist which could affect sales by the firm and by competitors?
	Does the customer also buy competitor products?
	To what extent may purchases be postponed?
The financial performance of the customer	How successful is the customer?

2   You can see below that the profit earned by Seth in servicing Narayan is greater, despite the increased discount.

	Kipling	Narayan
Number of shoes	500	420
	£	£
Revenue after discount	22,500	17,850
Transport	(5,000)	
Administration	(250)	(500)
Net profit	17,250	17,350

3   You may be quite surprised by the Acorn profile of your neighbours. Try to think about the reasons behind the profile. Next time you walk around your neighbourhood try to remember the Acorn profile to see if this sheds more light on the situation.

1   The value proposition can be said to be "what the customer gets for his money"

2   Performance, relative to competitors; price

3   Product quality, price, delivery times, product reliability (these are just a few!)

4   The identification of customer groups that respond differently from other groups to competitive offerings

5   Market attractiveness, and the overall ability to address segment needs

6   Rent is a fixed cost, because it remains the same regardless of how many units of a product are produced

7   (a)   Established customers do not require as much customer service assistance as new ones.
    (b)   Established customers are more likely to generate new business through referrals.
    (c)   Established customers tend to purchase more as their relationship with the brand or supplier lengthens.

8   Customer profitability analysis is an analysis of the total sales revenue generated from a customer or customer group, less all the costs that are incurred in servicing that customer group

9   Building accurate and up-to-date profiles of customers enables a company to:

    •   Extend help to a company's target audience
    •   Stimulate further demand
    •   Stay close to them

10 Today; future

References

Aaker, D. & McLoughlin, D. (2007) Strategic Market Management, John Wiley, Chichester.

Blythe, J. (2006), Principles and Practice of Marketing, Thomson Learning, London.

Blythe, J. (2005), Essentials of Marketing, 3rd edition, FT Prentice Hall, London.

Brassington, F & Pettitt, S, (2003), Principles of Marketing, 3rd edition, FT Prentice Hall, London.

Drummond, G. Ensor, J. & Ashford, R. (2008) Strategic Marketing Planning and Control, (3rd edition), Elsevier, Oxford.

Quelch, J.A & Jocz, K.E. 'Keeping a keen eye on consumer behaviour' FT.com Special Reports, 5 February 2009.

Chapter 3

The internal marketing environment

Topic list

1   Products and resources
2   Organisational culture and performance

Introduction

A look at the internal environment of an organisation is a way of identifying strengths and weaknesses. It therefore covers all aspects of the organisation. This is because the other functions of the organisation effectively act as constraints over what marketing personnel can achieve.

A company needs to evaluate its ability to compete and satisfy customer needs. The firm's resources, once identified, must be harnessed to a market orientation to ensure that those resources are directed at satisfying those needs.

There are a number of approaches to be taken with regard to corporate capability. In this chapter we conduct an overview of resources in the context of organisational effectiveness. The key issues are what resources the organisation has and how they are deployed.

An analysis of corporate/marketing resources (section 1) covers three main areas:

1   What the organisation currently has or owns
2   What the organisation has access to, even if it currently does not own the resources
3   How effectively it **deploys** its resources

The culture (section 2) of an organisation is strategically important. Culture is to some extent formed by past strategic success, and influences the development of strategy for the future. An awareness and understanding of the interaction between culture and strategy is therefore an important part of internal strategic assessment.

Syllabus-linked learning objective

By the end of the chapter you will be able to:

Learning objective	Syllabus link
1 Utilise a range of models and techniques to undertake a strategic audit of the internal environment	1.2.1

1   Products and resources

"In addition to external threats and opportunities, strategy development must be based on the objectives, strengths and capabilities of a business." Aaker & McLoughlin (2007) p.111

1.1 Resources and competences

 KEY CONCEPTS

concept

The **resource audit** covers technical resources, financial resources, managerial skills, the organisation and its information system. It is a review of assets of all kinds which are available to the organisation.

Resources are deployed as **competences** which support a competitive position. A distinctive competence is hard to imitate.

(a)   Technical resources

(i)   Technical ability
(ii)   Processes for NPD
(iii)   Ability to convert new technology into new marketing products

(b)   **Financial standing**. Firms with a good financial standing find it easier to raise money.

(c)   **Managerial skills**. An effective management is a key organisation resource in planning activities, controlling the organisation and motivating staff.

(d)   **Organisation**. Organisation structure can be a resource for marketers, for example, product divisionalisation or brand management control at brand level. The organisation structure should facilitate communication and decision-making.

(e)   **Information systems**. Information systems have a strategic role.

Resources are of no value unless they are organised into systems, and so a **resource audit** should go on to consider how well or how badly resources have been utilised, and whether the organisation's systems are **effective** and **efficient** in meeting customer needs profitably.

1.2 Portfolio analysis

KEY CONCEPTS

concept

Portfolio: A collection of products/SBUs reporting to one entity. Each product or SBU can be separately identified for decision-making and performance measurement.

Portfolio analysis compares the marketing and financial performance of a firm's products and/or SBUs with a view to decision-making.

Portfolio planning analyses the current position of an organisation's products or SBUs in their markets, and the state of growth or decline in each of those markets. Several matrices have been developed to analyse market share, market growth and market position.

1.2.1 Market share, market growth and cash generation: the Boston classification

The **BCG matrix**, illustrated below, classifies products (or businesses) in terms of potential cash generation on the basis of their **market share relative to that of their competitors** and the **rate of growth in the market** as a whole. The split on the horizontal axis is based on a market share identical to that of the firm's **nearest competitor**, while the precise location of the split on the vertical axis will depend on the rate of growth in the market.

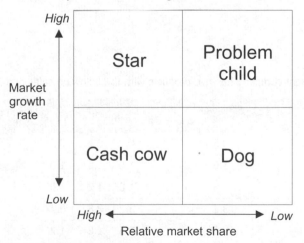

You should note that BCG analysis can also be applied to:

*   Individual products
*   Whole strategic business units (SBUs)

On the basis of this classification, each product (or, working at a higher level, each strategic business unit) will then fall into one of four broad categories.

(a) A **problem child** has a small relative market share in a high growth industry. The generic product is clearly popular, but customer support for the company brand is limited. A small market share implies that competitors are in a strong position and that if the product is to be successful it will **require substantial funds**, and a new marketing mix. If the market looks good and the product is viable, then the company should consider a **build** strategy to increase market share. This would require the commitment of funds to permit more active marketing. If the future looks less promising then the company should consider the possibility of withdrawing the product. The problem child is sometimes referred to as the **question mark**.

(b) A **star** is a product with a high relative market share in a high growth industry. By implication, **the star has potential for generating significant earnings** currently and in the future. However, at this stage it may still require substantial marketing expenditures to maintain this position, but would probably be regarded as a **good investment for the future**.

(c) A **cash cow** has a high relative market share but in a mature slow growth market. Typically, it is a well established product with a high degree of consumer loyalty. Product development costs are low and the marketing campaign is well established. The cash cow will normally make a **substantial contribution to overall profitability**. The appropriate strategy will vary according to its precise position. If market growth is reasonably strong then a **hold** strategy will be appropriate, but if growth or share are weakening, then a **harvest** strategy may be more sensible, cutting back on marketing expenditure and maximise short-term cash flow.

(d) A **dog** is a product characterised by low relative market share and low growth. Also, typically a well established product, it is apparently losing consumer support and may have cost disadvantages. The usual strategy would be to consider **divestment** unless cash flow position is strong, in which case the product would be **harvested** in the short-term prior to deletion from the product range.

Implicit in the matrix is the notion that **markets are dynamic**. The typical new product is likely to appear in the problem child category to begin with; if it looks promising and is given effective marketing, it might be expected to become a star, then, as markets mature, a cash cow and finally a dog. The suggestion that most products will move through these stages does not weaken the role played by marketing. On the contrary, it strengthens it, since poor marketing may mean that a product moves from being a problem child to a dog without making any substantial contribution to profitability. Equally, of course, good marketing may enable the firm to **prolong** the star and cash cow phases, thus maximising **cash flow** from the product.

The framework provided by the matrix can offer guidance in terms of developing **appropriate strategies** for products and in maintaining a **balanced product portfolio**, ensuring that there are enough cash generating products to match the cash-using products.

ACTIVITY 1

evaluation

An industrial equipment company has five products with the following sales and market characteristics.σ

Product	Sales £m	£m sales Top 3 firms			Market growth rate %	Relative share
A	0.5	0.7	0.7	0.5*	15%	0.71
B	1.6	1.6	1.6*	1.0	18%	1.0
C	1.8	1.8*	1.2	1.0	7%	1.5
D	3.2	3.2*	0.8	0.7	4%	4.0
E	0.5	2.5	1.8	1.7	4%	0.2

* Company sales within the market

The circles indicate the contribution the product makes to overall turnover. The centre of circles indicates their position on the matrix:

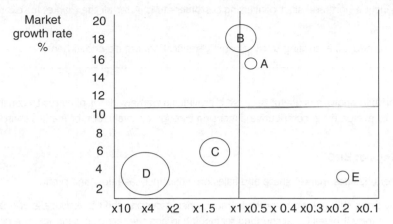

What can you deduce about the company's product portfolio from this diagram?

MARKETING AT WORK

Google

Until recently, the weight of investor opinion held that Google's only significant business – delivery of context-specific online advertising – was a star and was positioned to remain one for many years to come.

The Internet has so far attracted only about $US10 billion of the $US250 billion spent worldwide on advertising each year, and Google has proved its ability to translate its dominant position in the online ad market into a river of cash.

But context-specific online ad placement may not quite be the business that Google's more fervent admirers believe it to be.

In fact, it may be already well on the way to becoming a cash cow (for Google at least, given its already dominant share) rather than a star.

Future revenue growth for Google's core business is likely to be organic, that is, to come from higher traffic, higher online advertising spending or increased market share.

Stephen Ellis, *The Australian,* 4 March 2006

In early 2009, Google reported increased revenues in fourth quarter 2008 financial results, but reduced profits after taking strategic stakes in Clearwire and AOL. Total revenue was $5.7bn, which represents an 18% increase over the same period in 2007 and a 3% increase on the **third quarter of 2008**.

"Google performed well in the fourth quarter, despite an increasingly difficult economic environment," said Google chief executive Eric Schmidt.

He said it was unclear how long the downturn would last, but Google's focus would remain on the long term. "We will continue to invest in the core search and **ads business**, as well as strategic growth areas such as display, mobile and enterprise," Schmidt said.

ACTIVITY 2

The marketing manager of Juicy Drinks Ltd has invited you in for a chat. Juicy Drinks Ltd provides fruit juices to a number of supermarket chains, which sell them under their own label. 'We've got a large number of products, of course. Our freshly squeezed orange juice is doing fine – it sells in huge quantities. Although margins are low, we have sufficient economies of scale to do very nicely in this market. We've got advanced production and bottling equipment and long-term contracts with some major growers. No problems there. We also sell freshly squeezed pomegranate juice: customers loved it in the tests, but producing the stuff at the right price is a major hassle: all the seeds get in the way. We hope it will be a winner, once we get the production right and start converting customers to it. After all the market for exotic fruit juices generally is expanding fast.

What sort of products, according to the Boston classification, are described here?

The BCG portfolio analysis is useful because it provides a framework for planners to consider and forecast potential market growth and to evaluate the competitive dimension through an evaluation of market share and the likely changes in cash flow.

Shortcomings of BCG

(a)   Factors besides market share and sales growth affect cash flow and profit.

(b)   Many firms still use return on investment when assessing the attractiveness of a business opportunity, despite the opportunity it gives for accounting manipulation and the fact that it ignores the time value of money.

(c)   The model provides no real insight into how to compare one opportunity with another when considering which opportunity should be allocated investment resources, eg how does a star in one segment compare with a question mark in another?

(d)   As we have seen, in the right conditions a firm can profit from a low share of a low-growth market.

(e)   The techniques do not tell you how to generate new businesses.

(f)   Defining the market or segment is difficult.

(g)   Market share appears to be a significant advantage in high technology industries, where the learning effect is most apparent, but may bring diseconomies of scale in service industries.

1.2.2 Competitiveness of products

The **GE Business Screen** is a more complex analytical model using similar but more complex criteria: market attractiveness and business strength. It examines a company's competences in market sectors, without reference to individual products.

(a)   **Determinants of industry/market attractiveness**

    (i)   Market factors (eg size, growth)
    (ii)   Competitors
    (iii)   Investment factors
    (iv)   Price elasticity
    (v)   Technological change
    (vi)   Other PEST factors
    (vii)   Growth rate
    (viii) Bargaining power of buyers

(b)   **Determinants of business strength**

    (i)   Product quality and range
    (ii)   Distribution
    (iii)   Brand reputation
    (iv)   Proprietary technology
    (v)   Production capacity
    (vi)   Management skill
    (vii)   Market share
    (viii) Perceived differentiation

These factors can then be scored and weighted. For example, a market with a low size and intense competition based on price might receive a lower weighting than a market with high growth and limited competition.

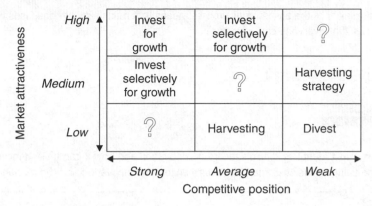

Each 'cell' requires a different management approach.

(a)   Each SBU can be plotted in one of the cells and the appropriate management approach adopted.

(b)   It is possible that SBUs might move around the matrix. Changes in PEST (political, economic, social, technological) factors may change an industry/market's attractiveness.

(c)   The matrix ignores the possibility of **knowledge generation** and **competence** sharing between SBUs.

Applications in one SBU may be of value elsewhere.

1.2.3 Shell Directional Policy Matrix

Another example is the **Shell Directional Policy Matrix**, which is based on prospects for sector profitability and the enterprise's competitive capabilities.

Prospects for sector profitability

	Unattractive	Average	Attractive
Weak	Disinvest	Phased withdrawal	Double or quit
Average	Phased withdrawal	Custodial Growth	Try harder
Strong	Cash generation	Growth Leader	Leader

(Enterprise's competitive capabilities)

1.2.4 The advantages and disadvantages of portfolio planning

Portfolio planning provides an excellent framework for analysis, and a starting point for developing a product-market mix strategy.

Drawbacks

(a)   Portfolio models are simple: they do not reflect the uncertainties of decision-making.

(b)   BCG analysis, in particular, does not take risk into account.

(c)   They ignore opportunities for creative segmentation or identifying new niches.

(d)   They assume a market is given rather than something that can be created and nurtured. After all, markets may be unattractive because customer needs have not been analysed sufficiently.

(e)   A lot of complicated analysis is needed to come up with relevant data. How do you decide whether an industry is attractive or not?

(f)   The complexity of the assessment process means that management consensus will tend to focus upon medium categories that everyone can agree on.

1.3 Innovation audit

 KEY CONCEPT

concept

An **innovation audit** identifies a firm's record of innovation and how it can be enhanced. It covers the organisation climate and culture, the value to the customer, policies to encourage innovation and the management team.

The chief object of being innovative is to ensure organisational success in a changing world. It can also have the following advantages.

(a)   Improvements in quality of **products** and **service**

(b)   A **leaner structure** – layers of management or administration may be removed

(c)   Prompt and imaginative **solutions to problems**

(d)   **Less formality** in structure and style, leading to better communication

(e)   **Greater confidence** inside and outside the organisation in its ability to cope with change. Innovation and new product development (NPD) is essential for many firms to survive and prosper. It is an increasingly important area.

A firm needs to assess how well it is able to deliver the level and type of innovation necessary to continue to meet customer needs and expectations. Drummond & Ensor (1999) identify **four key areas** for the innovation audit.

*   The current organisational climate
*   Measures of the organisation's **current performance** with regard to innovation
*   Review of **policies and practices** supporting innovation and facilitating it
*   The balance of **styles** of the management team

1.3.1 Organisational climate

Barriers to innovation in marketing

(a)   **Resistance to change**: Any new method of management thinking can experience some resistance from established managers. This resistance may be due to concern to protect the *status quo*, or because managers are ignorant of the new thinking. Integrating marketing communications seems so obvious that it may be overlooked or seen as a superficial approach.

(b)   **Old planning systems**: have sometimes downgraded marketing decisions to the tactical level. Advertising expenditure is decided on the basis of what the company can afford rather than what is strategically required. Promotion is seen as a series of short-term actions rather than as a long-term investment.

(c)   **Old structures/functional specialists**: Complementing traditional planning systems are traditional organisation structures. These structures freeze out new thinking on integrated marketing strategy. Individuals have limited specific responsibilities – just for advertising, say, or just for public relations – and this inhibits new thinking on integration.

(d)   **Centralised control**: If the chief executive keeps tight control of the organisation and of its planning and is unconvinced of the benefits of innovation then it will not happen.

(e)   **Cost considerations**: Innovation usually requires investment.

Disney and Pixar

Organisational culture is an extremely important influence on innovation. A Financial Times report on Disney's purchase of Pixar in 2006 contrasted their distinct organisational styles. *"Disney has become a pathologically dysfunctional organisation. Like IBM of the 1970s or AT&T in the 1980s, Disney grew fat and bureaucratic in the 1990s, long after cementing its lucrative entertainment franchise. Some of Disney's problems are endemic to large corporations. When a company has 133,000 employees, it cannot be governed by human beings. Instead, it must rely on a culture to preserve its earlier entrepreneurialism, while focusing workers on the continuing mission.*

Unfortunately, Disney's culture, like that of IBM and AT&T, encouraged inefficiency and stifled creativity. Over the past five years, Disney's shares have lost a third of their value and the company has become a corporate governance pariah. Many thought the low point was the fiasco surrounding Michael Ovitz, who left Disney with $140 million after just 14 months. But more troubling was the release of the abysmal Treasure Planet, a film that cost about as much as Mr Ovitz and avoided universal ignominy only because so few people saw it.

To survive and prosper, large organisations must be divided into manageable pods, whose workers have independence and incentive. In contrast to Disney, Pixar was just such a free-standing, freespirited group with a relaxed, open-plan office and no signs of managerial hierarchy. John Lasseter, Pixar's creative leader, wore Hawaiian shirts and rode a scooter inside. When Pixar won Oscars, employees displayed the statues proudly but dressed them in Barbie doll clothing. Whereas Disney executives micromanaged films, including those with Pixar, Mr Lasseter let his crew run free and encouraged ideas".

Methods of overcoming these barriers

(a) **Top management commitment**: The most effective way of overcoming these barriers to change is through the commitment of top management. The chief executive in particular needs to be convinced of the appropriateness of the new thinking and be enthusiastic about its implementation throughout the organisation.

(b) **Training and development**: It is one thing to change attitudes. It is another thing to be in a position to know exactly what to do. It needs the services of individuals trained in strategic thinking. The individuals chosen to implement any new program must be enthusiasts capable of overcoming resistance to change.

(c) **Marketing as a competitive advantage**: Those with responsibility for implementing an integrated marketing programme must do so with the objective of developing it as a sustainable, long-term competitive advantage.

(d) **Producing the results**: Nothing succeeds like success. Producing the business results as a consequence of effective marketing communications will boost confidence and gain management converts to the new thinking on an integrated approach.

1.3.2 Stages of an innovation audit

If asked to describe the innovation **audit**, here is a possible approach.

Step 1   **Benchmark with leading competitors**. For example, many motor firms regard the rate and speed of NPD as something they must emulate.

Step 2   **Assess reactivity: identify performance indicators** for innovation and compare with previous years

- Rate of NPD
- Number of innovations
- Success rate (more important than quantity)
- Percentage of revenue derived from innovations (3M has a target)
- Incremental sales resulting from innovation
- Average annual sales per new product/service
- Customer satisfaction ratings
- Staff turnover, if this affects climate of innovation

Note that if a higher percentage of revenue comes from **innovation** a **incremental** products, it looks as if innovatory products are **cannibalising** existing sales.

Step 3 Identify obstacles to innovation which typically reside in the corporate cultural structure.

Step 4 Recommend innovation objectives.

1.4 Product life cycle

concept

The **product life cycle** assumes that the marketing and financial characteristics of a product change over time, in relation to the market and in relation to other products. It is an attempt to recognise distinct stages in a product's sales history.

Many firms make a number of different products or services. Each product or service has its own **financial, marketing and risk characteristics**. The combination of products or services influences the profitability of the firm.

Marketing managers distinguish between product class, form and brand.

(a) **Product class**: this is a broad category of product, such as cars, washing machines, newspapers, also referred to as the generic product.

(b) **Product form**: within a product class there are different forms that the product can take, for example five-door hatchback cars or two-seater sports cars, twin tub or front-loading automatic washing machines, national daily newspapers or weekly local papers etc.

(c) **Brand**: the particular type of the product form (for example Ford Fiesta, Vauxhall Astra; Financial Times, Daily Mail, Sun).

The product life cycle applies in differing degrees to each of the three cases. A **product class** (eg cars) may have a long maturity stage, but a particular make or brand within the class might have an erratic life cycle. **Product forms**, however, tend to conform to the classic life cycle pattern, which is illustrated by the diagram below.

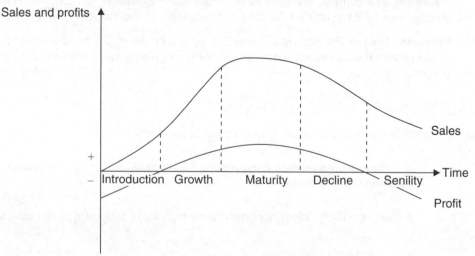

Introduction

(a) A new product takes time to find acceptance by would-be purchasers and there is a slow growth in sales. Unit costs are high because of low output and expensive sales promotion.

(b) There may be early teething troubles with production technology.

(c) The product for the time being is a loss-maker.

Growth

(a)   If the new product gains market acceptance, sales will eventually rise more sharply and the product will start to make profits.

(b)   Competitors are attracted. As sales and production rise, unit costs fall.

Maturity. The rate of sales growth slows down and the product reaches a period of maturity which is probably the longest period of a successful product's life. Most products on the market will be at the mature stage of their life. Profits are good.

Decline. Some products reach a stage of decline, which may be slow or fast. Eventually, sales will begin to decline so that there is over-capacity of production in the industry. Severe competition occurs, profits fall and some producers leave the market. The remaining producers seek means of prolonging the product life by modifying it and searching for new market segments. Many producers are reluctant to leave the market, although some inevitably do because of falling profits.

The product lifecycle concept has implications for many aspects of business, including all of the four Ps in the basic marketing mix, as is shown in the table.

| | Phase | | | |
	Introduction	Growth	Maturity	Decline
Products	Initially, poor quality. Product design and development are a key to success. No standard product and frequent design changes (eg microcomputers in the early 1980s).	Competitors' products have marked quality technical differences. Quality improves. Product reliability may be important.	Products become more standardised and differences between competing products less distinct.	Products even less differentiated. Quality becomes more variable.
Customers	Initial customers willing to pay high prices. Customers need to be convinced about buying.	Customers increase in number.	Mass market. Market saturation. Repeat-buying of products becomes significant. Brand image also important.	Customers are 'sophisticated' buyers of a product they understand well.
Promotion	High advertising and sales promotion costs.	High advertising costs still, but as a % of sales, costs are falling.	Markets become segmented. Segmentation and extending the maturity phase of the life cycle can be key strategies.	Less money spent on advertising and sales promotion.
Competition	Few or no competitors.	More competitors enter the market. Barriers to entry can be important.	Competition at its keenest: due to high sales volume. Higher prices in some market segments.	Competitors gradually exit from the market. Exit barriers can be important.

	Phase			
	Introduction	Growth	Maturity	Decline
Prices and costs	High prices but losses due to high fixed costs.	High prices. High contribution margins, and increasing profit margins. High P/E ratios for quoted companies in the growth market.	Falling prices but good profit margins due to high sales volume. Higher prices in some market segments.	Still low prices but falling profits as sales volume falls, since total contribution falls towards the level of fixed costs. Some increase in prices may occur in late decline stage.
Manufacturing	Over-capacity. High production costs.	Under-capacity. Move towards mass production and less reliance on skilled labour.	Optimum capacity. Low labour skills.	Over-capacity because mass production techniques are still used.
Place	Few distribution channels.	Distribution channels flourish and getting adequate distribution channels is a key to marketing success.	Distribution channels fully developed, but less successful channels might be cut.	Distribution channels dwindling.

In reviewing outputs, planners should assess the following.

(a)   The **stage of its life cycle** that any product has reached.

(b)   The **product's remaining life**, ie how much longer the product will be able to contribute significantly to profits.

(c)   How **urgent is the need to innovate**, to develop new and improved products in time?

1.4.1 Difficulties of the product life cycle concept

The product life cycle has been extensively criticised.

(a)   **Recognition**. How can managers recognise where a product stands in its life cycle?

(b)   **Not always true**. The traditional curve of a product life cycle does not always occur in practice.

Some products have no maturity phase, and go straight from growth to decline. Some never decline if they are marketed competitively (eg certain brands of breakfast cereals).

(c)   **Changeable**. Strategic decisions can change or extend a product's life cycle.

(d)   **Competition varies** in different industries. The financial markets are an example of markets where there is a tendency for competitors to copy the leader very quickly, so that competition has built up well **ahead** of demand.

Also, the concept has been denounced as promoting a product orientation at the expense of a market orientation.

 EXAM TIP   application

Exam questions are likely to concentrate on the marking strategies relevant to individual stages of the life cycle, as each stage involves different strategic choices. Each stage involves configuring the marketing mix in a particular way, to meet the firm's objectives. The examiner is unlikely to want mere descriptions of the model. Questions are more likely to focus upon specific stages of the life cycle and their implications for marketing strategy.

(a)   **Introduction and launch**

(i)   Does the firm lead in NPD or copy competitors?

(ii)   Penetration or skimming: should the firm seek to get as much market share as early as possible or should it seek to recoup as much profit as possible?

(b)   **Growth stage**

    (i)   What competitive strategy is most appropriate in the market place? Will the firm have to differentiate its offer?

    (ii)   How long should the firm continue the intense marketing support needed at this stage to build a market?

(c)   **Maturity**. Higher profits can be achieved by segmenting the market and modifying the product. Market share objectives and distribution are strategically important. Should you rejuvenate a mature product or finish it off? If so, what strategies can you use for rejuvenation: product enhancement, segmentation and so on?

(d)   **Decline** is probably the hardest to negotiate.

    (i)   Manage decline. Sales will be falling, so costs should be cut to maintain dealer loyalty. Decline needs to be managed slowly and smoothly, so that the firm can redirect its resources elsewhere.

    (ii)   Rejuvenation involves 'fining new needs or uses for the product and fitting the product to them to produce new sales.' This involves modifying the mix, producing new versions of the product or positioning the product for another group. For example Campbell's condensed soups have been additionally positioned as ingredients for cooking sauces.

(e)   As a general rule, any answer about the PLC should cover its drawbacks as well as its merits.

1.4.2 The PLC and cash generation

It is essential that firms plan their portfolio of products to **ensure that new products are generating positive cash flow** before existing 'earners' enter the decline stage.

The **product life cycle** concept can be added to a market share/market growth classification of products, as follows.

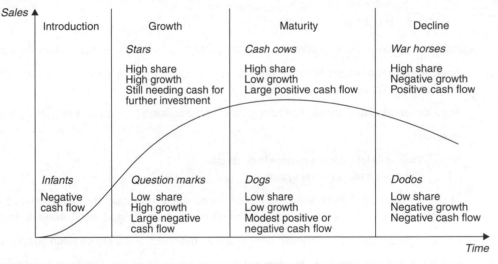

The product life cycle concept probably has more value as a **control tool** than as a method of **forecasting** a product's life. Control can be applied to speeding up the growth phase, extending the maturity phase and recognising when to cease making a product altogether.

The management of a product should fit its prevailing life cycle stage, as each stage has different financial characteristics.

(a)   **Development**. Money will be spent on market research and product development. Cash flows are negative and there is a high business risk.

(b)   **Launches** require expensive promotion campaigns.

(c)   **Growth**. The market grows, as does the demand for the product. Risks are competitor action.

    (i)   The market price mix might turn out to be inappropriate for the product (eg the price is set too high).
    (ii)   Competitors will enter, thereby reducing the profits that can be earned.

(d)   **Maturity**. Few new competitors will enter the market. Risk is low, so the concentration is on profit.

	Launch	Growth	Maturity	Decline
Characteristics	High business risk. Negative net cash flow. DCF evaluation for overall investment.	High business risk. Neutral net cash flow.	Medium business risk. Positive cash flow.	Low risk. Neutral-positive cash flow.
Critical success factors	Time to launch.	Market share growth. Sustaining competitive advantage.	Contribution per unit of scarce resource. Customer retention.	Timely exit.
Information needs	Market research into size and demand.	Market growth, share. Diminishing returns. Competitor marketing strategies.	Comparative competitor costs. Limiting factors.	Rate of decline; best time to leave; reliable sale values of assets.
Financial and other controls	Strategic 'milestones'. Physical evaluation. Mainly non-financial measures owing to volatility (eg rate of take up by consumers).	Discounted cash flow Market share Marketing objectives	ROI Profit margin Maintaining market share.	Free cash flow (for investment elsewhere).

2 Organisational culture and performance

"Four key organisational components are structure, systems, people and culture. All must be in sync with each other and with the business strategy." Aaker & McLoughlin (2007) p.340

2.1 Vision, mission and values

Strategic analysis is concerned with understanding the strategic position of the organisation via the following tools.

(a)   **Environmental analysis** (external appraisal) is the scanning of the business's environment for factors relevant to the organisation's current and future activities.

(b)   **Position or situation audit**. The current state of the business in respect of resources, brands, markets etc.

(c)   **Mission**

(i)   The firm's long-term approach to business
(ii)   The organisation's value system

"A primary purpose of an organisational vision – what a future strategy should be – and objectives is to help make strategic decisions. Thus, it is appropriate to look toward them for guidance." Aaker & McLoughlin, op. cit., p.32

A firm might decide upon its mission *after* assessing the needs of the organisation and its environmental situation.

(d)   **Goals** interpret the mission to the needs of different stakeholders (eg customers, employees, shareholders).

(e)   **Objectives** should embody mission and goals. Generally, they are **quantitative** measures, against which actual performance can be assessed.

(f)   **Corporate appraisal**. A critical assessment of strengths, weaknesses, opportunities and threats (SWOT) existing in the internal and environmental factors affecting an organisation.

(g)   **Gap analysis**. A projection of current activities into the future to identify if there is a difference between the firm's objectives and the results from the continuation of current activities.

Organisational culture is considered in more detail in Chapter 4.Organisational vision, mission and values are also covered in Chapter 5 in the context of strategic management and strategic direction.

2.2 Customer and market orientation

The Toyota Way

Spend some time with Toyota people and after a time you realise there is something different about them. The rest of the car industry raves about engines, gearboxes, acceleration, fuel economy, handling, ride quality and sexy design. Toyota's people talk about 'The Toyota Way' and about customers. In truth, when it is written down the Toyota creed reads much like any corporate mission statement. But it seems to have been absorbed by Japanese, European and American employees alike.

Mr Cho thinks something of the unique Toyota culture comes from the fact that the company grew up in one place, Toyota City, 30 minutes drive from Nagoya in central Japan, where the company has four assembly plants surrounded by factories of suppliers. In this provincial, originally rural setting, Toyota workers in the early days would often have small plots of land that they tended after their shift. Mr Cho, who made his career in the company by being a pupil of Mr Ohno and becoming a master of production control, thinks that the fact that Toyota managers and their suppliers see each other every day makes for a sort of hothouse culture – rather like Silicon Valley in its early days.

Jim Press is boss of Toyota's sales in North America. He left Ford in frustration 35 years ago, because he did not think it handled customer relations properly and he suspected that the upstart Japanese company making its way in the American market might do better. He was right. Toyota has shared a production plant in California with GM since 1984, under the name New United Motor Manufacturing Inc., known as Nummi. Identical cars come off the line, some badged as GM, the rest as Toyotas: after five years, according to one study by Boston Consulting Group, the trade-in value of the Toyota was much higher than that of the American model, thanks to the greater confidence people had in the Toyota dealer and service network.

Mr Press talks with a quiet, almost religious, fervour about Toyota, without mentioning cars as such. 'The Toyota culture is inside all of us. Toyota is a customer's company,' he says. "Mrs Jones is our customer; she is my boss. Everything is done to make Mrs Jones's life better. We all work for Mrs Jones."'

The Economist, 29 January 2005

With the bankruptcy of GM in 2009, doubts were raised about the future of the California plant joint venture, but it has been reported that Toyota is considering making Prius hatchbacks there. Toyota expects strong demand in the U.S., where the new model went on sale in June 2009, and is raising output in Japan. Prius was Japan's top-selling model in May.

In December 2008, Toyota halted work on its $1.3 billion Mississippi factory after plunging U.S. sales created excess capacity at its North American plants.

The marketing concept of business is to put the customer at the heart of the organisation's activities.

Customer focus should be present in all departments and functions. The organisation is thus **market-led**.

2.2.1 Marketing-led and market-led orientation

A **market** is a customer or a group of customers.

A **market-led firm** is a company in which everyone puts the customer at the centre of decision-making. The customer is not owned by the marketing department.

Market orientation is 'an organisational culture where beating the competition through the creation of superior customer value is the paramount objective throughout the business'.

(Piercy, 2008)

In a company with a market orientation, the aim of **providing superior customer value** dominates all thinking:

- What the business is
- Which markets to serve
- Investments and acquisitions
- Which people to employ and how to promote them

In **market-led** organisations, the marketing department is not in a world of its own. Customer value is designed and created by **multi-function** product teams supporting **all the business functions**.

Hooley *et al* identify the following components of a market orientation.

- **Customers**: know them well enough to give superior value.
- **Competition**: what are their short- and long-term capabilities?
- **Inter-functional**: mobilise the entire company to create superior customer value.
- **Culture**: employee behaviour should be managed to ensure customer satisfaction.
- **Long-term profit focus**: have a strategic but realistic vision.

 MARKETING AT WORK  application

Tata Motors

Tata is a major Indian industrial conglomerate. Tata Motors was until recently a lorry-manufacturing company. When the company decided to enter the car market, it developed the Indica from nothing in three years and at a cost only one-third as great as a European or US equivalent project. However, when the product was launched there were immediate problems with the suspension and air conditioning and most of all with after-sales service. The initial, corporate-culture conditioned response was 'we haven't done anything wrong'. However, the CEO insisted that the customer had to be put first. Five hundred engineers were sent out into the market place to talk to buyers. Customers were invited into the factory to describe their experiences.

The next generation Indica was ready three years later and quickly became a big seller in the small car segment. Version 3 was launched in early 2008 and offered three versions each with four sub-models. The Indica is now an established and popular product.

The type, or model, of marketing practiced in any organisation depends on a number of factors, not least of which are the nature of the business context and the organisation's dominant orientation. Marketing activities in organisations can be grouped broadly into four models:

(a) **Sales support** – The emphasis in this model is essentially reactive: marketing supports the direct sales force. It may include activities such as telesales or telemarketing, responding to enquiries, co-ordinating diaries, customer database management, organising exhibitions or other sales promotions, and administering agents. These activities usually come under a sales and marketing director or manager. This form of marketing is common in SMEs and some organisations operating in a B2B context.

(b) **Marketing communications** – The emphasis in this model is more proactive: marketing promotes the organisation and its product/service at a tactical level, either to customers (pull) or to channel members (push). It typically includes activities such as providing brochures and catalogues to support the sales force. Some B2C organisations may use marketing to perform the 'selling' role using direct marketing techniques and to manage campaigns based on a mix of media to raise awareness, generate leads and even take orders. In B2B markets, larger organisations may have marketing communications departments and specialists to make efficient use of marketing expenditures and to co-ordinate communications between business units.

(c) **Operational marketing** – The emphasis in this model is for marketing to support the organisation with a co-ordinated range of marketing activities including market research, brand management, product development and management, corporate and marketing communications, and customer relationship management. Given this breadth of activities, planning is also a function usually performed in this role but at an operational or functional level. Typically part of FMCG or B2C organisations, the operational marketing role is increasingly used in B2B organisations.

(d)   **Strategic marketing** – The emphasis in this model is for marketing to contribute to the creation of value and competitive customer strategy. As such, it is practised in customer focused and larger organisations. In a large or diversified organisation, it may also be responsible for the co-ordination of marketing departments or activities in separate business units. Strategic marketing decisions, when not made by professional marketers, are taken by business leaders.

2.3 Comparative and best practice analysis

2.3.1 Benchmarking and the market environment

 KEY CONCEPT

concept

Benchmarking: an external target of performance against which a firm measures its activities.

Benchmarks can be set on a variety of key performance indicators as an objective form of control. Marketing research and competitor intelligence would be needed to establish benchmarks and to monitor progress.

The practice of benchmarking is becoming increasingly popular. **Competitor benchmarking** focuses on the performance and relative strengths of direct competitors using information from customer and supplier interviews and published data from any source available. A firm tries to be as good as its competitors.

2.3.2 Monitoring competitor performance

When an organisation operates in a competitive environment, it should try to obtain information about the financial performance of competitors, to make a comparison with the organisation's own results. It might not be possible to obtain reliable competitor information, but if the competitor is a public company it will publish an annual report and accounts.

Financial information that might be obtainable about a competitor

(a)   Total profits, sales and capital employed.

(b)   ROCE, profit/sales ratio, cost/sales ratios and asset turnover ratios.

(c)   The increase in profits and sales over the course of the past twelve months (and prospects for the future, which will probably be mentioned in the chairman's statement in the report and accounts).

(d)   Sales and profits in each major business segment that the competitor operates in.

(e)   Dividend per share and earnings per share.

(f)   Gearing and interest rates on debt.

(g)   Share price, and P/E ratio (stock exchange information).

2.4 Cost efficiency and financial performance

There is a relationship between the quantity of products produced and the cost per unit. There are many routes to cost advantage (Aaker, 2007). They include:

* Economies of scale
* The experience curve
* Product design innovations
* The use of 'no-frills' offerings

KEY CONCEPT

Economy of scale. The more you produce and sell, the cheaper each successive unit will be.

ACTIVITY 3

A publisher contracts with a printer to print Study Texts.

Quantity printed	Cost £	Cost per book £
100	500	5.00
1,000	2,500	2.50
2,000	4,720	2.36

There are the same **fixed costs** incurred (for example, in setting-up the press) no matter how many or few books are printed.

The quantity produced affects the cost per unit. For example, if customers are unwilling to pay more than £3 for their books, and the publisher wants to make £0.50p profit on top of print cost, then the publisher has to sell **at least** 1,000 books.

How is this relevant to considerations of market share?

2.4.1 Experience curves

The **experience curve** takes it further. The more units **over time** that a firm produces, the cheaper each unit will be to produce. Why?

(a)   **Economies of scale**, as identified above.

(b)   **Learning**: the more people do a task, the more efficient they become (up to a point), and it takes them less time.

(c)   **Technological** improvements: firms can improve their production operations and make better use of equipment.

(d)   **Simplifying products can cut costs**. For example, car manufacturers are cutting costs by ensuring that the same components can be used in different marquees.

MARKETING AT WORK

Japanese firms pioneered target costing. They identified a customer need and specified a product to satisfy that need.

The production department and its accountants then worked out:

- How the product could be built
- The volume needed to reach the market price
- How quickly costs could be driven down

2.4.2 Market share performance

 concept

Market share is 'one entity's sales of a product or service in a specified market expressed as a percentage of total sales by all entities offering that product or service'. Thus, a company may have a 30% share of a total market, meaning that 30% of all sales in the market are made by that company.

Relative market share is the share of the market relative to that of the manufacturer's largest competitor.

An evaluation of market shares helps to identify **who the true competitor really is**, and avoids trying to outdo the wrong competitor.

Such an approach serves as a basis for marketing strategy, with a firm seeking as a target to build up an x% share of a particular market.

When a market manager is given responsibility for a product or a market segment, the product or market segment will be a profit centre, and measures of performance for the centre will include profits and cost variances etc. However, another useful measure of performance would be the **market share** obtained by the organisation's product in the market. A market share performance report should draw attention to the following.

(a)   The link between **cost and profit** and market performance in both the short- and the long-term.

(b)   The performance of the **product or market segment** in the context of the product life cycle.

(c)   Whether or not the product is gaining or losing ground, as its market share goes up or down.

Changes in market share have to be considered against the change in the **market as a whole**, since the product might be increasing its share simply when the market is declining, but the competition is losing sales even more quickly. (The reverse may also be true. The market could be expanding, and a declining market share might not represent a decline in absolute sales volume, but a failure to grab more of the growing market.)

2.4.3 Profit impact of market strategies (PIMS)

PIMS analysis attempts to establish the profitability (ie return on capital) of various marketing strategies, and identifies a link between the size of **return on capital** and **market share** so that companies in a strong competitive position in the markets for their base products would be earning high returns.

In general, profits increase in line with market share.

Three possible reasons have been put forward for this correlation.

(a)   **Economies of scale** and experience curve effects enable a market leader to produce at lower unit costs than competitors, and so make bigger profits. A company with the highest market share, especially if this company is also the innovator with the longest experience, will enjoy a considerable competitive advantage. This is referred to as the experience curve.

(b)   **Bargaining power**. A strong position in the market gives a firm greater strength in its dealings with both buyers and suppliers.

(c)   **Quality of management**. Market leaders often seem to be run by managers of a high caliber.

MARKETING AT WORK

application

Reebok

Reebok was a best-selling trainer brand but competition from Nike and Adidas saw its market share plummet and its share price fall from over $50 in 1997 to $7 at the start of 2001. Reebok sought to bounce back as a 'sports brand that operates' in a fashion market, with an ad campaign designed to appeal to 16 to 24-year olds. Other outdoor brands, such as Timberland and Caterpillar, also eroded Reebok's market share with Timberland capturing 2.9% of the US trainer market (2.1% in 1999). Fashion brands such as Hermes and DKNY also muscled in on the market.

In 2005 Reebok were bought out by former rival Adidas, and have struggled to regain market share. It is still a highly recognisable presence in the market however, and in 2009 launched an iPhone app that allows users to customise and purchase a pair of trainers through their mobile phones. Your Reebok uses the iPhone's touch, motion and GPS features to create personalised trainers with a selection of styles, materials, colours and text. Users can then purchase the shoe online, which will range between £80-£110 depending on the materials selected, or share their creations with friends.

The app is available for free from the iPhone App Store, launching initially in the UK and US, with plans to expand to Germany, France, Belgium, the Netherlands, Austria and Ireland in the coming months.

Dusan Hamlin, managing director of Inside Mobile, said: "Reebok has been quick to grasp the potential of iPhone apps as a compelling route to market that can fuse branding and direct response goals. By marrying visually stunning design, personalised content and advertising, Inside Mobile has enabled Reebok to engage consumers as well as drive sales."

www.revolutionmagazine.com [accessed 18 June 2009]

EXAM TIP

application

It is not enough to know by heart the theory of each of the tools described in this chapter, so do not spend all your study time on that. At the post-graduate level, you are expected to be able to deploy **higher skills**.

These include the sensible selection of a tool and the interpretation of the results it produces. Both depend totally on an understanding of and familiarity with the strengths, weaknesses and applications of a given tool in a given context.

Learning objective review

Learning objective	Covered
1 Utilise a range of models and techniques to undertake a strategic audit of the internal environment	☑ Resources and competences (1.1)
	☑ Portfolio analysis (1.2)
	☑ Innovation audit (1.3)
	☑ Product life cycle (1.4)
	☑ Vision, mission and values (2.1)
	☑ Customer and market orientation (2.2)
	☑ Comparative and best practice analysis (2.3)
	☑ Cost efficiency and financial performance (2.4)

Quick quiz

1 What is covered by the resource audit?

2 "Resources are of no value unless they are organised into ...." Fill in the blank.

3 What are the criteria used by the General Electric Business Screen?

4 What is covered by an innovation audit?

5 Distinguish between product class, form and brand

6 What are the four broad groupings of marketing activity in organisations?

7 What is benchmarking?

8 Why might economies of scale promote a cost advantage against competitors?

9 "In general, profits increase in line with ...." Fill in the blank.

10 How is the PLC related to marketing orientation?

 BPP LEARNING MEDIA

1   The evaluation and resulting strategic considerations for the company in the diagram above are that:

(a)   There are two 'cash cows', thus the company should be in a cash-positive state.

(b)   New products will be required to follow on from A.

(c)   A is doing well (15%) but needs to gain market share to move from position 3 in the market – continued funding is essential. Similar for B.

(d)   C is a market leader in a maturing market – strategy of consolidation is required.

(e)   D is the major product which dominates its market; cash funds should be generated from this product.

(f)   E is very small. Is it profitable? Funding to maintain the position or selling-off are appropriate strategies.

2   (a)   Orange juice is a cash cow.
    (b)   Pomegranate juice is a question mark, which the company wants to turn into a star.

3   It shows that high market share can, by spreading fixed costs over many units of production, be more profitable.

Higher sales volumes can mean lower costs per unit, hence higher profits. The Boston Consulting Group estimated that as production volume doubles, cost per unit falls by up to 20%.

High market share therefore gives cost advantages.

1   The resource audit covers technical resources, financial resources, managerial skills, the organisation and its information system

2   Systems

3   Market attractiveness and business strength

4   It covers the organisation climate and culture, the value to the customer, policies to encourage innovation and the management team

5   'Class' is a broad category; form is an example within a class; brand is the offering (or group of offerings) from a particular supplier.

6   Sales support; marketing communications; operational marketing and strategic marketing

7   Benchmarking is an external target of performance, against which a firm measures its activities. Benchmarks can be set on a variety of key performance indicators as a form of control

8   Economies of scale enable a market leader to produce at lower unit costs than competitors, and so make bigger profits

9   Market share

10 It may be that over-attention to the PLC actually produces a product orientation.

Aaker, D. & McLoughlin, D. (2007) <u>Strategic Market Management</u>, John Wiley, Chichester.

Blythe, J. (2006), <u>Principles and Practice of Marketing,</u> Thomson Learning, London.

Blythe, J. (2005), <u>Essentials of Marketing</u>, (3rd edition), FT Prentice Hall, Harlow.

Brassington, F. & Pettitt, S. (2003<u>), Principles of Marketing</u>, (3rd edition), FT Prentice Hall, Harlow.

Drummond, G., Ensor, J. & Ashford, R. (2008) <u>Strategic Marketing Planning and Control</u>, (3rd edition), Elsevier, Oxford.

Drummond, G. & Ensor, J. (1999) <u>Strategic Marketing – Planning and Control</u>, Butterworth-Heinemann, Oxford.

Hooley, G., Saunders, J., Piercy, N., & Nicoulaud, B., (2007) <u>Marketing Strategy and Competitive Positioning</u>, (4th edition), FT Prentice Hall, Harlow.

Leahul, D. "*Reebok targets trainer addicts with iPhone app*", available online at: www.revolutionmagazine.com, 13 May 2009 [accessed 18 June 2009].

Piercy, N.F. (2008) <u>Market-Led Strategic Change – Transforming the Process of Going to Market</u>, (4th edition), Butterworth-Heinemann, Oxford.

Porter, M.E (2004) <u>Competitive Advantage</u>, Free Press, London.

Chapter 4

Developing organisational capability

Topic list

Introduction

As we saw in Chapter 1, competitive advantage distinguishes the successful business from the average, enabling it to earn an **above average level of profit**.

There are two main approaches to achieving competitive advantage, each encompassing several strands of strategic thinking.

(a)   **The positioning approach**

The positioning approach to strategy is closely related to the traditional concept of marketing orientation. It starts with an assessment of the commercial environment and positions the business so that it fits with environmental requirements.

(b)   **The resource-based approach**

The resource-based approach starts with the idea that competitive advantage comes from the possession of distinctive and unique resources, or 'organisational capability'. This approach forms the topic of this chapter.

Syllabus-linked learning objectives

By the end of the chapter you will be able to:

Learning objectives	Syllabus link
1 Critically evaluate the resource-based view of an organisation and the value of this approach in developing resource and capability to deliver an organisation's vision and mission	1.2.2
2 Critically evaluate the fit between an organisation's culture and its current strategy, and assess its ability to be flexible and agile in a changing marketing environment	1.2.3
3 Utilise a range of internal information and assessment tools to evaluate an organisation's strengths and weaknesses in order to assess its readiness for development	1.2.4
4 Critically assess strategic alternatives against pre-determined criteria for an organisation	3.1.1

1   The resource-based view of strategy

"Assets and competencies can involve a wide spectrum, from buildings and locations to research and development expertise or a metaphorical symbol, such as the Mercedes star. Though a strong asset or competency is often difficult to build, it can result in an advantage that is significant and enduring." Aaker & McLoughlin (2007) p.8

1.1 Resources, capabilities and competences

The resource-based approach to strategy begins from a consideration of strengths and weaknesses and, in particular, of **distinctive competences**. It was developed in response to two issues:

(a)   Many environments are **too complex and dynamic** to permit continuing effective analysis and response.

(b)   Once an opportunity is discerned and an offering made, it is very easy for **competitors to make similar offerings**, thus rapidly eroding competitive advantage.

The resource-based view is that sustainable competitive advantage is only attained as a result of the **possession of distinctive resources**. These may be physical resources, such as the effective monopolisation of diamonds by De Beers, or, more typically in today's service economies, they may be **core competences**. Core competences critically underpin an organisation's competitive advantage.

Sometimes, often in what are exceptional circumstances, a strength may disappear, signaling trouble ahead if an alternative is hard to find.

MARKETING AT WORK

BA's big strength has always been the Heathrow hub and its dominance of the lucrative business traffic across the Atlantic. In 2006/07, the final year of the financial-services boom, BA posted a record result. Corporate Lawyers. merchant bankers and other masters of the universe thought nothing paying £4,000 and more for a return trip to America, and the cash rolled in.

The airline announced a record profit of £922 million, achieved an operating margin of 10% (something that had eluded BA managers for the previous two decades) and paid a dividend to shareholders for the first time since 2001.

Then the music stopped. The credit crunch and recession revealed the reliance on Heathrow and Atlantic business traffic to be not a strength but a weakness. Business traffic dried up with companies, and in particular the big banks, slashing their travel budgets.

"Companies are travelling less and spending less per trip," said Amon Cohen, a business travel expert and contributing editor of Business Travel News. "With so many empty seats, airlines are falling over themselves to offer discounts of as much as 70% in business class. Looking ahead, it does not get much brighter. A survey of British corporate travel buyers published by the Institute of Travel & Meetings last week found that three-quarters of them expected their spending to fall even further over the next 12 months."

BA's results for the 2007/08 financial year showed how hard and fast the downturn had hit. The airline recorded a £401 million loss – £331 million of which came in the final quarter of the year alone – scrapped the dividend.

BA's lifeblood "premium traffic – first and business class – fell 17% in April and by the same amount in May. Business class fares across the Atlantic have dropped sharply.

Sunday Times, 21 June 2009

ACTIVITY 1

What can BA do to respond to such conditions?

1.1.1 Competences

Competences develop in a variety of ways.

- **Experience** in making and marketing a product or service
- The talents and potential of **individuals** in the organisation
- The **quality of co-ordination**

Johnson *et al* (2007) divide competences into two types.

(a) An organisation must achieve at least a **threshold level** of competence in **everything** it does.
(b) Its **core competences** are those where it **outperforms competitors** and that are **difficult to imitate**.

Hamel and Prahalad (1996) suggest that an important aspect of strategic management is the determining of the competences the company will require **in the future** in order to be able to provide new benefits to customers. They say a **core competence** must have three qualities.

- It must make a **disproportionate** contribution to the **value** the customer perceives.

- It must be '**competitively unique**', which means one of three things: actually unique; superior to competitors; or capable of dramatic improvement.

- It must be **extendable**, in that it must allow for the development of an array of new products and services.

Bear in mind that **relying on a competence is no substitute for a strategy**. However, a core competence can form **a basis for a strategy**. Here it is important to reiterate that a core competence must be **difficult to imitate** if it is to confer lasting competitive advantage. In particular, skills that can be bought-in are unlikely to form the basis of core competences, since competitors would also be able to buy them in just as easily. Core competences are more about what the organisation *is* than about what it *does*. So it is possible to regard a strong **brand** as a kind of core competence: it is a unique resource that confers a distinct competitive advantage.

To some extent, the resource-based approach is diametrically opposed to the marketing concept since, instead of approaching strategy on the basis of giving customers what they want, it concentrates on exploiting what the business already has to offer. In fact, this distinction is largely theoretical, but it leads to some important ideas.

(a)   Where the marketing concept is adopted, it will still be necessary to deploy threshold capabilities in all critical areas and the possession of unique resources and core competences will enhance the market offering.

(b)   Conversely, where strategy is built on unique resources and core competences, marketing activities must be carried out with at least threshold competence if the customer is to be satisfied.

1.1.2 Organisational capability

Organisational capabilities and culture will have great influence on success and failure. An important variable is **organisational structure**. In the days of mass marketing, a vertically organised hierarchical form was appropriate for achieving economies of scale and expertise. Companies now seeking to cut overheads, achieve fast response to changing markets and competition and exploit the advantages of a mass customisation approach need something better. Increasingly, advances in IT are producing organisations based on **networks**.

(a)   **Internal networks** take the form of horizontally-oriented, cross-functional teams with responsibility for processes that deliver customer satisfaction. Communication flows freely, making the best use of resources whatever their functional label. This style of working reduces costs, speeds response and improves motivation.

(b)   **External networks** are created when companies withdraw from activities that are not fundamental to their specific value-creating strategy and **concentrate on their core competences**. They buy-in the services they no longer perform for themselves, using the core competences of other companies to support their own. This type of organisation arises under the pressure of new technologies, new markets and new processes that make it difficult for any organisation to do everything well.

The **McKinsey 7S model**, as illustrated below, was designed to show how the various aspects of a business relate to one another. It is a useful example of the way culture fits into an organisation. In particular, it shows the links between the organisation's behaviour and the behaviour of individuals within it.

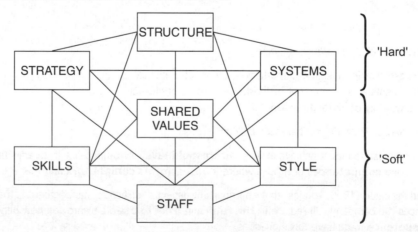

Three of the elements were originally considered 'hard', but in today's context they are becoming more flexible.

(a)   **Structure**. The organisation structure determines division of tasks in the organisation and the hierarchy of authority from the most senior to junior. Today's company is likely to be made up of flat, empowered networks.

(b)   **Strategy**. Strategy is the way in which the organisation plans to outperform its competitors; it will be market-led.

(c)   **Systems**. Systems include the technical systems of accounting, personnel, management information and so on, with particular emphasis on how market-related information is distributed and used.

The McKinsey model suggests that the 'soft' elements are equally important.

(a) **Shared values** lie at the heart of the organisation and are the guiding principles for the people in it. They are vital for developing the motivation to drive the organisation to achieve.

(b) **Staff** are the people in the organisation. They have their own complex concerns and priorities. The successful organisation will recruit the right staff and develop their motivation to pursue the right goals.

(c) **Style** is another aspect of the **corporate culture**, and includes the shared assumptions, ways of working and attitudes of senior management.

(d) **Skills** are the core competences that enable the company to create value in a particular way.

1.1.3 Marketing contexts

It is worth remembering at this point that organisations operate in a variety of contexts using different marketing activities, and this has a large impact on structure and capabilities. There is no 'one size fits all' approach.

Organisations and their marketers have to select and use techniques appropriate to their specific context. Typical marketing contexts are summarized as:

FMCG: Used in organisations with a strong market orientation, the 'standard' model of marketing is based on identification of customers' needs and techniques of segmentation, targeting and positioning supported by branding and customer communications.

B2B: The model of marketing adopted depends on factors such as the importance of face-to-face selling, the dominant orientation and power of buyers. Markets are often less information-rich than FMCG markets, which constrains marketing decisions.

Capital projects: A variant of the B2B model where opportunities for positioning are few and the value of any single order constitutes a significant proportion of turnover in a period

Not-for-profit: The organisation is not driven by shareholder value and competition may not be a significant factor in strategy

SMEs: Operating in any of the above sectors, SMEs are characterised by their limited marketing resources and the limited use of marketing techniques.

 ACTIVITY 2   application

What would the effects of introducing a marketing approach to a charity?

1.2 Knowledge as a resource

 KEY CONCEPTS   concept

Knowledge is information within people's minds. It may or may not be recorded in the form of generally accessible information.

Knowledge management (KM) involves the identification and analysis of available and required knowledge, and the subsequent planning and control of actions to develop knowledge assets so as to fulfil organisational objectives.

Knowledge assets are the sum of the knowledge regarding markets, products, technologies, resources, skills and systems that a business owns or controls and which enable it to achieve its objectives.

Knowledge management entails identifying knowledge and using a variety of organisational and technological means to ensure that it is **shared**.

A **knowledge-based economy** is an economy based on application of knowledge. Organisations' capabilities and efficiency in using their knowledge override other, more traditional, economic factors such as land and capital. We are living in an age in which the competitiveness of organisations depends on the accumulation of knowledge and its rapid mobilisation to produce goods and services.

(a)   Producing unique products or services or producing products or services at a lower cost than competitors is based on superior knowledge.

(b)   Knowledge is especially valuable as it may be used to create new ideas, insights and interpretations and for decision-making.

(c)   Knowledge, like information, is of no value unless it is applied.

As the importance of knowledge increases, the success of an organisation becomes increasingly dependent on its ability to gather, produce, hold and disseminate knowledge.

1.2.1 Where does knowledge reside?

There are various actions that can be taken to try to determine the prevalence of knowledge in an organisation. One is the identification and development of informal networks and communities of practice within organisations. These self-organising groups share common work interests, usually cutting across a company's functions and processes. People exchange what they know and develop a shared language that allows knowledge to flow more efficiently.

Another means of establishing the prevalence of knowledge is to look at knowledge-related business outcomes. One example is product development and service innovation. While the knowledge embedded within these innovations is invisible, the products themselves are tangible.

1.2.2 Knowledge management

Knowledge management is a relatively new concept in business theory. It is connected with the theory of the learning organisation and founded on the idea that knowledge is a major source of competitive advantage in business. The aim of knowledge management is to exploit existing knowledge and to create new knowledge so that it may be exploited in turn. This is not easy. All organisations possess a great deal of data, but it tends to be unorganised and inaccessible. It is often locked up inside the memories of people who do not realise the value of what they know. Even when it is recorded in some way it may be difficult and time consuming to access, as is the case with most paper archives.

In a knowledge-based economy, knowledge, therefore, has to be actively managed. Knowledge includes tacit knowledge in employees' heads as well as formally recorded facts (known as codified knowledge) and transactions.

Knowledge management programmes are attempts at:

(a)   Designing and installing techniques and processes to create, protect and use **explicit knowledge** (codified knowledge that the company knows that it has). Explicit knowledge includes facts, transactions and events that can be clearly stated and stored in management information systems.

(b)   Designing and creating environments and activities to discover and release **tacit knowledge** (explained below).

Tacit knowledge is expertise held by people within the organisation that has not been formally documented.

(a)   Tacit knowledge is a difficult thing to manage because it is **invisible** and **intangible**. We do not know what knowledge exists within a person's brain, and whether he or she chooses to share it is a matter of choice.

(b)   The **motivation to share** hard-won experience is sometimes low; the individual is 'giving away' their value and may be very reluctant to lose a position of influence and respect by making it available to everyone.

For these two reasons an organisation may never fully know what knowledge it possesses and could exploit. Knowledge management is an attempt to address this problem. It attempts to turn all relevant knowledge, including personal knowledge, into corporate **knowledge assets** that can be easily and widely shared throughout an organisation and appropriately applied.

Examples of tacit and explicit knowledge in a company

Tacit knowledge	Explicit knowledge
Practical and unwritten procedures.	Costing procedures codified in company accounting manuals.
Informal networks and procedures for sales order processing.	New product development through formal company review procedures.
Multifunctional team working on new projects that rely on informal contacts.	Company patents and legal contracts.
Experience of what has worked in practice in branding development over a number of years.	A company's written history of its past events and experience, successes and failures – often very limited.
Specific company treatment of some detailed aspects of management accounting.	Training schemes and apprenticeship programmes that develop and teach best practice.

Knowledge management covers a variety of aspects.

Creation	How is knowledge created?
Capture	How is knowledge obtained by the system?
Storage	How is knowledge stored?
Availability	How is knowledge made available?
Utilisation	How is knowledge used?

The purpose of the process is to build on what is already known, and extend further the knowledge available to the organisation.

Knowledge is now commonly viewed as another source of **competitive advantage**. Producing unique products or services or producing products or services at a lower cost than competitors is based on **superior knowledge**. As the importance of knowledge increases, the success of an organisation becomes increasingly dependent on its ability to gather, produce, hold and disseminate knowledge. This is vastly facilitated by information technology.

1.2.3 Customer knowledge within the organisation

Many business functions deal with customers, including marketing, sales, service, logistics and financial functions. Each function will have its own reasons for being interested in customer information, and may have its own way of recording what it learns and even its own customer information system. The diverse interests of different departments make it difficult to pull together customer knowledge in one common format and place and the problem is magnified because all have some political reason to keep control of what they know about customers.

Organisational means of encouraging sharing include emphasising it in the corporate culture, evaluating people on the basis of their knowledge behaviour and rewarding those who display good knowledge-sharing practice.

On a more practical level, information and communications technology can be of great assistance too.

The more information that a firm can obtain about competitors and customers, the more it should be able to adapt its product/service offerings to meet the needs of the market place through strategies such as differentiation. For example, mail order companies that are able to store data about customer buying habits can exploit this data by recognising patterns of buying behaviour, and offering products at likely buying times that are in line with the customer's profile.

Good information systems may alter the way business is done and may provide organisations with new opportunities. The very term 'information' has strong links with IT, and the role of IT in helping marketers to make decisions is ever growing.

Marketers often face 'information overload' where they have too much information thrown at them from multiple sources. IT systems can help alleviate this by helping to store and structure the information to hand. The key point to remember, however, is that technology alone does not help to cut through the sheer amount of information. Marketers need to understand the decisions that have to be made, define them well and then clearly identify the information that is then required. No IT system to date has been able to do that: human intervention and planning is always required.

2 Organisational culture

"If the fundamental principles of marketing are not accepted by the organisation, any move towards being market-led and customer orientated could be dismissed as 'not the way we do it'." Drummond *et al* (2008) p.248

 KEY CONCEPT

concept

Organisation culture may be defined as:

* 'The collection of traditions, values, policies, beliefs and attitudes that constitute a pervasive context for everything we do and think in an organisation' (Mullins, 2007)

* 'The way we do things around here'

2.1 Environmental influences on organisational culture

Culture is *"the collective programming of the mind which distinguishes the members of one category of people from another"*(Hofstede, 1984). It may be identified as ways of behaving, and ways of understanding, that are shared by a group of people.

Schein (2004) defines organisational culture as 'the set of shared, taken-for-granted implicit assumptions that a group holds and that determines how it perceives, thinks about and reacts to its environment'. He also suggests that the culture of an organisation is grounded in the founder's basic beliefs, values and assumptions, and embedded in the organisation over time – what Schein calls 'the residue of success'.

Culture may therefore be identified as ways of behaving, and ways of understanding, that are shared by a group of people. Referring to it as: 'The way we do things round here', Schein says that organisational culture matters because cultural elements determine strategy, goals and modes of operating.

Examples of organisation culture include the following.

Item	Example
Beliefs and values, which are often unquestioned	'The customer is always right'.
Behaviour	In the City of London, standard business dress is still generally taken for granted and even 'dress down Fridays' have their rules.
Artefacts	Microsoft encourages communication between employees by setting aside spaces for the purpose.
Rituals	In some firms, sales people compete with each other, and there is a reward, given at a ceremony, for the salesperson who does best in any period.
Symbols	Corporate logos are an example of symbols, but they are directed outwards. Within the organisation, symbols can represent power: dress, make and model of car, office size and equipment and access to facilities can all be important symbols.

Manifestations of culture in an organisation may thus include:

* How formal the organisation structure is
* Communication: are senior managers approachable?
* Office layout
* The type of people employed
* Symbols, legends, corporate myths
* Management style
* Freedom for subordinates to show initiative
* Attitudes to quality
* Attitudes to risk
* Attitudes to the customer
* Attitudes to technology

Influences on organisational culture include:

(a)   The organisation's **founder**. A strong set of values and assumptions is set up by the organisation's founder, and even after he or she has retired, these values have their own momentum. Or, to put it another way, an organisation might find it hard to shake off its original culture.

(b)   The organisation's **history**.

    (i)   Culture reflects the era when the organisation was founded.

    (ii)   The effect of history can be determined by stories, rituals and symbolic behaviour. They legitimise behaviour and promote priorities.

(c)   **Leadership and management style**. An organisation with a strong culture recruits and develops managers who naturally conform to it, who perpetuate the culture.

(d)   The **organisation's environment**. As we have seen, nations, regions, occupations and business types have their own distinctive cultures, and these will affect the organisation's style.

Cultural values can be used to guide organisational processes without the need for tight control. They can also be used to motivate employees, by emphasising the heroic dimension of the task. Culture can also be used to drive change, although – since values are difficult to change – it can also be a powerful force for preserving the *status quo*.

2.2 Mintzberg's organisational structures

Mintzberg (1979) believes that all organisations can be analysed into five components, according to how they relate to the work of the organisation, and how they prefer to co-ordinate.

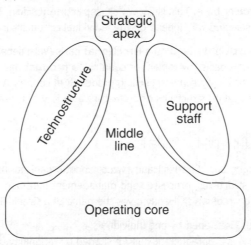

Component	Job	Preferred means of co-ordination
Strategic apex	Ensures the organisation follows its mission. Manages the organisation's relationship with the environment.	Direct supervision (especially in small businesses).
Operating core	People **directly** involved in the process of obtaining inputs, and converting them into outputs.	Mutual adjustment; standardisation of skills.
Middle line	Converts the desires of the strategic apex into the work done by the operating core.	Standardisation of outputs (results).
Technostructure	• Analysers determine the best way of doing a job. • Planners determine outputs (eg goods must achieve a specified level of quality). • Personnel analysts standardise skills (eg training programmes).	Standardisation of work processes or outputs.

Component	Job	Preferred means of co-ordination
Support staff	Ancillary services such as public relations, legal counsel, the cafeteria. Support staff do not plan or standardise production. They function independently of the operating core.	Mutual adjustment

These **components are linked** in five ways.

(a) **Organisation hierarchy** and formal authority.

(b) **Flow of regulated activity**. Inputs are processed into outputs.

(c) **Informal communications** supplement or bypass the formal communication system and formal hierarchy.

(d) **System of work constellations**. Groups of people work together on distinct tasks.

   (i) For example, in producing a set of annual financial statements, people from the finance department (for the numbers), the sales department (for detailed statistics) and public relations (for presentation) need to be involved.

   (ii) On a more on-going basis, the members of the accounts department work together to produce financial information.

(e) ***Ad hoc* decision processes**. A decision process involves recognising a problem, diagnosing its causes, finding a solution and implementing it. For any one decision, these activities occur in a number of different places in the organisation.

In most organisations, tasks and people are grouped together in some rational way: on the basis of specialisation, say, or shared technology or customer base. This is known as **departmentation**. Different patterns of departmentation are possible, and the pattern selected will depend on the individual circumstances of the organisation.

Organisations can be **departmentalised** on a **functional** basis (with separate departments for production, marketing, finance etc), a **geographical** basis (by region, or country), a **product** basis (eg worldwide divisions for product X, Y etc), a **brand** basis, or a **matrix** basis (eg someone selling product X in country A would report to both a product X manager and a country A manager). Organisation structures often feature a variety of these types, as **hybrid** structures.

2.3 Handy's cultural styles

In his book 'Gods of Management', Charles Handy wrote about organisational classification under four types. The four types are differentiated by their structures, processes and management methods. The differences are so significant as to create **distinctive cultures**, to each of which Handy gives the name of a Greek God.

* Power culture (Zeus) is shaped by one individual.
* Role culture (Apollo) is a bureaucratic culture shaped by rationality, rules and procedures.
* Task culture (Athena) is shaped by a focus on outputs and results.
* Existential/person culture (Dionysus) is shaped by the interests of individuals.

Zeus: Power culture	**Apollo: Role culture**
The organisation is controlled by a key central figure, owner or founder. Power is direct, personal, informal. Suits small organisations where people get on well.	Classical, rational organisation: bureaucracy. Stable, slow-changing, formalised, impersonal. Authority based on position and function.

Athena: Task culture	**Dionysus: Person culture**
Management is directed at outputs: problems solved, projects completed. Team-based, horizontally-structured, flexible, valuing expertise – to get the job done.	The purpose of the organisation is to serve the interests of the individuals who make it up: management is directed at facilitating, administering.

2.3.1 Power culture

Zeus is the god representing the **power culture** or **club culture**. Zeus is a dynamic entrepreneur who rules with snap decisions. Power and influence stem from a central source, perhaps the owner-directors or the founder of the business. The degree of formalisation is limited, and there are few rules and procedures. Such a firm is likely to be organised on a functional basis.

(a)   The organisation is capable of adapting quickly to meet change.

(b)   Personal influence decreases as the size of an organisation gets bigger. The power culture is therefore best suited to smaller entrepreneurial organisations, where the leaders have direct communication with all employees.

(c)   Personnel have to get on well with each other for this culture to work. These organisations are clubs of 'like-minded people introduced by the like-minded people, working on empathetic initiative with personal contact rather than formal liaison.'

2.3.2 Role culture

Apollo is the god of the **role culture** or **bureaucracy**. There is a presumption of logic and rationality.

(a)   These organisations have a formal structure, and operate by well-established rules and procedures.

(b)   Individuals are required to perform their job to the full, but not to overstep the boundaries of their authority. Individuals who work for such organisations tend to learn an expertise without experiencing risk; many do their job adequately, but are not over-ambitious.

(c)   The bureaucratic style, as we have seen, can be very efficient in a stable environment, when the organisation is large and when the work is predictable.

2.3.3 Task culture

Athena is the goddess of the **task culture**. Management is seen as completing a succession of projects or solving problems.

(a)   The task culture is reflected in project teams and task forces. In such organisations, there is no dominant or clear leader. The principal concern in a task culture is to get the job done. Therefore the individuals who are important are the experts with the ability to accomplish a particular aspect of the task.

(b)   Performance is judged by results.

(c)   Task cultures are expensive, as experts demand a market price.

(d)   Task cultures also depend on variety, and to tap creativity requires a tolerance of perhaps costly mistakes.

2.3.4 Person culture

Dionysus is the god of the **existential** or **person culture**. In the three other cultures, the individual is subordinate to the organisation or task. An existential culture is found in an organisation whose purpose is to serve the interests of the individuals within it. These organisations are rare, although an example might be a partnership of a few individuals who do all the work of the organisation themselves (with perhaps a little secretarial or clerical assistance): for example, barristers (in the UK) work through chambers.

Management positions in these organisations are often lower in status than the professionals and are labelled secretaries, administrators, bursars, registrars or clerks.

The organisation depends on the talent of the individuals; management is derived from the consent of the managed, rather than the delegated authority of the owners.

Handy cites a pharmaceutical company which at one time had all its manufacturing subcontracted, until the turnover and cost considerations justified a factory of its own. The company hired nine talented individuals to design and run the factory. Result:

(a)   The design team ran on a task culture, with a democratic/consultative leadership style, using project teams for certain problems. This was successful while the factory was being built.

(b)   After its opening, the factory, staffed by 400, was run on similar lines. There were numerous problems. Every problem was treated as a project, and the workforce resented being asked to help sort out 'management' problems. In the end, the factory was run in a slightly more autocratic way. Handy states that this is a classic case of a task culture (to set something up) being superseded by a role culture (to run it). Different cultures suit different businesses.

Handy also matched appropriate cultural models to Anthony's (1965) classification of managerial activity.

(a)   **Strategic management** (carried out by senior management) is concerned with direction-setting, policy-making and crisis handling. It therefore suits a **power culture**.

(b)   **Tactical management** (carried out by middle management) is concerned with establishing means to the corporate ends, mobilising resources and innovating (finding new ways of achieving goals). It therefore suits a **task culture**.

(c)   **Operational management** (carried out by supervisors and operatives) is concerned with routine activities to carry out tactical plans. It therefore suits a **role culture**.

 ACTIVITY 3
application

Review the following statements. Ascribe each of them to one of Handy's four corporate cultures.

People are controlled and influenced by:

(a)   The personal exercise of rewards, punishments or charisma.

(b)   Impersonal exercise of economic and political power to enforce procedures and standards of performance.

(c)   Communication and discussion of task requirements leading to appropriate action motivated by personal commitment to goal achievement.

(d)   Intrinsic interest and enjoyment in the activities to be done, and/or concern and caring for the needs of the other people involved.

"If the [chosen] strategy goes against the dominant culture it is likely to fail unless a major effort is made to develop and maintain support. This could be achieved through staff training, appraisal and restructuring." Drummond et al (2008) p.260

3   Assets

"The organisation's current and potential capabilities have to be identified and this can be achieved by evaluating the assets and competencies that make up the company's resources." Drummond *et al, op.cit.,* p.89

 KEY CONCEPTS
concept

*"**Assets** are organisational attributes, tangible or intangible, that can be utilised to gain advantages in the market."* Drummond *et al, op.cit.,* p.260

Specifically, a **marketing asset** is something that a firm can use to advantage in the market place.

Examples of assets that create competitive advantage include:

(a)   Scale advantages (market share, leverage, global presence, specialist skills)
(b)   Production processes (flexibility, innovation, capacity, uniqueness)
(c)   Customer franchises (relationships, patents, brands)
(d)   Working capital (access, amount, location)
(e)   Distribution networks (coverage, relationships, size)
(f)   Relationships (suppliers, banks, JVs)
(g)   Property (type, location, quality)

3.1 The asset-based approach

An **asset-based approach** identifies the types of assets the marketer will use: customer; distribution and internal assets. It matches 'marketing assets' with customer requirements. There are four types of marketing assets (Hooley *et al*, 2007).

* **Customer-based** assets
* **Distribution-based** assets
* **Internal** assets
* **Alliance-based** assets

3.1.1 Customer-based assets

These exist in the customer's mind.

(a)   Corporate **image and reputation** can be an asset or a liability, depending on the received wisdom.
(b)   A **brand** is an asset.
(c)   **Market domination**. High market share is an asset because of the economies of scale it brings.
(d)   **Better products/services** as perceived by the customer.

3.1.2 Distribution-based assets

(a)   **Distribution network**. This covers sites and access to customers. For many years banks regarded their branch networks as an asset, but branches are costly to maintain and Barclays in the UK has recently attracted criticism for its decision to close many of its small local branches.

(b)   **Distribution control**. Control of distribution constitutes a barrier to entry to other competitors.

(c)   **Pockets of strength**. Where a company cannot serve a wide market, it can build strength in specific regions or through selected distribution outlets.

(d)   **Uniqueness**. A unique or hard-to-copy distribution channel is an asset.

3.1.3 Internal assets

(a)   **Low costs** give a firm the flexibility to choose low prices or to benefit from better margins.

(b)   **Information systems and market intelligence**. Customer databases are built up over time and can enable offers to be targeted.

(c)   The **existing customer base**. Satisfied customers are more likely to be repeat customers.

(d)   Other assets include **technological skills** which can support marketing activities, production **expertise**, **intellectual property**, partnerships and corporate culture.

3.1.4 Alliance based assets

Many firms are expanding through alliances. For example, airlines have code sharing arrangements. Such assets include:

- Market access
- Management skills
- Shared technology
- Exclusivity (eg shutting out competitors)

 MARKETING AT WORK

application

Many airlines have alliances in which they 'share' passengers for flights on certain legs. For example, a passenger flying BA might, on certain journeys, be transferred to a Qantas flight.

In theory this can be an asset to both companies, provided that customer expectations are met (ie that BA and Qantas offer similar standards of service quality).

 EXAM TIP

concept

To some extent, the resource-based approach is diametrically opposed to the marketing concept since, instead of approaching strategy on the basis of giving customers what they want, it concentrates on exploiting what the business already has to offer.

In fact, this distinction is largely theoretical, but it leads to some important ideas that you could use in the exam.

(a)   when the marketing concept is adopted, it will still be necessary to deploy threshold capabilities in all critical areas and the possession of unique resources and core competences will enhance the market offering.

(b)   Conversely, where strategy is built on unique resources and core competences, marketing activities must be carried out with at least threshold competence if the customer is to be satisfied.

In the same case study , low cost airlines are giving the customers what they want (low cost air travel, opening up air travel to people who may not have thought they could afford to fly overseas) and they are able to do this by exploiting their assets through their particular business model:

- Modern fleets
- Single class cabins
- Point-to-point routes (reduce complexity)
- Few frills, with 'extras' charged for
- Direct sales (online, with no use of travel agents)
- Good fleet utilisation
- Use of secondary airports
- Simple ground facilities
- Short haul only
- Performance- based compensation for employees

Learning objectives	Covered
1 Critically evaluate the resource-based view of an organisation and the value of this approach in developing resource and capability to deliver an organisation's vision and mission	☑ Resources, capabilities and competences (1.1) ☑ Knowledge as a resource (1.2)
2 Critically evaluate the fit between an organisation's culture and its current strategy, and assess its ability to be flexible and agile in a changing marketing environment	☑ Organisational culture (section 2)
3 Utilise a range of internal information and assessment tools to evaluate an organisation's strengths and weaknesses in order to assess its readiness for development	☑ Assets (section 3)
4 Critically assess strategic alternatives against pre-determined criteria for an organisation	☑ This chapter looks at the resource-based view of strategy as one aspect of strategy formulation, and how organisational culture and an analysis of organisational assets can shape the strategy and often give rise to alternatives.

1   How do Johnson & Scholes categorise competences?

2   What qualities are required of a core competence by Hamel & Prahalad?

3   The resource-based view of strategy is that sustainable .... is only attained as a result of the possession of .... Fill in the blanks.

4   Give the seven elements of the McKinsey 7S model.

5   Effective knowledge management requires a range of aspects. What are they?

6   Define 'organisational culture'.

7   What are Mintzberg's five organisational components?

8   How did Anthony categorise the hierarchy of management activity?

9   What are the four types of marketing asset defined by Hooley et al?

10   What is a marketing asset?

1   An obvious option is to embark upon a round of cost cutting, and BA is working on exactly that at the time of writing in an attempt to cope with the huge losses it is sustaining. Staff have been asked to work for one month for free. Other options are unpaid leave, and reduced hours. In the words of the chief executive: "Our survival depends on everyone contributing to changes that permanently remove costs from every part of the business."

2   (a)   The reasons for the organisation's existence should be expressed in terms of the consumer or client.

       (b)   Marketing research should be used to find out:

            (i)   Who needs help, and in what ways, and how satisfactory is the current help provided
            (ii)   Where funds should be raised, and what the best approaches should be
            (iii)   Which political figures are susceptible to lobbying and how such lobbying should best be conducted

       (c)   Target markets would be identified for charitable acts, fund-raising and influencing.

       (d)   The charity might also wish to promote an image to the public, perhaps by means of public relations work.

       (e)   The management of the charity will be aware that they are in competition for funds with other charities, and in competition with other ways of spending money in trying to obtain funds from the public. It should organise its 'sales and marketing' systems to raise funds in the most effective way.

            (i)   Many charities now engage in telemarketing.
            (ii)   Many charities have acquired logos – even NHS hospitals have acquired them.

3   (a)   Zeus/power culture
       (b)   Apollo/role culture
       (c)   Athena/task culture
       (d)   Dionysus/person culture

1 Johnson et al (2007) divide competences into two types.

(i) An organisation must achieve at least a threshold level of competence in everything it does.

(ii) Its core competences are those where it outperforms competitors and that are difficult to imitate.

2 It must make a disproportionate contribution to the value the customer perceives.

It must be 'competitively unique'.
It must be extendable, in that it must allow for development of new products

3 Competitive advantage; distinctive resources

4 Structure; Strategy; Systems; Shared values; Staff; Style; Skills

5 Creation; capture; storage; availability; utilisation

6 Organisational culture may be identified as ways of behaving, and ways of understanding, that are shared by the group of people working for an organisation

7 Strategic apex; operating core; middle line; technostructure; support staff

8 Strategic management: concerned with direction-setting, policy-making and crisis handling

Tactical management: concerned with establishing means to the corporate ends, mobilising resources and innovating

Operational management: concerned with routine activities to carry out tactical plans

9 Customer-based assets

Distribution-based assets

Internal assets

Alliance-based assets

10 A marketing asset is something that a firm can use to advantage in the market place.

Aaker, D. & McLoughlin, D. (2007) <u>Strategic Market Management</u>, John Wiley, Chichester.

Anthony, R.N. (1965) <u>Planning and Control Systems</u>, Harvard Business, Boston.

Drummond, G. Ensor, J. & Ashford, R. (2008) <u>Strategic Marketing Planning and Control,</u> (3rd edition), Elsevier Ltd, Oxford.

Hamel, G. & Prahalad, C.K. (1996) <u>Competing for the Future</u>, new edition, Harvard Business School Press, Boston.

Handy, C. (2009) *Gods of Management: The Changing Work of Organisations*, Souvenir Press Ltd, London.

Hofstede, G. (1984) *Culture's* <u>Consequences: International Differences in Work-Related Values</u>, (abridged edition), Sage Publications Inc, Thousand Oaks California.

Hooley, G., Saunders, J., Piercy, N., & Nicoulaud, B., (2007) <u>Marketing Strategy and Competitive Positioning</u>, (4th edition), FT Prentice Hall, Harlow.

Johnson, G., Scholes, K., & Whittington, R. (2007*) Exploring Corporate Strategy*, (8th edition), FT Prentice Hall, Harlow.

Mintzberg, H (1979) <u>The Structuring of Organisations</u>, US edition, FT Prentice Hall, Harlow.

Mullins, L.J., (2007) <u>Management and Organisational Behaviour</u>, (8th edition), FT Prentice Hall, Harlow.

O,Connell, D. '*Could British Airways really go bust or not?*', Sunday Times, 21 June 2009.

Schein, E. (2004) <u>Organisational Culture and Leadership</u>, (3rd edition), Jossey Bass, San Francisco.

Chapter 5

Developing strategy

Topic list

Introduction

This chapter develops the wide subject of the development of corporate strategy. For the purposes of your Analysis & Decision studies, an important aspect is an explanation of the way that 'strategy' and 'marketing' relate to one another. To quote from the syllabus guidance, it is vital to "recognise the importance of coordinating the often disparate functions of an organisation."

The Analysis & Decision syllabus requires you to have a good grasp of the evolving nature of strategic processes. In this chapter we discuss ways in which strategy is made in organisations. There are many approaches, each with something to offer, but the important this is to have a consistent framework to make sure that all influences can be taken account of.

We review the **rational model**. This is the classic approach; it has its weaknesses, but its great strength is that it is thorough. As a result, this method actually forms a good checklist of the things that strategists should consider, if only brief.

There are other approaches to strategy. These are, generally speaking, **descriptive** rather than **prescriptive**; that is to say, they are based on observation of what real world organisations actually do when making their strategies.

It is important to be aware that the terminology commonly used in this area of study is rather imprecise: 'strategy', 'corporate strategy', 'business strategy', 'marketing' and 'marketing strategy' are terms that are often used as if they were interchangeable.

Syllabus-linked learning objectives

By the end of the chapter you will be able to:

Learning objectives	Syllabus link
1 Critically evaluate an organisation's current strategic intent, based upon its vision, mission, values and stakeholder expectations	1.3.1
2 Critically analyse the role of strategic intent in shaping an organisation's strategy development	1.3.2

1   Evaluating the current direction

"A primary purpose of an organisation's vision – what a future strategy should be – and objectives is to help make strategic decisions. Thus, it is appropriate to look toward them for guidance". Aaker & McLoughlin, 2007) p.32

1.1 Organisational mission

The terminology of strategic management is not universally defined. There is a number of words that are used almost interchangeably: strategy, tactics, mission, purpose, values, object, aim, target, goal, policy.

The organisational purpose, also known as the **mission** can be understood as the firm's long-term approach to business, and a reflection of the organisation's value system. **Goals** interpret the mission to the needs of different stakeholders (eg customers, employees, shareholders), and **objectives** should embody mission and goals!

KEY CONCEPTS

concept

Strategic analysis is concerned with understanding the strategic position of the organisation.

Mission denotes values, the business's rationale for existing

Vision refers to where the organisation intends to be in the future.

Customers and the mission statement

In the increasingly competitive service sector, it is no longer enough to promise customer satisfaction. Today, customer 'delight' is the stated aim for companies battling to retain and increase market share.

British Airways, which lists delighting customers among its goals, says ensuring the safety of passengers and meeting all their needs drives everything it does. 'Other airlines fly the same routes using similar aircraft. What BA must do is provide a superior standard of efficiency, comfort and general service which persuades passengers to fly with us again and again,' says Mike Street, director of customer services at BA.

Kwik-Fit, the car repair group, is another company that has included customer delight in its mission statement. Its forecourt promises to deliver '100% customer delight' in the supply and fitting of vehicle brakes, tyres and exhausts leaves little margin for mistakes – and none at all for making any customer unhappy. Staff attend courses at company-run centres covering *"all practical aspects of their work, customer care and general management techniques"*. Commitment is encouraged by 'job security', opportunities for promotion and a reward package that includes profit-related pay and shares in the company. Customer satisfaction is monitored via reply-paid questionnaires distributed after work is carried out and through a freephone helpline that is open 24 hours a day. Kwik-Fit also says its customer survey unit *"allows us to make contact with 5,000 customers a day, within 72 hours of their visit to a Kwik-Fit Centre"*.

What the organisation wishes to achieve – its mission – is fundamental to any focused control of its activities. One aspect of this control is analysis of those groups with an interest in what the organisation does. The organisation needs to satisfy the agendas of these various groups. As mentioned in the syllabus guidance notes, the 'best' strategy (measured using accepted business criteria) may not be acceptable to them, or may not fit with the current direction.

1.2 Stakeholder analysis and relationships

Mendelow (1985) classifies stakeholders on a matrix whose axes are 'power held' and 'likelihood of showing an interest' in the organisation's activities. These factors will help define the type of relationship the organisation should seek with its stakeholders.

Mendelow's stakeholder matrix

Level of interest

	Low	High
Power Low	A	B
Power High	C	D

How should a company treat stakeholders in the various segments?

Stakeholder analysis identifies the interest groups in an enterprise. Different stakeholders will have their own views as to strategy. As some stakeholders have negative power, in other words power to impede or disrupt the decision, their likely response might be considered. An analysis of stakeholder risk has two elements.

(a) The risk that any particular strategic option poses to the interests of the different stakeholders.

(b) The risk that stakeholders might respond in such a way as to make a proposed strategy less attractive.

Stakeholder	Interests at stake	Response risk
Management	Pay, status, power, promotion	Subtle sabotage, procrastination, internal politics
Employees	Pay, security, expertise	Strike action, resignation
Shareholders	Return on investment	Sell shares, or refuse to invest more
Bankers	Loan security; profits	Refusal to continue lending arrangements
Customers	Product	Switch to another supplier
Suppliers	Business	Will fail to deliver
Government	Public interest; election; taxes	Will regulate or tax

The firm can make strategic gains from managing stakeholder relationships. Studies have revealed:

(a) Correlation between employee retention and customer loyalty (eg, low staff turnover in service firms generally results in more repeat business).

(b) Continuity and stability in relationships with employees, customers and suppliers is important in enabling organisations to respond to certain types of change.

These soft issues are particularly pertinent for industries where creativity is important and for service businesses. Knowledge-based and service industries are likely to be the growth industries of the future.

1.3 Organisational configuration

The importance of organisational structure was discussed in Chapter 4. The way that an organisation is structured has a significant influence upon its strategic direction.

As we saw in Chapter 4, the **McKinsey 7S model** shows how the various aspects of a business relate to one another. It is a useful illustration of the influences upon an organisation's behaviour. To recap:

McKinsey 7S framework

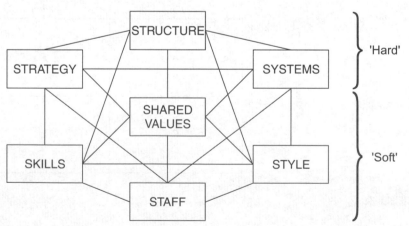

The organisation structure determines division of tasks in the organisation and the hierarchy of authority from the most senior to junior.

1.4 Ethics

The conduct of an organisation, its management and employees will be measured against ethical standards by the customers, suppliers and other members of the public with whom they deal. Types of ethical problem a manager may meet with in practice are listed below.

(a) **Production practices**. Attempts to increase profitability by cutting costs may lead to dangerous working conditions, inadequate safety standards in products or reprehensible practices (eg child labour). This is a problem for firms which outsource production to low cost factories overseas.

(b) **Gifts**. There is a fine line to be drawn between gifts, accepted as part of a way of doing business, and bribes.

(c) **Social responsibility**. Companies are being held to account for their influences upon such matters as pollution levels and human rights issues.

(d) **Competitive behaviour**. There is a distinction between competing aggressively and competing unethically and illegally.

  ACTIVITY 2   application

The Heritage Carpet Company is a London-based retailer which imports carpets from Turkey, Iran and India. The company was founded by two Europeans who travelled independently through these countries in the 1970s. The company is the sole customer for carpets made in a number of villages in each of the source countries. The carpets are hand woven. Indeed, they are so finely woven that the process requires that children be used to do the weaving, thanks to their small fingers. The company believes that it is preserving a 'craft', and the directors believe that this is a justifiable social objective. Recently, a UK television company has reported unfavourably on child exploitation in the carpet weaving industry. There were reports of children working twelve-hour shifts in poorly lit sheds and cramped conditions, with consequent deterioration in eyesight, muscular disorders and a complete absence of education. The examples cited bear no relation to the Heritage Carpet Company's suppliers although children are used in the labour force, but there has been a spate of media attention. The regions in which the Heritage Carpet Company's supplier villages are found are soon expected to enjoy rapid economic growth.

What social and ethical issues are raised for the Heritage Carpet Company?

Mission, discussed at the beginning of this chapter, should incorporate recognition of the ethical dimension.

  EXAM TIP   application

It is important to understand that if ethics is applicable to corporate behaviour at all, it must be a fundamental aspect of mission, since everything the organisation does flows from that. Managers responsible for strategic decision-making cannot avoid responsibility for their organisation's ethical standing.. Ethics and environmental considerations can conflict with business objectives, however. In the sample case study, Ryanair and other low cost carriers (indeed the whole airline industry) face pressure from environmentalists to cut carbon emissions. This will increase their costs, and not all airlines are happy to take part

Ryanair boss Michael O'Leary has hit back at criticism from the climate change minister, saying his airline was *"the greenest in Europe"*.

In a broad attack on airlines' efforts to tackle carbon emissions, Ian Pearson said Ryanair was the "irresponsible face of capitalism". In an interview with the Guardian, Mr Pearson said: "When it comes to climate change, Ryanair are not just the unacceptable face of capitalism, they are the irresponsible face of capitalism."

Mr O'Leary defended his company and the industry as a whole. He said the "silly" minister and "eco-lunatics" were targeting the aviation industry when it accounted for 2% of the problem.

Even though his company was growing, the new planes it had invested £10bn in the last five years had cut its emissions and fuel consumption by 50%, Mr O'Leary said.

Friends of the Earth said if the government was serious about fighting climate change it should scrap airport expansion plans and tax breaks for the air industry.

A proposed EU emissions trading scheme will see airlines pay for exceeding their current level of emissions from 2011/2012. Airlines would be issued with pollution permits - those that cut emissions would be able to sell their surplus while an airline that increased its emissions would have to buy more permits.

Although Ryanair is opposing these efforts, Toby Nicol, spokesman for Budget airline Easyjet, said that the company *"stands full-square with the government"* on the proposal to include EU internal flights and international flights in the carbon trading scheme.

www.bbc.co.uk – 5 January 2007

1.4.1 The scope of corporate ethics

Corporate ethics may be considered in three contexts.

- The organisation's interaction with national and international society
- The effects of the organisation's routine operations
- The behaviour of individual members of staff

(a) **Influencing society**. Businesses operate within, and interact with, the political, economic and social framework of wider society. It is both inevitable and proper that they will both influence and be influenced by that wider framework. Governments, individual politicians and pressure groups will all make demands on such matters as employment prospects and executive pay. Conversely, businesses themselves will find that they need to make their own representations on such matters as monetary policy and the burden of regulation. International variation in such matters and in the framework of corporate governance will affect organisations that operate in more than one country. It is appropriate that the organisation develops and promotes its own policy on such matters.

(b) **Corporate behaviour**. The organisation should establish corporate policies for those issues over which it has direct control. Examples of matters that should be covered by policy include health, safety, labelling, equal opportunities, environmental effects, political activity, bribery and support for cultural activities.

(c) **Individual behaviour**. Policies to guide the behaviour of individuals are likely to flow from the corporate stance on the matters discussed above. The organisation must decide on the extent to which it considers it appropriate to attempt to influence individual behaviour. Some aspects of such behaviour may be of strategic importance, especially when managers can be seen as representing or embodying the organisation's standards. Matters of financial rectitude and equal treatment of minorities are good examples here.

Business ethics are also relevant to competitive behaviour. This is because a market can only be free if competition is, in some basic respects, fair. There is a distinction between competing aggressively and competing unethically. The dispute between British Airways and Virgin centred around issues of business ethics.

It is unethical for US researchers to test expensive treatments on people in Third World countries who would be unable to afford those drugs, a bioethics commission warned on Thursday in a published report.

In an article in the New England Journal of Medicine, the National Bioethics Advisory Commission also said it was unethical to give volunteers placebos instead of treatments that are known to work.

These warnings by Harold Shapiro and Eric Meslin, the chairman and executive director respectively of the presidential commission, mark the latest round in a debate over the rules for conducting studies in countries where ethical standards may be less stringent than in the United States.

The issue surfaced in the Journal in 1997 when Drs. Peter Lurie and Sidney M Wolfe of Public Citizen's Health Research Group cited 15 government-financed studies that, they said, were using unethical methods to test whether various treatments could block the spread of the AIDS virus from a woman to her newborn child. All were being done in developing countries.

Some of the women in those studies were given placebos, even though the GlaxoSmithKline drug AZT had been shown to prevent babies from contracting AIDS from their infected mothers. At the time, it was regarded as unethical in the United States and other countries to test alternative AIDS treatments by giving pregnant volunteers a placebo.

Supporters of the studies had argued that giving placebos was valid because the radically different economic conditions in developing countries, where AZT was not widely available, made it virtually impossible to do the type of research that had become the standard in developed countries.

Shapiro and Meslin, who lead the 17 member advisory council established by former President Bill Clinton in 1995, wrote in the Journal that the experimental treatment should be tested against the best established treatment, "whether or not that treatment is available in the host country."

Giving placebos when an effective treatment exists "is not ethically acceptable," they said. Shapiro and Meslin also said it was important to "avoid the exploitation of potentially vulnerable populations in developing countries."

If an experiment is testing a drug or device that " is not likely to be affordable in the host country or if the health care infrastructure cannot support its proper distribution and use, it is unethical to ask persons in that country to participate in the research, since they will not enjoy any of its potential benefits," they said.

There have been suggestions that researchers or drug companies may be testing products in poor countries because the cost is less and the rules are less stringent.

"Conducting a trial in a developing country because it is more convenient or efficient or less troublesome to do is never a sufficient justification," said Shapiro and Meslin. The two also said that if tests show that the experimental treatment turns out to be more effective, it should be made available to all the people who participated in the study.

Researchers should not abandon their volunteers after the study is completed, they said.

1.4.2 Ethics and marketing

The marketing function has its own specific areas of ethical responsibility, as acknowledged by the 'societal marketing concept' and the CIM's own Code of Professional Standards.

KEY CONCEPT

concept

The societal marketing concept is a management orientation that holds that the key task of the organisation is to determine the needs and wants of target markets and to adapt the organisation to delivering the desired satisfactions more effectively and efficiently than its competitors in a way that preserves or enhances the consumer's and society's well-being.

Application of ethical considerations to the marketing mix

(a)   **Product/service**

   (i)   Failure to inform customers about risks associated with the use of the product: dishonesty. Currently, there are lawsuits in the US in which people are suggesting that the tobacco companies, despite their denials, have known for some time that nicotine is addictive.

   (ii)   Using materials of a poorer quality in a bid to cut costs.

   (iii) Does manufacture involve an unacceptable environmental cost?

(b)   **Pricing**. In economic terms, price is a matter of supply and demand and, in the pursuit of profit, prices are what the market will bear. Ethics come into the discussion when:

   (i)   Cartels attempt to fix prices by rigging the market
   (ii)   Consumers are sometimes charged extras, not officially disclosed

(c)   **Promotion**

   (i)   Advertising: honest, legal, decent and truthful
   (ii)   Tastefulness of imagery (eg violence, sexual stereotyping)

(d)   **Place.** Ethical concerns regarding relationships with intermediaries can involve the use of power, or delays in payment.

1.4.3 Corporate social responsibility (CSR)

The behaviour of organisations may also be considered in the light of notions of corporate social responsibility. This is a rather poorly defined concept. However, there does now seem to be widespread acceptance that commercial organisations should devote some of their resources to the promotion of wider social aims that are not necessarily mandated by either law or the rules of ethics.

There is a fundamental split of views about the nature of corporate responsibility.

*   The stakeholder view that a range of goals should be pursued
*   The view that the business organisation is a purely economic force, subject to law

Businesses, particularly large ones, are subject to increasing expectations that they will exercise social responsibility. This is an ill-defined concept, but appears to focus on the provision of specific benefits to society in general, such as charitable donations, the creation or preservation of employment, and spending on environmental improvement or maintenance. A great deal of the pressure is created by the activity of minority action groups and is aimed at businesses because they are perceived to possess extensive resources. The momentum of such arguments is now so great that the notion of social responsibility has become almost inextricably confused with the matter of ethics. It is important to remember the distinction. Social responsibility and ethical behaviour are not the same thing.

In this context, you should remember that a business managed with the sole objective of maximising shareholder wealth can be run in just as ethical a fashion as one in which far wider stakeholder responsibility is assumed. On the other hand, there is no doubt that many large businesses have behaved irresponsibly in the past and some continue to do so.

2   Models of strategic management

"Strategic market management is often frustrating because the environment is so difficult to understand and predict. The communication and choices required within the organisation can create strain and internal resistance. The most valuable organisational resource, management time, is absorbed. The alternative of simply waiting for and reacting to exceptional opportunities often seems efficient and adequate. Despite these costs and problems, strategic market management has the potential to:

*   *Precipitate the consideration of strategic choices*
*   *Force a long-range view*
*   *Make visible the resource allocation decision ...*
*   *Aid strategic analysis and decision making*

- *Provide a strategic management and control system*
- *Provide both horizontal and vertical communication and coordination systems*
- *Help a business cope with change."*   Aaker & McLoughlin (2007) p.14

2.1 Strategic marketing

The primary role of strategic marketing is to identify and create value for the business through strongly differentiated positioning. It achieves this by influencing the strategy and culture of the organisation in order to ensure that both have a strong customer focus.

In organisations where strategic marketing does not exist as a function, the process or decisions are still undertaken by senior managers or business leaders. Where it is an explicit function, the strategic marketing role will usually be performed by a marketing function in a business unit and by a corporate level marketing function, which may also have a responsibility for co-ordinating the activities of marketing departments in business units.

When this role is carried out by a marketing specialist, it is called 'marketing director' or 'strategic marketing manager', sometimes based in a department called 'marketing' rather than 'strategic marketing'. Strategic marketers should champion the customer experience and exert a strong influence on the organisation to adopt a customer orientation, contribute along with other directors and senior managers to its competitive strategy, align the organisation's activities to the customer, and manage the organisation's marketing activities.

During strategy formulation, strategic marketing is about choices that customer-focused organisations make on where and how to compete and with what assets. It is also about developing a specific competitive position using tools from the marketing armoury including brands, innovation, customer relationships and service, alliance, channels and communications, and increasingly, price. Strategic marketing does not own the business strategy but, like other departments and functions, should contribute to it and control the operational levers that make a strategy effective. However, marketing has an exceptional contribution to make in identifying opportunities and determining ways to create value for customers and shareholders.

During implementation, strategic marketing is the 'glue' that connects many aspects of the business. It will often manage one or a portfolio of brands. Increasingly, it works with HR to ensure that the culture and values in the organisation are consistent with the brand and to ensure that marketing competences are part of the overall framework for staff development across the business. Strategic marketing also has responsibility for directing the implementation of marketing activities needed to execute the organisation's strategy. Other key tasks of strategic marketing in today's organisations are:

(a)   Contributing to strategic initiatives being undertaken by the organisation, for example marketing input to a 'due diligence' evaluation of a prospective merger or acquisition. In some cases, strategic marketers will be managing multi-disciplinary teams.

(b)   Co-ordinating and managing customer information across the organisation within the data protection and privacy legislation. This involves close relationships with the IT function.

(c)   Advising on competitive positioning: that is, determining target market segments and how they will be approached. This will include developing and driving the business case for investment in brands, new products and services

(d)   Championing and developing innovation and entrepreneurship within the organisation

(e)   Ensuring that the marketing function is appropriately skilled and resourced

(f)   Providing input with finance on the valuation of brands for reporting and disclosure

This concept of strategic marketing draws heavily on theory and practice of strategic management, not just of marketing. This is an important distinction since strategic marketing is as much a part of directing how the organisation competes as it is a part of marketing itself. Professional marketers engage in relationships with most functions within the organisation and are 'business people' rather than 'technical marketers'. This is particularly so at the strategic level. It requires participants at this level to embrace a wider range of management theory and practice than has been the case in the past.

In addition to traditional marketing theory, strategic marketing also embraces:

- Business and corporate strategy
- Investment decisions
- Culture and change management

- Quality management
- Programme and project management

Marketers still have an essential role to play in contributing their specialist marketing skills to the formulation, implementation and control of strategy.

EXAM TIP

application

It goes without saying that strategic marketing operates in a global context – take the example of Ryanair in the sample case study. That is not to say that the Analysis and Decision syllabus has nothing to offer the organisation pursuing a domestic strategy or entering its first foreign market. Even if an organisation is not operating across borders, it is likely to be working in a market in which competitors based in other countries are operating – in other words, a global context

2.1.1 The role of marketing in market-led strategic management

Ohmae (1991) summarises business strategy as a triangular relationship involving the three Cs: the corporation, the customers and the competition. The corporation and its competitors will seek to provide value to customers and incur costs in doing so.

Marketing plays a vital role in the management of this strategic triangle via the creation of an advantageous marketing mix. Such a mix will match the needs of the customer with the strength of the corporation and effectively differentiate the resulting value offered from those of the competitors. Marketing expertise and personnel are important drivers in taking a firm to the customer and making the organisation '**market-led**' (focusing on the customer).

In short, the pursuit of **customer satisfaction** is at the heart of the market-led company, but there are issues arising from this (Piercy *et al*, 2008):

New customers	• **Rising expectations**: customers exposed to world class service will expect it everywhere
	• **Sophistication**: customers can see through marketing-speak, and want transparency
	• Increased **cynicism** about marketing
New competitors	• From **overseas**
	• **Reinventing** the business (eg Direct Line Insurance)
New type of organisation	• **Outsourcing** arrangements
	• **Collaboration** arrangements
	• **Alliances** (eg airlines)
	• **Stakeholder** influences
New ways of doing business	• **Customer-specific** marketing
	• **Databases** are used to develop profiles of individual customers to entice them into a **relationship**
	• **Internet marketing**: buyers and sellers can conduct a dialogue as the Internet is interactive
	• **Customer co-operatives**: Internet newsgroups and chatrooms enable customers to get together perhaps to negotiate discounts or to share experience of a brand

2.2 Strategic intent, vision and leadership

concept

Strategy: a course of action including the specification of resources required to meet a specific objective.

Corporate strategy is concerned with the overall purpose and scope of the organisation and how value will be added to the different parts (business units) of the organisation.

Tactics: the deployment of resources to execute an agreed strategy.

Policy: a general statement providing guidelines for management of decision-making.

Strategic management: the development, implementation and control of agreed strategies. There is more to strategy than merely deciding what you want to achieve and how you are to achieve it.

Synergistic planning is a rational process of determining further action based on realistic consideration of the current situation and desired outcome.

Any level of the organisation can have objectives and devise strategies to achieve them. The strategic management process is multi-layered, as illustrated in the diagram, below.

Levels of strategy

CORPORATE STRATEGY

What businesses are we (or want to be) in?

How do we enter or exit?

| BUSINESS STRATEGY | BUSINESS STRATEGY | BUSINESS STRATEGY |

Strategies relevant to a particular area

Strategic Business Unit (SBU)   SBU   SBU

FUNCTIONAL STRATEGIES

R&D	OPERATIONS	MARKETING	HRM	IT/IS	FINANCE
• Products	• Capacity	• Orientation	• Recruitment	• Systems	• Sources
• Processes	• Process technology	• Marketing mix	• Selection	• Technology	• Uses
• Design	• Work flows	• Product planning	• HRD	• Management	
• Development	• Quality	• Marketing information	• Appraisal		
• Testing	• Outsourcing	• Segmentation	• Reward		
		• Services			

Strategies involving many functions (eg change management, total quality, re-engineering)

Corporate decisions relate to the scope of a firm's activities, the long-term direction of the organisation, and allocation of resources. The 'planning' model of strategy formation suggest a logical sequence which involves

- Analysing the current situation
- Generating choices (relating to competitors, products and markets) and
- Implementing the chosen strategies

It is important to recognise the hierarchical level of planning and control decisions, because decision-makers can only make plans or take control action within the sphere of the authority that has been delegated to them.

Synergistic planning, introduced above, has been described in several ways. We will discuss it under four main headings.

(a)   Determining the desired outcome
(b)   Analysing the current situation
(c)   Designing possible courses of action
(d)   Deciding what to do and how to do it

2.2.1 The synergistic planning process

(a)   **The desired outcome**. Any process of planning must start with a clear definition of what is to be achieved. This process of objective setting is frequently undertaken in a very superficial manner in the real world and sometimes hardly performed at all. There may be an assumption that 'everybody knows what we are trying to achieve' or reference back to long-established objectives that have lost some or all of their relevance under current circumstances. Only when objectives are clearly defined can possible courses of action be assessed and eventual success or failure be measured. The process of definition is not complete until everyone concerned has agreed on a single clear statement of what is to be attained. Vagueness and imprecise of language are to be avoided, but appear all too often for political purposes, since they allow different interpretations to be used by parties pursuing different agendas. Vagueness and ambiguity hamper affective action.

(b)   **The current situation** (Part 1 of this syllabus). Any plan must take into account circumstances that will affect attainment of the objective. The first step is to establish just where the individual or organisation stands to begin with. Current circumstances will include a vast array of factors, some of far more immediate importance than others. An important aspect of the current situation is the potential that exists for future developments that may affect possible future action. You should be familiar with the idea of SWOT – strengths, weaknesses, opportunities and threats. Strengths and weaknesses exist now; opportunities and threats have potential for the future. SWOT is a very common model for analysing the existing situation and widely used in marketing.

(c)   **Possible courses of action** (Part 2 of this syllabus). Simple problems, when analysed, often suggest a single, fairly obvious route to a satisfactory solution. If you come home from a skiing holiday and find that a cold snap has left you with a burst pipe, you have little alternative to turning off the water at the main and trying to find a plumber. The analysis of more complex problems will tend to suggest a range of possible courses of action. There is a requirement for both experience and imagination here. Experience will suggest routes that have proved satisfactory in similar circumstances in the past. Imagination suggest both modifications to such plans and completely new ones.

(d)   **Deciding what to do and how to do it** (Part 3 of this syllabus). When a range of possible plans has been outlined, it then becomes necessary to undergo a process of selection, normally by considering such matters as those below.

Probability of success
Resources required
Acceptability of the proposed action and its implications
Potential obstacles

The process of planning is not complete when a course of action has been chosen. It is then necessary to prepare detailed plans for all the groups and individuals involved. These must be integrated in such a way that all action undertaken supports the attainment of the overall objective. Performance measures and control mechanisms must also be established so that effort is not wasted and obstacles can be overcome.

2.2.2 Levels of strategy

We have already identified three levels of strategy in a large organisation.

- **Corporate strategies**. Corporate strategy might involve diversifying into a new line of business or closing a business down. It might mean global expansion or contraction.

- **Business strategies**. Business strategy might involve decisions as to whether, in principle, a company should:

- **Operational and functional strategies**, eg:

  - Segment the market and specialise in particularly profitable areas
  - Compete by offering a wider range of products
  - Offer a differentiated product

Some large, diversified firms have separate strategic business units dealing with particular areas. Functional/operational strategies deal with specialised areas of activity.

MARKETING AT WORK

application

Management of real estate is an important aspect of strategy for retailers; some have very large holdings in prime locations, which represent major capital assets. The *Financial Times* had this to say about one such retailer.

'J Sainsbury announced the formation of a 10-year, £1.2 billion property joint venture with British Land as it reported robust fourth-quarter trade. 'The supermarket operator, which has been under pressure to release value from its property portfolio, said it was investing £273 million in the 50:50 securitised joint venture, which owns 39 retail sites with a value of £1.2 billion, representing a net equivalent yield of 5.1 per cent.

'Sainsbury said the venture "unlocked significant development potential and value creation". It is aiming to extend up to 25 sites by about 500,000 square feet of net selling area following the deal.'

As at 31 March 2009, the portfolio held by the British Land/J Sainsbury joint venture had a valuation of £964 million, with annual net rent of £63 million.

www.britishland.com [accessed 21 June 2009]

2.2.3 A corporate strategic planning model

A model of the **corporate strategic planning process** appears below. There are three stages., as illustrated below.

Strategic analysis

Strategic analysis is concerned with understanding the strategic position of the organisation.

(a) **Environmental analysis** (external appraisal) is the scanning of the business's environment for factors relevant to the organisation's current and future activities.

(b) **Position or situation audit**. The current state of the business in respect of resources, brands, markets etc.

(c) **Mission**

    (i)   The firm's long-term approach to business
    (ii)   The organisation's value system

(d) **Goals** interpret the mission to the needs of different stakeholders (eg customers, employees, shareholders).

(e) **Objectives** should embody mission and goals. Generally, they are quantitative measures, against which actual performance can be assessed.

(f) **Corporate appraisal**. A critical assessment of strengths, weaknesses, opportunities and threats (SWOT) existing in the internal and environmental factors affecting an organisation.

(g) **Gap analysis**. A projection of current activities into the future to identify if there is a difference between the firm's objectives and the results from the continuation of current activities.

Note that you might decide the mission after assessing the needs of the organisation and its environmental situation.

Strategic choice

Strategic choice is based on strategic analysis.

(a) **Strategic options generation**. Here are some examples.

    (i)   Increase market share
    (ii)   International growth
    (iii)   Concentration on core competences
    (iv)   Acquisition

(b) **Strategic options evaluation**. Alternative strategies are developed and each is then examined on its merits.

    (i)   Acceptability to the organisation's stakeholders
    (ii)   Suitability
    (iii)   Feasibility

(c) **Strategy selection**

    (i)   Competitive strategy is the generic strategy determining how you compete.
    (ii)   Product-market strategy determines where you compete.
    (iii)   Institutional strategies determine the method of growth.

Strategic implementation

The implementation of the strategy has to be planned. This is the conversion of the strategy into detailed plans or objectives for operating units.

(a) Some plans detail specifications as to how the activities should be carried out.

(b) Others will specify targets which managers are expected to reach on their own initiative.

(c) The planning of implementation has several aspects.

    (i)   Resource planning (ie finance, Human Resources (HR). This involves assessing the key tasks, and the resources to be allocated to them.

    (ii)   Systems. Systems are necessary to provide the necessary strategic information, as well as essential operational procedures. Control systems are used to assess performance.

    (iii)   Organisation structure.

  ACTIVITY 3   application

Ganymede Ltd is a company selling widgets. The finance director says 'We plan to issue more shares to raise money for new plant capacity – which will enable us to enter the vital and growing widget markets of Latin America. After all, we've promised the shareholders 5% profit growth this year, and trading is tough'.

Identify the corporate, business and functional strategies in the above statement.

The rational strategic planning model

ENVIRONMENTAL ANALYSIS

eg PEST factors
Competitive forces
Turbulence

MISSION

• Why the business exists at all.
• What business are we in?
• Values

POSITION OR SITUATION AUDIT

Company's internal resources and facilities: current performance, comparatives

GOALS

The relevance of the mission to different stakeholders

OBJECTIVES

How the mission can be achieved. Desirable outcomes of corporate activity

Strategic analysis:
• Where are we now?
• Where do we want to be?

CORPORATE APPRAISAL

eg Strengths, Weaknesses, Opportunities, Threats; Gap analysis

CORPORATE STRATEGIC CHOICE

(1) Options generation
(2) Options evaluation
(3) Choice

Strategic choice:
Which way is best?

FUNCTIONAL STRATEGIES

Implementation and control:
How can we ensure arrival?

STRATEGY IMPLEMENTATION

REVIEW & CONTROL

Assess actual performance in the light of plans

KEY CONCEPT

concept

Leadership is the process of influencing others to work willingly towards a goal, and to the best of their capabilities. 'The essence of leadership is followership. In other words it is the willingness of people to follow that makes a person a leader'

Koontz, O'Donnell, Weihrich (1988)

Leadership comes about in a number of different ways.

(a)   A manager is **appointed** to a position of authority within the organisation. Leadership of subordinates is a function of the position.

(b)   Some leaders are **elected**.

(c)   Other leaders **emerge** by popular choice or through their personal drive. The personal, physical or expert power of leaders is more important than position power alone. Within teams and groups of equal colleagues leadership can and does change.

If a manager has indifferent or poor leadership qualities then the team would still do the job, but not efficiently. A good leader can ensure more than simply a compliance with orders. Leadership and management are different but linked activities; two sides of the same coin. Managing is concerned with logic, structure, analysis and control. If done well, it produces predictable results on time.

Leadership requires a different mind set and the leader has different tasks.

- Creating a sense of direction
- Communicating the vision
- Energising, inspiring and motivating

All of these activities involve dealing with people rather than things. A manager needs leadership skills to be effective.

One of the key features of a system of strategic planning is that it requires leadership. Specifically, it encourages the following:

(a)   **Forces managers to think**. Strategic planning can encourage creativity and initiative by tapping the ideas of the management team.

(b)   **Forces decision-making**. Companies cannot remain static – they have to cope with changes in the environment. A strategic plan helps to chart the future possible areas where the company may be involved and draws attention to the need to keep on changing and adapting, not just to 'stand still' and survive.

(c)   **Better control.** Management control can be better exercised if targets are explicit.

(d)   **Enforces consistency at all levels**. Long-term, medium-term and short-term objectives, plans and controls can be made consistent with one another. Otherwise, strategies can be rendered ineffective by budgeting systems with performance measures which have no strategic content.

(e)   **Public knowledge**. An entrepreneur who builds a long-lasting business has 'a theory of the business' which informs his or her business decisions. In large organisations that theory of the business has to become public knowledge, as decisions cannot be taken by only one person.

(f)   **Time horizon**. Some plans are needed for the long-term.

(g)   **Co-ordinates**. Activities of different business functions need to be directed towards a common goal.

(h)   **Clarifies objectives**. Managers are forced to define what they want to achieve.

(i)   **Allocates responsibility**. A plan shows people where they fit in.

2.3 Strategic intent and flexibility: taking account of other influences

KEY CONCEPTS

concept

Intended strategies are plans. Those plans or aspects of plans which are actually realised are called deliberate strategies.

Emergent strategies are those that develop out of patterns of behaviour. The task of strategic management is to control and shape these emergent strategies as they develop.

Johnson & Scholes (2006) anchor plans in the behaviour of the organisation and the people in it. They suggest an approach which follows a similar outline to the rational model, but which recognises the need for some flexibility in taking account of, among other influences, the political and cultural influences on managers. They discuss two other ways in which strategy can arise through deliberate management intent.

2.3.1 The command view

Here strategy develops through the direction of an individual or group, but not necessarily through formal planning. In this model there is a person or group with acknowledged strategic power and responsibility.

The mechanisms by which this authority arises are reminiscent of Weber's analysis of legitimate authority into legal-rational, charismatic and traditional. Johnson & Scholes mention the autocratic leader; the charismatic leader whose reputation or personality gives control of strategic direction; and the making of economic and social strategy in the public sector by elected politicians.

2.3.2 Paradigm and politics

(a)   The word **paradigm** may be used to signify the basic assumptions and beliefs that an organisation's decision-makers hold in common. Note that this is a slightly different concept from culture. The paradigm represents collective experience and is used to make sense of a given situation; it is thus essentially conservative and inhibiting to innovation, while an innovative culture is entirely feasible.

(b)   The **politics** of the organisation may also influence strategy. 'The political view of strategy development is that strategies develop as the outcome of processes of bargaining and negotiation among powerful internal or external interest groups (or stakeholders).'

Johnson & Scholes (2006) describe the processes by which paradigm and politics influence the process of strategy development.

Step 1   **Issue awareness**

- Internal results, customer responses or environmental changes can make individuals aware of a problem.

- A trigger alerts the formal information system to the problem, so that organisational activity takes over from the individual's consideration of the problem.

Step 2   **Issue formulation**

Managers try to analyse and get to the root of the problem. Information may be used to rationalise, rather than challenge, management's existing view of the situation. Formal analysis, in practice, plays a small role.

Step 3   **Solution development**

Some possible solutions are developed and one is selected.

- Memory search: solutions which worked in the past
- Passive search: wait for a solution to suggest itself

Solutions begin with a vague idea, which is further refined and explored by internal discussion.

Step 4   Solution selection

- Eliminate unacceptable plans. This screening process involves bargaining, diplomacy and judgement rather than formal evaluation according to the business case. ('Unacceptable' might mean unacceptable in terms of organisational politics, rather than in terms of business sense.)

- Endorsements. Many strategic decisions originate from management subsystems, which senior managers authorise. Junior managers might filter strategic information, or ignore certain options, to protect themselves.

 MARKETING AT WORK   application

Enron is now notorious for its unethical practices. However, its collapse is traceable to a failure of strategic control. In the early 1990s, Enron was extremely successful as a market-maker in the supply of gas and electricity. Its strategy was 'asset light': it did not produce gas, or very much electricity, but it used its financial expertise and its control of gas pipe lines and electricity grids to make large profits from the integration of supply and demand.

Unfortunately, early success bred hubris and quite junior executives were allowed to make major investments in industries whose characteristics were totally different from the homogeneity of product and ease of distribution of gas and electricity. In each case, the strategies failed because they made large demands for capital and low utilisation of Enron's core trading competences.

2.3.3 Criticisms of formal strategic planning

Criticisms of the strategic planning model concern how it has worked in practice and more fundamental problems of theory. They can be summed up as a recognition of the need to be flexible when making strategic plans and decisions.

Criticisms of strategic planning in practice

Criticism	Comment
Practical failure	Empirical studies have not proved that formal planning processes (the delineation of steps, the application of checklists and techniques) contribute to success.
Routine and regular	Strategic planning occurs often in an annual cycle. But a firm cannot allow itself to wait every year for the appointed month to address its problems. It may need to 'do something' straight away.
Reduces creative initiative	Formal planning discourages strategic thinking. Once a plan is locked in place, people are unwilling to question it.
Internal politics	The assumption of objectivity in evaluation ignores political battles between different managers and departments.
Exaggerates power	Managers are not all-knowing, and there are limits to the extent to which they can control the behaviour of the organisation.

Criticism of the rational model in theory

Criticism	Comment
Formalisation	We have no evidence that any of the strategic planning systems – no matter how elaborate – succeed in capturing (let alone improving on) the messy informal processes by which strategies really do get developed.
Detachment: divorcing planning from operations	Managers manage by remote control. Senior managers at the top 'think great thoughts' while others scurry beneath them. This implies that managers do not really need day-to-day knowledge of the product or market.

Criticism	Comment
Formulation precedes: **Implementation**	A strategy is planned – then it is implemented. But defining strengths and weaknesses is actually very difficult in advance of testing them.
Formulation precedes: **Predetermination**	Planning assumes that the environment can be forecast, and that its future behaviours can be controlled, by a strategy planned in advanced and delivered on schedule. This is only true of stable environments.

MARKETING AT WORK

application

This is a classic example of what can go unexpectedly right.

Honda is now one of the leading manufacturers of motorbikes. The company is credited with identifying and targeting an untapped market for small 50cc bikes in the US, which enabled it to expand, trounce European competition and severely damage indigenous US bike manufacturers. By 1965, Honda had 63% of the US market. But this occurred by accident.

On entering the US market, Honda had wanted to compete with the larger European and US bikes of 250ccs and over. These bikes had a defined market, and were sold through dedicated motorbike dealerships. Disaster struck when Honda's larger machines developed faults – they had not been designed for the hard wear and tear imposed by US motorcyclists. Honda had to recall the larger machines.

Honda had made little effort to sell its small 50cc motorbikes – its staff rode them on errands around Los Angeles. Sports goods shops, ordinary bicycle and department stores had expressed an interest, but Honda did not want to confuse its image in its 'target' market of men who bought the larger bikes.

The faults in Honda's larger machines meant that, reluctantly, Honda had to sell the small 50cc bikes just to raise money. They proved very popular with people who would never have bought motorbikes before.

Eventually the company adopted this new market with enthusiasm with the slogan: 'You meet the nicest people on a Honda'. The strategy had emerged, against managers' conscious intentions, but they eventually responded to the new situation.

2.4 Alternatives to planning

2.4.1 No strategic planning: 'freewheeling opportunism'

The **freewheeling opportunism approach** suggests firms should not bother with strategic plans and should exploit **opportunities** as they arise, judged on their individual merits and not within the rigid structure of an overall corporate strategy.

(a) **Advantages**

    (i)   Opportunities can be seized when they arise, whereas a rigid planning framework might impose restrictions so that the opportunities are lost.

    (ii)   It might encourage a more flexible, creative attitude among lower-level managers.

(b) **Disadvantages**

    (i)   **No co-ordinating framework** for the organisation as a whole.

    (ii)   The firm ends up **reacting** all the time rather than acting purposively.

MARKETING AT WORK

application

Commercial property

Freewheeling opportunism is not uncommon in the commercial property market. Much building of offices, hotels and retail outlets is largely speculative: where trading results fail to live up to expectations, important assets may be sold off at bargain prices. This is especially the case in the event of an economic downturn.

2.4.2 Strategic 'drift'

Vision versus opportunism

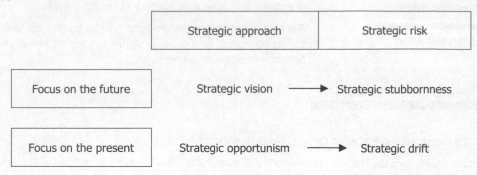

| Strategic approach | Strategic risk |

Focus on the future → Strategic vision ⟶ Strategic stubbornness

Focus on the present → Strategic opportunism ⟶ Strategic drift

This diagram demonstrates the risks associated with the different types of strategic focus. With a focus on the future, a company can be said to have 'strategic vision', but there is the risk that this becomes a kind of stubbornness and misguided determination to forge ahead with a strategy that may not be justified by events or business circumstances. On the other hand, a concentration on the present , exploiting opportunities as they arise, can lead to what is known as 'strategic drift'

Under conditions of strategic drift, decisions are made incrementally (see below) rather than as the result of being directed by some unifying and overarching 'vision'. Short lived opportunities may be mistaken for ones that truly merit long-term strategic investment. Expected synergies may fail to materialise. New business areas will have been put in place without any sustainable business advantage.

2.4.3 No strategic planning: incrementalism

Herbert Simon (1970) suggested that managers do not optimise (ie, get the best possible solution), but instead they satisfice. Managers are limited by time, by the information they have and by their own skills, habits and reflexes. They do not in practice evaluate all the possible options open to them in a given situation, but choose between relatively few alternatives. This is called bounded rationality.

(a)   Strategy-making tends to involve **small scale extensions of past policy – incrementalism** – rather than radical shifts following a comprehensive rational 'search' and evaluation of the alternatives.

(b)   In marketing terms, small scale adjustments of current marketing programmes *may* not be enough either to:

 (i)   **Move** with existing customers and their needs
 (ii)   **Identify** new markets or sets of customers

 On the other hand, an incremental approach may be both safe and satisfactory.

 MARKETING AT WORK   application

Tesco.com and Webvan

Tesco.com, the online shopping operation set up by the UK supermarket giant is an excellent example of successful incrementalism. Tesco decided to test the potential for online grocery shopping with a website based on a single store at Osterley in West London. Over the next two years the business model was refined and the crucial decision to impose a delivery charge was made. This had the beneficial effect of leading customers to place fewer, larger orders so as to derive the greatest benefit from the flat-rate charge. Tesco.com has grown successfully each year since its launch, partly because costs have been held down by making deliveries from existing stores. Tesco is now involved in a joint venture in the USA to create a similar home shopping operation.

Tesco's approach was markedly different from that of Webvan, which set out to completely remodel the US grocery retailing industry. It aimed to create a chain of highly automated warehouses in order to increase worker productivity and offered free delivery. Unfortunately, Webvan was never really in control of its costs and it was estimated that the company lost US$130 on every order. After four years of operation, the company was declared insolvent after burning its way through US$1.2 billion.

2.4.4 No strategic planning: crafting emergent strategies

Some strategies do not arise out of **conscious** strategic planning, but result from a number of **ad hoc choices**, perhaps made lower down the hierarchy, which may not be recognised at the time as being of strategic importance. These are called **emergent strategies**. They develop out of **patterns of behaviour**, in contrast to planned strategies which are imposed from above.

ACTIVITY 4

application

Aldebaran Ltd is a public relations agency founded by an entrepreneur, Estella Grande, who has employed various talented individuals from other agencies to set up in business. Estella Grande wants Aldebaran Ltd to become the largest public relations agency in North London. Management consultants, in a planning document, have suggested 'growth by acquisition'. In other words, Aldebaran should buy up the other public relations agencies in the area. These would be retained as semi-independent business units, as the Aldebaran Ltd group could benefit from the goodwill of the newly acquired agencies.

When Estella presents these ideas to the Board there is general consensus with one significant exception. Livia Strange, the marketing director, is horrified. 'How am I going to sell this to my staff? Ever since we've been in business, we've won business by undercutting and slagging off the competition. My team have a whole culture based on it. I give them champagne if they pinch a high value client. Why acquire these new businesses – why not stick to pinching their clients instead?'

What is the source of the conflict?

Mintzberg uses the metaphor of **crafting strategy** to help understand the idea. Emergent strategies can be shaped by managers. Strategies are shaped as they develop, with managers giving help and guidance, devoting more resources to some, exploiting new opportunities and responding to developments. For example, Honda's management reacted to the emergent strategy, eventually, and shaped its development.

Separating 'thinking' and 'doing' has the following result.

(a)   A purely deliberate strategy hampers rapid learning from experience.

(b)   A purely emergent strategy defies control. It may in fact be a bad strategy, dysfunctional for the organisation's future health.

Deliberate strategies introduce strategic change as a sort of quantum leap in some organisations. In this case, a firm undergoes only a few strategic changes in a short period, but these are very dramatic.

However, managers cannot simply let emerging strategies take over. Why?

*   **Direction**. The emergent strategy may be inappropriate for the long-term direction of the organisation and may have to be corrected. An insistence on carrying it through is the 'strategic stubbornness' we saw earlier.

*   **Resources**. It may have future implications for resource use elsewhere: in most organisations, different parts of the business compete for resources. Managers might wish to build on the strategy by actively devoting more resources to it.

No realised strategy will be wholly deliberate or wholly emergent. The line between deliberate and emergent elements within each strategy will be in part influenced by organisation structure and culture. The environment is uncertain and there are limits on what managers can achieve. Small steps may be a more practical way to move forward than to attempt to follow a grand plan: as already mentioned this is known as 'incrementalism' and is characterised by small scale extensions of past practice.

The assumption is that planning is a 'good thing' – but you need to be aware of the potential limitations of plans, if only to understand what might go wrong or to suggest alternative ways of developing strategy. Where there is high uncertainty, your plans will, inevitably, be tentative, and you may need to develop contingency plans – or at least identify the need to develop them – in your answer.

2.4.5 Deliberate and emergent strategies

The diagram below should help explain material in this section.

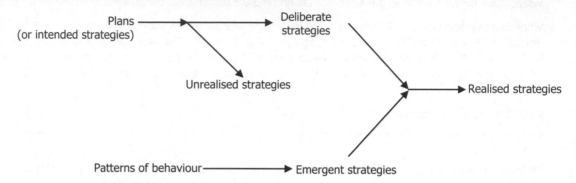

MARKETING AT WORK

application

BPP began life as a training company. Lecturers had to prepare course material. This was offered for sale in a bookshop in the BPP building. Owing to the demand, BPP began offering its material to other colleges, in the UK and worldwide. BPP Learning Media, which began as a small offshoot of BPP's training activities, is now a leading publisher in the market for targeted study material for the examinations of several professional bodies. It is unlikely that this development was anticipated when the course material was first prepared.

EXAM TIP

concept

The great thing about the rational model is that it is comprehensive. Even if it is unrealistic to think of a given organisation moving with stately deliberation through an annual planning cycle, the rational model does give us a checklist that can be used to identify areas in which a company's strategy-making may be capable of improvement. You may well find it a useful source of ideas.

Learning objectives	Covered
1 Critically evaluate an organisation's current strategic intent, based upon its vision, mission, values and stakeholder expectations	☑ Organisational mission (1.1)
	☑ Stakeholder analysis and relationships (1.2)
	☑ Organisational configuration (1.3)
	☑ Ethics (1.4)
2 Critically analyse the role of strategic intent in shaping an organisation's strategy development	☑ Strategic marketing (2.1)
	☑ Strategic intent, vision and leadership (2.2)
	☑ Strategic intent and flexibility (2.3)
	☑ Alternatives to planning (2.4)

1   What do you understand by the term 'strategic analysis'?

2   What are the two elements of stakeholder risk?

3   What is the 'societal marketing' concept?

4   What is 'strategic marketing'?

5   List Ohmae's three 'Cs'.

6   What are the three layers of strategy?

7   List the three stages of strategic planning.

8   Contrast intended and emergent strategies.

9   What is 'strategic drift'?

10   What are some of the practical criticisms of strategic planning?

11   How do 'leaders' come about?

12   "The pursuit of .... is at the heart of the market-led company", Fill in the blank.

1   (a)   Key players are found in segment D: strategy must be acceptable to them, at least. An example would be a major customer.

     (b)   Stakeholders in segment C must be treated with care. While often passive, they are capable of moving to segment D. They should, therefore, be kept satisfied. Large institutional shareholders might fall into segment C.

     (c)   Stakeholders in segment B do not have great ability to influence strategy, but their views can be important in influencing more powerful stakeholders, perhaps by lobbying. They should therefore be kept informed. Community representatives and charities might fall into segment B.

     (d)   Minimal effort is expended on segment A.

2   **Many**. This is a case partly about boundary management and partly about enlightened self-interest and business ethics. The adverse publicity, although not about the Heritage Carpet Company's own suppliers, could rebound badly. Potential customers might be put off. Economic growth in the area may also mean that parents will prefer to send their children to school. The Heritage Carpet Company as well as promoting itself as preserving a craft could reinvest some of its profits in the villages (eg by funding a school), by enforcing limits on the hours children worked. It could also pay a decent wage. It could advertise this in a 'code of ethics' so that customers are reassured that the children are not simply being exploited. Alternatively, it could not import child-made carpets at all. (This policy, however, would be unlikely to help communities in which child labour is an economic necessity.)

3   The corporate objective is profit growth. The corporate strategy is the decision that this will be achieved by entering new markets, rather than producing new products. The business strategy suggests that those markets include Latin America. The functional strategy involves the decision to invest in new plant (the production function) which is to be financed by shares rather than loans (the finance function).

4   Livia Strange's department has generated its own pattern of competitive behaviour. It is an emergent strategy. It conflicts directly with the planned strategy proposed by the consultants. This little case history also makes the additional point that strategies are not only about numbers, targets and grand plans, but about the organisational cultures influencing people's behaviour.

1   Strategic analysis is concerned with understanding the strategic position of the organisation.

2   The risk that any particular strategic option poses to the interests of different stakeholders. The risk that stakeholders might respond in such a way as to make a proposed strategy less attractive

3   The societal marketing concept holds that the key task of the organisation is to determine the needs of target markets and to deliver them more effectively and efficiently than its competitors, in a way that promotes the consumer's and society's well-being.

4   The primary role of strategic marketing is to identify and create value for the business through strongly differentiated positioning. It achieves this by influencing the strategy and culture of the organisation in order to ensure that both have a strong customer focus.

5   Company; customers; competition

6   Corporate; business; tactical/operational

7   Strategic analysis; strategic choice; strategic implementation

8   Intended strategies are plans. Those plans or aspects of plans which are actually realised are called deliberate strategies. Emergent strategies are those that develop out of patterns of behaviour.

9   Too much concentration on the present , exploiting opportunities as they arise, can lead to what is known as 'strategic drift' . Under conditions of strategic drift, decisions are made incrementally rather than as the result of direction from a unifying and overarching 'vision'

10   Practical failure: Empirical studies have not proved that formal planning contribute to success.
     Routine and regular: A firm cannot allow itself to wait every year for the appointed month to address its problems.
     Reduces creative initiative: Formal planning discourages strategic thinking.
     Internal politics: The assumption of objectivity ignores internal political battles
     Exaggerates power: Managers are not all-knowing

11   They can be appointed; they are elected; they might emerge by popular choice

12   Customer satisfaction

Aaker, D. & McLoughlin, D. (2007) <u>Strategic Market Management</u>, John Wiley, Chichester.

Anon (2009) *'Ryanair hits back in 'green' row'*, available from: http://news.bbc.co.uk/2/hi/uk_news/politics/6233019.stm (accessed 21 June 2009).

Drummond, G., Ensor, J. & Ashford, R. (2008) <u>Strategic Marketing Planning and Control</u>, (3rd edition), Elsevier, Oxford.

Johnson, G. & Scholes, K., (2006) <u>Exploring Corporate Strategy</u>, (7th edition), FT Prentice Hall, Harlow.

Koontz, H., O'Donnell, C. & Weihrich, H. (1988) <u>Management</u>, (revised edition), McGraw-Hill Education, Maidenhead.

Mendelow, A. (1985) *'Stakeholder analysis for strategic planning and implementation'* in *Strategic Planning & Management Handbook*, King & Cleland (eds) Van Nostrand Reinhold, NY.

Mintzberg, H. (2000) <u>The Rise and Fall of Strategic Planning</u>, FT Prentice Hall, Harlow.

Ohmae, K. (1991) <u>The Mind Of The Strategist: The Art of Japanese Business</u>, McGraw-Hill Professional, London.

Piercy, N.F (2008) <u>Market-Led Strategic Change – Transforming the Process of Going to Market</u>, (4th edition), Butterworth-Heinemann, Oxford.

Simon, H. (1970) <u>Sciences of the Artificial</u>, MIT Press, New York.

Chapter 6

Assessing strategic marketing options

Topic list

Introduction

Any plan must take into account circumstances that will affect attainment of its objectives. As we have already seen, the first step is to establish just where the individual or organisation stands to begin with, and an important aspect of the current situation is the potential that exists for future developments.

Strategic choice is based on strategic analysis, and has three aspects

(a) **Strategic options generation**. Here are some examples.

   (i)   Increase market share
   (iii)   International growth
   (iii)   Concentration on core competences
   (iv)   Acquisition

(b) **Strategic options evaluation and development**. Alternative strategies are developed and each is then examined on its merits.

   (i)   Acceptability to the organisation's stakeholders
   (ii)   Suitability
   (iii)   Feasibility

(c) **Strategy selection**

   (i)   Competitive strategy is the generic strategy determining how you compete.
   (ii)   Product-market strategy determines where you compete.
   (iii)   Institutional strategies determine the method of growth.

To be successful, strategic options should contain both real and perceived value propositions and be relevant, sustainable and feasible.

This chapter looks at the different approaches to generating and evaluating strategic options.

Syllabus-linked learning objectives

By the end of the chapter you will be able to:

Learning objectives	Syllabus link
1 Critically evaluate the determinants of strategic options and choices	2.1.1
2 Critically evaluate how strategic options can be developed	2.1.2
3 Critically assess the impact of changing an organisation's strategic position within the market place	2.2.8
4 Critically assess strategic alternatives against pre-determined criteria for an organisation	3.1.1

1 Determinants of strategic options

"What characteristics of a business make some options unfeasible without a major organisational change? What characteristics will be pivotal in choosing among strategic options?" Aaker & Mcloughlin (2007) p.119

1.1 Past and current strategies

It is important to make an accurate profile of past and current strategies. Strategy is a pattern of senior management decisions, arising out of the general management process whereby senior managers direct and control the business. This general management process generates consistent decisions. For example, a firm's managers may prefer certain types of market opportunities (eg low risk) than others. Sometimes, however, a strategy evolves into something very different from what was planned.

Strategic opportunities must be related to the firm's resources. A strategic approach involves identifying a firm's competences. As we have already seen, the distinctive competence of an organisation is what it does well, uniquely, or better than rivals. For a relatively undifferentiated product such as cement, the ability of a maker to run a truck fleet more effectively than its competitors will give it competitive strengths (if, for example, it can satisfy orders quickly). These competences may come about in a variety of ways.

- Experience in making and marketing a product or service
- The talents and potential of individuals in the organisation
- The quality of co-ordination

1.2 Organisational capabilities and constraints

Organisations are successful when they intentionally achieve internal harmony and external adaptation to their environment. Managers should use analytical techniques to identify the relationship between the organisation's internal capability and competences, and the external outputs. In very basic terms, the need for the fit is identified by the SWOT analysis and strategies are undertaken to secure the fit.

Arguably, the choice of strategy should follow a strategic logic.

- It must be consistently related to the objectives of the organisation.
- It must match the organisation's capability (including its structure, control systems and culture) to its environment.

The idea is that all the pieces of the strategic puzzle should fit together in a predetermined manner.

A business needs to identify those business processes that have the greatest impact on customer satisfaction, such as quality and employee skills.

(a)   Companies should also attempt to identify and measure their distinctive competences and the critical technologies they need to ensure continued leadership. Which processes should they excel at?

(b)   To achieve these goals, performance measures must relate to employee behaviour, to tie in the strategic direction with employee action.

(c)   An information system is necessary to enable executives to measure performance. An executive information system enables managers to drill down into lower level information.

While these perspectives identify the current parameters for competitive success, the company needs to learn and to innovate to satisfy future needs. This might be one of the hardest items to measure.

(a)   How long does it take to develop new products?

(b)   How quickly does the firm climb the experience curve to manufacture new products?

(c)   What percentage of revenue comes from new products?

(d)   How many suggestions are made by staff and are acted upon?

(e)   What are staff attitudes? Some firms believe that employee motivation and successful communication are necessary for organisational learning.

(f)   Depending on circumstances, the company can identify measures for training and long-term investment.

1.3 Financial capabilities and constraints

" ... a growth strategy, even if it simply involves greater penetration of the existing product market, usually requires working capital and other assets, which may exceed the funds available from operations." Aaker & McLoughlin, op.cit, p.120

Financial performance indicators indicate whether the company's strategies, implementation, and execution are contributing to bottom-line management and the generation of investment resources. A realistic appraisal of the resources (probable, actual and potential) that are required by the business can make strategy development itself more realistic.

Financial issues do not take care of themselves.

(a)   Money is a resource, and financial measures will ultimately effect a firm's ability to obtain that resource (eg by raising the firm's cost of capital, if shareholders perceive greater risk).

(b)   Well designed financial control systems can actually assist in TQM programmes (eg by identifying variances).

EXAM TIP

application

The financial perspective on a business is one of the four key perspectives that make up the balanced scorecard of business performance. See Durmmond *et al* (2008) pp. 144-145 for more on this. An exercise, apply the scorecard to the performance of Ryanair.

1.4 Organisational strengths and weaknesses

"A strategic option is a particular value proposition for a specific product market with supporting assets and competencies and functional strategies and programmes." Aaker & McLoughlin, op.cit, p.10

Common and important value propositions include:

*   Quality
*   Customer relationships
*   Value
*   Innovation
*   Focus
*   Being global
*   Developing brand equity

You should also be familiar with the idea of **SWOT** – strengths, weaknesses, opportunities and threats. Strengths and weaknesses exist now; opportunities and threats have potential for the future. SWOT is a very common model for analysing the existing situation and widely used in marketing.

1.4.1 Corporate appraisal

SWOT analysis is a useful technique for organising information about an organisation's strengths and weaknesses (**internal** appraisal) and the opportunities and threats (**external** appraisal) which it encounters. SWOT can be enhanced by **ranking** items in order of significance, and it is always important not to confuse the level at which the analysis is conducted (eg corporate SWOT and marketing SWOT). The SWOT can be used to identify possible **strategies**.

The purpose of **corporate appraisal**, is to **combine** the assessment of the environment and the analysis of the organisation's internal resources and capabilities.

KEY CONCEPT

concept

Corporate appraisal: 'a critical assessment of the strengths and weaknesses, opportunities and threats in relation to the internal and environmental factors affecting the entity in order to establish its condition prior to the preparation of a long-term plan.'

1.4.2 SWOT analysis

A **strengths and weaknesses** analysis expresses which areas of the business have:

- Strengths that should be exploited
- Weaknesses which should be improved

It therefore covers the results of the position audit.

Opportunities

- What opportunities exist in the business environment?
- Their inherent profit-making potential
- The organisation's ability to exploit the worthwhile opportunities

Threats

- What threats might arise?
- How will competitors be affected?
- How will the company be affected?

The opportunities and threats might arise from PEST and competitive factors.

 ACTIVITY 1   application

Assess the company which is the subject of the following SWOT:

Strengths	Weaknesses
£10 million of capital available	Heavy reliance on a small number of customers
Production expertise and appropriate marketing skills	Limited product range, with no new products and expected market decline. Small marketing organisation.

Threats	Opportunities
A major competitor has already entered the new market	Government tax incentives for new investment
	Growing demand in a new market, although customers so far relatively small in number

Effective SWOT analysis does not simply require a categorisation of information, it also requires some **evaluation of the relative importance** of the various factors under consideration.

(a) These features are only of relevance if they are **perceived to exist by the customers**. Listing corporate features that internal personnel regard as strengths/weaknesses is of little relevance if customers do not perceive them as such.

(b) In the same vein, threats and opportunities are conditions presented by the external environment and they should be independent of the firm.

The SWOT can now be used to guide strategy formulation. The two major options are **matching** and **conversion**.

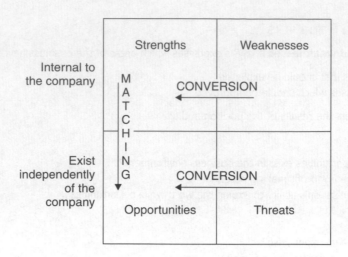

(a) **Matching**

This entails finding, where possible, a match between the strengths of the organisation and the opportunities presented by the market. Strengths which do not match any available opportunity are of limited use while opportunities which do not have any matching strengths are of little immediate value.

(b) **Conversion**

This requires the development of strategies which will convert weaknesses into strengths in order to take advantage of some particular opportunity, or converting threats into opportunities which can then be matched by existing strengths.

 ACTIVITY 2   application

Hall Faull Downes Ltd has been in business for 25 years, during which time profits have risen by an average of 3% per annum, although there have been peaks and troughs in profitability due to the ups and downs of trade in the customers' industry. The increase in profits, until five years ago, was the result of increasing sales in a buoyant market, but more recently, the total market has become somewhat smaller and Hall Faull Downes has only increased sales and profits as a result of improving its market share.

The company produces components for manufacturers in the engineering industry.

In recent years, the company has developed many new products and currently has 40 items in its range compared to 24 only five years ago. Over the same five-year period, the number of customers has fallen from 20 to nine, two of whom together account for 60% of the company's sales.

Give your appraisal of the company's future, and suggest what it is probably doing wrong.

 EXAM TIP   application

In practice (and for the purposes of analysing the pre-screen case study material) it helps if you rank the items of the SWOT in order of **importance** and **urgency**. Concentrate your resources on the essentials.

1.4.3 Weihrich's TOWS matrix

Weihrich, one of the earliest writers on corporate appraisal, originally spoke in terms of a TOWS matrix in order to emphasise the importance of threats and opportunities. Note that this is therefore an inherently **positioning** approach to strategy. A further important element of Weihrich's discussion was his categorisation of strategic options.

- SO strategies employ strengths to seize opportunities.
- ST strategies employ strengths to counter or avoid threats.
- WO strategies address weaknesses so as to be able to exploit opportunities.
- WT strategies are defensive, aiming to avoid threats and the impact of weaknesses.

One useful impact of this analysis is that the four groups of strategies tend to relate well to different time horizons. SO strategies may be expected to produce good short-term results, while WO strategies are likely to take much longer to show results. ST and WT strategies are more probably relevant to the medium-term.

This consideration of time horizon may be linked to the overall resource picture: SO strategies can be profitable in the short-term, generating the cash needed for investment in WT strategies, improving current areas of weakness so that further opportunities may be seized. ST and WT strategies are likely to be more or less resource-neutral, but care must be taken to achieve an overall balance.

1.4.4 Other approaches

Both the basic SWOT approach and Weihrich's more sophisticated method require careful thought.

- Apparently distinct factors may be linked.
- A single factor may seem to fit into more than one category.
- It is important to prioritise the various factors.

Less prescriptive frameworks may assist the process of synthesis and may even be satisfactory in themselves in simple circumstances.

(a)   **Issue analysis** avoids problems of classification by simply examining issues in depth.

(h)   **The 6 Cs framework** can be used to give structure to the rather open-ended issue analysis approach.

> (i)   Customers
> (ii)   Competitive position
> (ii)   Core competences
> (iv)   Chance and opportunity
> (v)   Critical success factors
> (vi)   Constraints

1.5 Product-market opportunities

Models such as the **Ansoff matrix** can also be applied, although its application might be more complex than in the single domestic market. To remind you, see diagram below.

		Product	
		Present	*New*
Market	*Present*	Market penetration: (for growth) or consolidation (to maintain position or withdrawal)	Product development
	New	Market development	Diversification

How can this be applied to international marketing strategy? Unfortunately the categories tend to shift.

(a)   It is obviously easy to suggest what the **new market** might be: another country.

(b)   What, however, do we mean by '**new product**'? Is the product new to the company? Has it only been developed? Is the company still on a learning curve in its domestic market? In this case there might be a choice.

> (i)   Introduce the new product **simultaneously** in domestic and overseas markets.

(ii)   Have a continuing rolling programme.

Year 1: the domestic market is dealt with first

Year 2: existing overseas markets are serviced

Year 3: genuinely new overseas markets are addressed

By year 3, the decision to introduce new products into new markets has effectively become one of market development, on the grounds that product has already been on sale at home and in existing overseas markets.

(c)   It would appear **unlikely** that a company would set up abroad in a completely unfamiliar market with a completely new product, when there are easy opportunities to minimise the risk.

Other strategic models such as the BCG matrix may also be applied to global operations.

 EXAM TIP

application

The Ansoff matrix, above, can be applied equally to a company looking for new international development or to an established global player. Many strategic developments are concerned with building on where the organisation currently sits in the global market, via current products and competences and stretching them to improve competitive position. There are a number of options for expanding or contracting operations. Try applying the matrix to Ryanair in the sample case study; task 2 on the sample exam paper asks candidates to evaluate two possible growth options.

1.6 Sources of competitive advantage

Competitive advantage has to be sustained. It can come from better products, customer perceptions, costs, competences, assets, economies of scale, attitudes and relationships, offensive and defensive.

(a)   Competitive advantage only really exists in the customer's mind.

(b)   Competitive advantage can be easily lost as a result of market changes or new ways of doing business.

Competitive advantage will be lost, gradually or rapidly, if the organisation's chosen strategy loses its relevance. Customers' needs are no longer met and market share declines.

1.6.1 Different types of advantage

Competitive advantage	Example/comment
Better product in some way	Renault –'safest car in its class'
Perceived advantage or psychic benefit	Exclusivity (eg Harrods)
Global skills	BA; HSBC
Low costs, via high productivity or focus	Discount retailers or supermarkets such as Lidl or Aldi
Better competences	Some firms are 'better' at marketing or aligning technologies to markets than others
Superior assets	Property, cash or brands
Economies of scale	Size can be a source of competitive advantage
Attitude	This is partly related to culture and management abilities
Superior **relationships**	Companies can exploit business alliances and develop personal relationships

The most important competitive advantages depend on the market and existing competitors.

TK Maxx

The first TK Maxx store opened in Bristol, and despite the fourth lowest score for customer satisfaction in a 2006 'Which?' survey, there are now almost 200 stores. The TK Maxx strategy is to sell genuine branded goods at deep discounts of 20 to 60%. This strategy depends on a core competence of opportunistic buying from both suppliers and retailers who have excess stock.

1.7 Warfare analogies

Firms can choose a variety of strategies to **attack or defend** their position. Different strategies are appropriate to challengers, followers, leaders and nichers.

The broad generic strategies outlined above have some flaws, as we have seen. We suggested a number of approaches to price and value. In this section we describe how marketing activities can be used against **competitors**.

Considering strategic options from a competitor rather than customer orientation is referred to as **competitive marketing strategy**.

1.7.1 Offensive warfare strategies

Offensive strategies can be used by all companies. In order to ensure success, a company must be able to gain an advantage over the competition in the segment or area of attack. Kotler (2001) describes the following **attack strategies**.

Strategy	Comment
Frontal attack	This is the direct, head-on attack meeting competitors with the **same product line**, **price**, **promotion and so on**. Because the aggressor is attacking the enemy's strengths rather than weaknesses, it is generally considered the riskiest and least advised of strategies.
Flanking attack	The aim is to engage competitors in those product markets where they are weak or have no presence at all. Its overreaching goal is to build a position from which to launch an attack on the major battlefield later without waking 'sleeping giants'.
Encirclement attack	Multi-pronged attack aimed at diluting the defender's ability to retaliate in strength. The attacker stands ready to block the competitor no matter which way he turns in the product market. • An attacker can encircle by **product proliferation** as Seiko did in the watch market, supplying 400 watch types in the UK out of 2,300 models worldwide. • **Market encirclement** consists of expanding the products into all segments and distribution channels.
Bypass attack	This is the most indirect form of competitive strategy as it **avoids confrontation** by moving into new and as yet uncontested fields. Three types of bypass are possible; develop **new products**, diversify into **unrelated products** or diversify into **new geographical markets**.
Guerrilla warfare	Less ambitious in scope, this involves making small attacks in different locations while remaining mobile. Such attacks take several forms: law suits, poaching personnel, interfering with supply networks and so on. The overriding aim is to **destabilise** by prods rather than blows.

1.7.2 Defensive warfare strategies

It is generally agreed that **only a market leader** should play defence in an attempt to hold on to its existing markets in the face of competitive attack.

Strategy	Comment
Position defence	Static defence of a current position, retaining current product-markets by consolidating resources within existing areas. **Exclusive reliance** on a position defence effectively means that a business is a **sitting target** for competition.
Mobile defence	A high degree of **mobility prevents the attacker's chances of localising defence** and accumulating its forces for a decisive battle. A business should seek market development, product development and diversification to create a stronger base.
Pre-emptive defence	**Attack is the best form of defence**. Pre-emptive defence is launched in a segment where an attack is **anticipated** instead of a move into related or new segments.
Flank position defence	This is used to occupy a position of **potential** future importance in order to deny that position to the opponent. Leaders need to develop and hold secondary markets to prevent competitors using them as a spring board into the primary market. (For example, Japanese manufacturers used the upper–end executive and coupe market to break into the volume car sector in the US.)
Counter-offensive defence	This is attacking where one is being attacked. This requires **immediate response** to any competitor entering a segment or initiating new moves. Examples are price wars, where firms try to undercut each other.
Strategic withdrawal	May be a last resort, but 'cutting your losses' can be the best option in the long run. Management resistance to what is seen as a drastic step is likely to be the biggest barrier.

The five attacking strategies for challenging market leaders and the six defensive strategies used to fight off challenges are not mutually exclusive. As contingent factors change, a successful company will reconsider and revise its core strategies.

 ACTIVITY 3

application

Hester Bateman plc (HB plc) is a manufacturing cutler: that is, the company makes knives, forks and spoons. HB is based in Sheffield in the United Kingdom which has been the centre of the UK cutlery industry for at least one hundred years. When the industry was first established, it was very fragmented and there were many small entrepreneurial businesses making cutlery. Often, these businesses were organised around a family and they usually employed between six and ten people. Hester Bateman was one such entrepreneur. The industry began to consolidate, in the late nineteenth century and early twentieth century, as a series of mergers were effected.

HB plc was constituted in its present form in the 1920s when it obtained its market listing on the Stock Exchange. It now consists of a large factory which employs 500 people and a Head Office employing 200 people. These are both in Sheffield.

In 1990 HB plc made a rights issue to finance a modernisation programme in its factory. At that time the Board reviewed the company's objectives. A statement was issued by the Board which said:

'HB plc is a UK manufacturing cutler based in Sheffield, the home of the cutlery industry. Our success is due to harnessing local skills in production and design and using these to deliver the finest quality product to our customers across the world. They know that the finest cutlery in the world is stamped "Made in Sheffield". We intend to continue with our fine traditions.'

HB plc has always made all its cutlery in Sheffield and attaches great importance to the fact that it can, therefore, be marked 'Made in Sheffield'.

HB plc usually spends approximately £150,000 a year on research and development. Five per cent of this spending is on new designs for the export market and the remainder is evenly split on designs for the home market and on improvements in production systems.

BQ plc

There is another UK manufacturing cutler of a similar size to HB plc, BQ plc, which is based in Birmingham.

Since 1991 BQ plc has followed a different production policy to HB plc. Approximately half of its cutlery is made in Korea and imported to the UK and marketed under BQ plc's brand names.

Markets

From the date of its formation until the late 1980s HB plc did very good business with countries across the world.

Since 1990 HB plc has experienced increasing competition from countries of the Pacific Rim – Korea, Taiwan, Hong Kong and Singapore. This competition has been conducted on the basis of cost. This has been possible because the production technology involved in making cutlery is a mature one. It is also comparatively cheap and readily available. Further, for many users cutlery has become a generic product.

Generics are unbranded, plainly packaged, less-expensive versions of products, purchased in supermarkets, such as spaghetti, paper towels and canned peaches.

HB plc has experienced a growing loss of market share in the UK to imports from the Pacific Rim. HB plc's export markets have largely disappeared. The only export business which it does is an annual sale of about £200,000 of very high quality cutlery to a department store in New York. HB plc makes a gross margin of 45% on this business.

Estimated market data at December 2008:

UK market share by:	Quantity %	Value %
HB plc	35	45
BQ plc*	30	35
Imports	35	20

* These percentages include all cutlery sold by BQ plc whether made in the UK or in Korea.

Financial performance

The increasingly competitive environment has had a marked effect on HB plc's profitability and stock market performance. After the publication of its latest annual results the following comment was made in an influential UK financial newspaper:

'HB plc's latest results which show a profit after tax of £2.25 million look deceptively good. However, these are flattered by the fact that HB plc has not made any major investments since the 1980s.

Its ROCE is about 4% and this could be beaten by any fixed return risk-free deposit investment. There seems to be little prospect of growth in any direction. These shares are really only a HOLD for the sentimental; otherwise SELL.'

Required

(a)   How can Porter's classification of generic strategies be used by HB plc to analyse its current competitive position?

(b)   Discuss the extent to which you believe that the statement of objectives made in 1990 is still applicable today.

(c)   Recommend possible marketing strategies for HB plc. Discuss the advantages and disadvantages of your recommendations.

We can apply these strategies to firms with different positions in the market.

- Pioneers
- Followers
- Challengers
- Nichers

1.7.3 Strategies for pioneers

- Position defence
- Mobile defence
- Flanking defence
- Contraction defence (withdrawal)
- Pre-emptive defence
- Counter-offence

1.7.4 Strategies for challengers

Challenges can either attack lenders, accept the *status quo*, or try and win market share from other smaller companies in the market.

- Frontal attack
- Flank attack
- Encirclement attack
- Bypass attack
- Guerrilla attack

Dolls

Between 2001 and 2004, Mattel lost 20% of its share of the worldwide fashion-doll segment to smaller rivals such as MGA Entertainment, creator of a hip new line of dolls called Bratz. MGA recognised what Mattel had failed to – that preteen girls were becoming more sophisticated and maturing more quickly. At younger ages, they were outgrowing Barbie and increasingly preferring dolls that looked like their teenage siblings and the pop stars they idolised. As the target market for Barbie narrowed from girls aged three to 11 to girls about three to five, the Bratz line cut rapidly into the seemingly unassailable Mattel franchise. Mattel finally moved to rescue Barbie's declining fortunes, launching a brand extension called My Scene that targeted older girls, and a line of hip dolls called Flavas to compete head-on with Bratz. But the damage was done. Barbie, queen of dolls for over 40 years, lost a fifth of her realm almost overnight – and Mattel didn't see it coming.

1.7.5 Strategies for followers

Many firms succeed by imitating the leaders. This is common in financial services markets where the basic functionality of a product is similar. Given that there are controls over monopoly status, most markets will have at least two players. Followers can follow:

- **Closely**, by imitating the marketing mix, and targeting similar segments
- **At a distance**, with more differentiating factors
- **Selectively** to avoid direct competition

Kotler makes the important point that 'followership is not the same as being passive or a carbon copy of the leader'. The follower has to define a path that does not invite competitive retaliation. He identifies three broad followership strategies.

(a) **Cloner**. This is a parasite that lives off the investment made by the leader in the marketing mix (such as in products or distribution). The **counterfeiter** is an extreme version of the cloner, who produces fakes of the original (eg fake Rolex watches for sale in the Far East).

(b) **Imitator**. This strategy copies some elements but differentiates on others (such as packaging).

(c) **Adapter**. This involves taking the leader's products and adapting or even improving them. The adapter may grow to challenge the leader.

1.7.6 Market nichers

This is associated with a **focus** strategy and relies partly on segmentation, and partly on specialising. There are several specialist roles open to market nichers.

(a) **End-user specialist**, specialising in one type of customer
(b) **Vertical level specialist**, specialising at one particular point of the production/ distribution chain
(c) **Specific customer specialist**, limiting selling to one or just a few customers
(d) **Geographic specialist** selling to one locality
(e) **Product or service specialist**, offering specialised services not available from other firms
(f) **Quality/price specialist** operating at the low or high end of the market
(g) **Channel specialist**, concentrating on just one channel of distribution

2 Assessing strategic options

"Which strategic option or set of options should form the basis for a business strategy? To answer this question, each option should be challenged with respect to whether it contains a real and perceived value proposition and whether it is relevant, sustainable and feasible." Aaker & McLoughlin *op. cit.* p.163

Strategies are evaluated according to their **suitability** to the firm's situation; their **feasibility** in terms of resources and competences; and their **acceptability** to key stakeholder groups, particularly shareholders and customers.

2.1 Suitability and sustainability

Suitability relates to the strategic logic of the strategy. The strategy should fit the situation of the firm over the longer term.

It should satisfy a range of requirements.

- Exploit strengths: that is, unique resources , core competences and points of difference over time
- Rectify company weaknesses
- Neutralise or deflect environmental threats
- Help the firm to seize opportunities
- Satisfy the goals of the organisation
- Fill the gap identified by gap analysis
- Generate/maintain competitive advantage
- Involve an acceptable level of risk
- Suit the politics and corporate culture

2.2 Feasibility

Feasibility asks whether the strategy can be implemented and, in particular, if the organisation has adequate resources.

- Enough money
- The ability to deliver the goods/services specified in the strategy
- The ability to deal with the likely responses that competitors will make
- Access to technology, materials and resources
- Enough time to implement the strategy

Strategies that do not make use of existing competences, and, therefore, call for new competences to be acquired, might not be feasible, since gaining competences takes time and can be costly.

Two important financial approaches to assessing the feasibility of particular strategies are **funds flow analysis** and **breakeven analysis**. Funds flow analysis examines the way money flows into the business and out of it; where it comes from, where it goes, what it is committed to and how much of it is available. Breakeven analysis is the study of the level of activity that has to be sustained if the firm is not to lose money.

Resource deployment analysis makes a wider assessment of feasibility in terms of resources and competences. The resources and competences required for each potential strategy are assessed and compared with those of the firm. A two-stage approach may be followed.

(a)   Does the firm have the necessary resources and competences to achieve the threshold requirements for each strategy?

(b)   Does the firm have the core competences and unique resources to maintain competitive advantage?

2.2.1 Elements of a feasibility study

1   **Corporate audit**

(a)   Objectives, five-year plan
(b)   Key criteria for project appraisal/evaluation

2   **The scenario or project**

3   **Assumptions**

4   **Feasibility research**

(a)   Experimental/technical research: design studies, performance specification, timings, costs.

(b)   Market research: demand analysis, competition, buying motives, pricing etc.

(c) Commercial potential (to include analysis of the feasibility research in terms of timing, cost, human resource needs). Outline income and expenditure analysis.

    (i)   Venture capital required
    (ii)   Cost of capital at current interest rate
    (iii)   Working capital
    (iv)   Short-term loans/overdraft requirements
    (v)   Cash flow projections – funding periods
    (vi)   Contingencies
    (vii)   Payback periods and net gains

2.3 Acceptability and relevance

The acceptability of a strategy depends on the views of **stakeholders**.

Strategies will be primarily evaluated by considering how far they contribute to meeting the dominant objective of increasing shareholder value. A wide range of measures is available to help assess financial viability.

- Return on investment
- Profits
- Growth
- EPS
- Cash flow
- Price/Earnings
- Market capitalisation
- Cost-benefit analysis

Specific projects and ventures can be assessed using a variety of financial techniques. The most satisfactory is the NPV approach, explained in Chapter 9.

There are several important stakeholder groups.

(a) The **workforce** constitutes an important stakeholder group that typically has an interest in the financial implications of strategy because of its links to job security. Successful strategies that enhance shareholder value tend to reduce or put on hold the search for economies in head count. However, the success of some strategies may derive from cost reductions achieved partly by reducing the need for labour.

(b) **Customers** may object to a strategy if it alters the perceived value they receive. Such an approach is likely to be followed rapidly by failure of the strategy in the targeted market segment.

(c) **Banks** are interested in the implications for cash resources, debt levels and so on.

(d) **Government**. A strategy involving a takeover may be prohibited under competition legislation.

(e) **The public**. The environmental impact may cause key stakeholders to protest. For example, out of town superstores are now frowned upon by national and local government in the UK.

(f) **Risk**. Different shareholders have different attitudes to risk. A strategy which changed the risk/return profile, for whatever reason, may not be acceptable.

How stakeholders relate to the management of the company depends very much on what type of stakeholder they are – internal, connected or external – and on the level in the management hierarchy at which they are able to apply pressure. Clearly a company's management will respond differently to the demands of, say, its shareholders and the community at large.

2.4 Levels of strategy

As we saw in the previous chapter, any level of the organisation can have objectives and devise strategies to achieve them. The strategic management process is multi-layered.

2.4.1 Corporate strategies

KEY CONCEPT

concept

Corporate strategy is concerned with the overall purpose and scope of the organisation and how value will be added to the different parts (business units) of the organisation.

Johnson, Scholes and Whittington (2007)

Defining aspects of corporate strategy

Characteristic	Comment
Scope of activities	Strategy and strategic management impact upon the whole organisation: all parts of the business operation should support and further the strategic plan.
Environment	The organisation counters threats and exploits opportunities in the environment (customers, clients, competitors).
Resources	Strategy involves choices about allocating or obtaining corporate resources now and in future.
Values	The value systems of people with power in the organisation influence its strategy.
Timescale	Corporate strategy has a long-term impact.
Complexity	Corporate strategy involves uncertainty about the future, integrating the operations of the organisation and change.

2.4.2 Business strategy

KEY CONCEPT

concept

Business strategy is about how to compete successfully in particular markets.

Johnson, Scholes and Whittington (2007)

Business strategy can involve decisions such as whether to segment the market and specialise in particularly profitable areas, or to compete by offering a wider range of products.

MARKETING AT WORK

application

Smartphones

In November 2007, The Financial Times reported that Nokia not only had the dominating share of the global mobile phone market generally, it also had 57% of the smartphone segment. Apple, which launched its iPhone in June 2007 sold 1.4 million units in the third quarter and seems set to become number two in the smartphone segment.

Some large, diversified firms have separate **strategic business units** (SBUs) dealing with particular areas. Business strategy for such large organisations is strategy at the SBU level.

2.4.3 Functional and operational strategies

KEY CONCEPT

concept

Operational strategies are concerned with how the component parts of an organisation deliver effectively the corporate and business-level strategies in terms of resources, processes and people.

Johnson, Scholes and Whittington (2007)

Individual operational strategies are often the concern of business functions, so they are also known as functional strategies. Here are some examples.

Functional area	Comment
Marketing	Devising products and services, pricing, promoting and distributing them, in order to satisfy customer needs at a profit. Marketing and corporate strategies are interrelated.
Production	Factory location, manufacturing techniques, outsourcing and so on.
Finance	Ensuring that the firm has enough financial resources to fund its other strategies by identifying sources of finance and using them effectively.
Human resources management	Secure personnel of the right skills in the right quantity at the right time, and ensure that they have the right skills and values to promote the firm's overall goals.
Information systems	A firm's information systems are becoming increasingly important, as an item of expenditure, as administrative support and as a tool for competitive strength. Not all information technology applications are strategic, and the strategic value of IT will vary from case to case.
R&D	New products and techniques.

EXAM TIP

application

The syllabus also mentions the importance of understanding the effects of *changing* strategic direction. The company might change its strategic position in the marketplace for a number of reasons:

1   To reflect a new business strategy (eg, producing cheaper products to appeal to customers with less to spend. See the General Electric example below)

2   To resonate with customers (eg, advertising of 'no frills' brands in a tougher economic climate)

3   To differentiate from competitors (eg through innovation and new product development)

4   To express organisational values and culture (eg Innocent Drinks selling orange juice to attract a new set of customers)

5   To express CSR, reputation, sustainability and ethics (eg EasyJet welcoming the EU emissions trading scheme, when other airlines are resisting)

It is important to understand the implications for the organisation of any decision to work outside its previously agreed strategy – namely in terms of compatibility, the resources required to fulfil the new approach and the organisation's capacity and capability to deliver.

"General Electric yesterday became the latest big manufacturer forced to change course and make cheaper and simpler products to cope with the decline in purchasing power around the world." The trend towards 'value for money' is affecting a broad swathe of business.

Over the next six years, GE Healthcare will devote half of its $1 billion R&D budget towards low cost products designed for use in emerging markets and remote areas (up from a mere 15%). There has been a sharp downturn in US health spending, and a profound change in the political mood. The new US administration is aiming to reduce the costs of healthcare.

In consumer electronics, Sony has brought out its own low-tech camcorder, the Webbie, priced at under $200 in response to the huge success of the low-priced Flip.

Times Online May 2009

Learning objectives	Covered
1 Critically evaluate the determinants of strategic options and choices	☑ Past and current strategies (1.1)
	☑ Organisational capabilities and constraints (1.2)
	☑ Financial capabilities and constraints (1.3)
	☑ Organisational strengths and weaknesses (1.4)
	☑ Product-market opportunities (1.5)
	☑ Sources of competitive advantage (1.6)
	☑ Warfare analogies (1.7)
2 Critically evaluate how strategic options can be developed	☑ Suitability and sustainability (2.1)
	☑ Feasibility (2.2)
	☑ Acceptability and relevance (2.3)
	☑ Levels of strategy (2.4)
3 Critically assess the impact of changing an organisation's strategic position within the market place	☑ See Exam Tip at end of chapter
4 Critically assess strategic alternatives against pre-determined criteria for an organisation	☑ Sources of competitive advantage (1.6)
	☑ Suitability, feasibility and acceptability (section 2)
	☑ Organisational capabilities and constraints (1.2)

1   Identify three categories of strategic choice.

2   Give some examples of means of obtaining competitive advantage.

3   Identify five offensive strategies.

4   Identify strategies for market followers.

5   Identify possible approaches to market development.

6   Why are past and current strategies a useful guide in strategy development?

7   Give some common value propositions.

8   What are the two major options under a SWOT analysis?

9   What measures might be used to assess financial viability?

10   Describe Weihrich's categorisation of strategic options.

1   The company is in imminent danger of losing its existing markets and must diversify its products and/or markets. The new market opportunity exists to be exploited, and since the number of customers is currently small, the relatively small size of the existing marketing force would not be an immediate hindrance. A strategic plan could be developed to buy new equipment and use existing production and marketing to enter the new market, with a view to rapid expansion. Careful planning of manpower, equipment, facilities, research and development would be required and there would be an objective to meet the threat of competition so as to obtain a substantial share of a growing market. The cost of entry at this early stage of market development should not be unacceptably high.

2   A general interpretation of the facts as given might be sketched as follows.

(a)   **Objectives.** the company has no declared objectives. Profits have risen by 3% per annum in the past, which has failed to keep pace with inflation but may have been a satisfactory rate of increase in the current conditions of the industry. Even so, stronger growth is indicated in the future.

(b)
Many new products developed	Products may be reaching the end of their life and entering decline.
Marketing success in increasing market share	
Possible decline in the end-product	New product life cycles may be shorter.
Smaller end-product market will restrict future sales prospects for Hall Faull Downes.	Reduction in customers.
	Excessive reliance on a few customers.
	Doubtful whether profit record is satisfactory
	None identified.

(c)   **Strengths.** The growth in company sales in the last five years has been as a result of increasing the market share in a declining market. This success may be the result of the following.

(i)   Research and development spending
(ii)   Good product development programmes
(iii)   Extending the product range to suit changing customer needs
(iv)   Marketing skills
(v)   Long-term supply contracts with customers
(vi)   Cheap pricing policy
(vii)   Product quality and reliable service

(d)   **Weaknesses**

(i)   The products may be custom-made for customers so that they provide little or no opportunity for market development.

(ii)   Products might have a shorter life cycle than in the past, in view of the declining total market demand.

(iii)   Excessive reliance on two major customers leaves the company exposed to the dangers of losing their custom.

(e)   **Threats.** There may be a decline in the end-market for the customers' product so that the customer demands for the company's own products will also fall.

(f)   **Opportunities.** No opportunities have been identified, but in view of the situation as described, new strategies for the longer-term would appear to be essential.

(g)   **Conclusions.** The company does not appear to be planning beyond the short-term, or is reacting to the business environment in a piecemeal fashion. A strategic planning programme should be introduced.

(h)   **Recommendations.** the company must look for new opportunities in the longer-term.

(i)   In the short term, current strengths must be exploited to continue to increase market share in existing markets and product development programmes should also continue.

(ii)   In the longer term, the company must diversify into new markets or into new products and new markets. Diversification opportunities should be sought with a view to exploiting any competitive advantage or synergy that might be achievable.

(iii)   The company should use its strengths (whether in R & D, production skills or marketing expertise) in exploiting any identifiable opportunities.

(iv)   Objectives need to be quantified in order to assess the extent to which new long-term strategies are required.

3   (a)   In Hester Bateman's (HB's) case, the issues are not particularly clear cut. The size of the market is changing. From being strictly demarcated on national lines, the market has become global. This trend is certain to continue. In this new global market, what strategies can HB pursue?

(i)   Cost leadership would seem out of the question, in the short term at least. This is because cutlery making technology can be easily imitated by countries in the Pacific. At the moment, their labour costs are much lower; how long this will remain is a different question.

(ii)   Differentiation. HB could differentiate the product on a global basis, on the basis of quality (by using special alloys) or by designing products that are attractive to users, or by introducing a range of new designs.

(iii)   Focus. HB could decide to serve the UK or European market only, but it will still be vulnerable to cheaper competition. On the other hand it could position itself as a luxury brand to serve wealthier consumers.

Clearly, differentiation or focus are the way forward, as HB will always be vulnerable to lower cost competition, from Pacific Rim countries first of all, and then from other countries as they industrialise.

(b)   **Statement of objectives**

The statement of objectives contains remarkably few of them! Nothing has been quantified. As a mission statement it addresses the past not the future, on the assumption that past traditions can be preserved as a guarantee for future success.

To some extent, having survived the recessions of the early 1980s and 1990s, HB is in a strong position, having obviously taken steps to maintain its competitiveness. It is still able to trade on its quality image, as it has 45% of the market by value, as opposed to only 35% by volume. This is still significantly more than its competitors from overseas, suggesting that they are fighting over a niche that is relatively unprofitable for UK companies. Concentrating on the higher end of the market, rather than battling over market share for cheap generic items has been a sound strategy.

However, can this strategy be continued? It is possible that competitors will do their best to raise quality and HB's premium position will no longer be secure. Furthermore, the lack of investment will begin to tell. Finally, although the firm has maintained its market position in the short term, it has lost the confidence of investors in its ability to deliver long-term improvements.

HB therefore needs to update its objectives with a proper mission statement to satisfy the needs of its various stakeholders.

*   To what extent can it continue to trade on its quality image?
*   What customers is it looking to satisfy?
*   What does it intend to do to address the concerns of its investors?

Clearly, the survival of the firm itself as an independent entity is in doubt. Investors are being advised to sell, yet the firm is still profitable and has a large share of the UK market. An argument perhaps is that it has failed to capitalise on the competitive strengths it has. If it is exporting to a New York department store, it is clear that there might be further export opportunities, which are not being satisfied, in the luxury goods market.

HB's position is therefore confused. On the one hand, it has survived two recessions, no mean feat. It has a commanding position in the British market, and its designs satisfy choosy US customers. Investors however have another viewpoint. The firm seems vulnerable to a take-over.

(c) **Marketing strategies**

HB must first of all decide which generic strategy it is to pursue. We have suggested that cost leadership is out of the question, and so either differentiation or focus should be pursued. Once this is decided, a suitable marketing mix must devised. We can suggest a focus strategy, exploiting product differentiation (ie a differentiation-focus strategy). HB already produces cutlery of a different quality (eg the highest quality is exported to the US). In order to improve profits, HB first of all needs to identify which product markets are the most profitable, and deal with them in a suitable way. Different strategies might be suggested for different market niches to ensure profit streams.

Furthermore, the firm needs to undertake a programme of market research to find out what its customers (both retailers such as the New York department store, and the end-consumer or user) think about HB, and how it can better satisfy their needs.

Product

'Made in Sheffield' goods enable the firm to charge a premium price. The firm should concentrate on exploiting the international luxury market for high quality 'designer' goods. For example, scotch whisky is exported to Japan, and HB can channel its R and D towards producing a variety of innovative designs that can combine premium prices at the high end of the market.

At the same time it needs to enhance the profits earned from the UK market where it is facing cheap generic competition. It has little scope for cutting prices, and so it might be a good idea to maintain its position but at a lower price. It could set up, therefore, a brand of cheap imported cutlery, to compete with BQ and the other importers. This would release resources to concentrate on higher quality premium-priced products which could still have the Made in Sheffield tag. HB can therefore set up two brands. There are obviously profits to be earned from the generic end of the market, and HB still has the opportunity to deliver.

Many firms sell low and high-quality versions of a product under different brand names. It is not so much the company that has to be positioned appropriately in the market, as its brands.

The firm could also use its expertise in quality metal work to expand its product range (using Ansoff's product development strategy) into the same market. Suggestions might include:

- Related products such as silver (soup tureens, trays, silver goblets)
- Less plausibly, perhaps, ornaments, jewellery, even cufflinks

Price

The price element of the mix is implicit in the product. To increase its profitability, HB is to manufacture premium products at premium prices. This is in order to increase the ROCE: the New York business earns a gross margin of 45%.

Under a different brand name, HB is to import cheap generic products from Pacific Rim or cheaper countries, and use its existing networks to take on the competition. This will hopefully generate more profits, or at least cover costs, as the expensive manufacturing capability will be directed elsewhere. HB will be able to compete more effectively.

Place

The distribution system is an important element of the marketing mix. HB has obviously no problem in the UK, but perhaps it needs to consider whether it is as effective and efficient as it could be. We are told little about HB's existing distribution and logistics systems.

However, the twin pronged strategy does require some new expertise.

(i)   If the company is importing its generic products from overseas, it will need to have suitable warehousing and storage facilities, and to have systems which can predict likely demand, so customers do not have to wait too long.

(ii)   It is hoped that many of the premium priced products will be exported. The US department store is a model for strategies that can be adopted in other countries in the EU and over the world. HB will need assistance, perhaps from one of the UK government's export advisory services, to find distributors for its product. The distributors will inevitably have a significant say in how the goods are to be positioned and sold. In a market such as Japan, HB will need a suitable partner to negotiate the thickets of the distribution system; in a country that uses chopsticks, demand for cutlery will be limited, but it can be sold as a luxury item.

However, the main markets would be the US where further expansion is obviously possible and the EU.

The company might consider offering an enhanced service to customers, for example a just-in-time delivery system.

Promotion

Promotional strategies will be an essential feature of HB's repositioning itself as a premium priced quality product. This means finding a suitable advertising agency, and researching the communications messages the company wishes to pursue. It might mean advertising in media it has not used before (eg magazines promoting luxury goods, or lifestyle magazines such as The World of Interiors).

Finally the firm needs to promote itself to another audience: investors, who have to be convinced that the new strategy will work. At the moment they are critical, and will sell to a bidder. To keep their jobs, the existing managers must work to convince investors that the company's existing and potential strengths can be better exploited in future.

1   How to compete; direction of growth; method of growth

2   Better product; perceived advantage; global skills; low costs; better competencies; superior assets; economies of scale; attitude; superior relations

3   Frontal; flanking; encirclement and bypass attacks and guerrilla warfare

4   Cloning, adaptation and imitations

5   New geographical areas; different package sizes; new distribution channels; differential pricing

6   Strategy is a pattern of senior management, and the process tends to generate consistent decisions. For example, a firm's managers may prefer certain types of market opportunities (eg low risk) than others. Such factors can be an important guide in evaluating the acceptability of potential future strategies.

7   Quality; customer relationships; value; innovation; focus; being global; developing brand equity

8   Matching and conversion

9   Return on investment
Profits
Growth
EPS
Cash flow
Price/Earnings
Market capitalisation
Cost-benefit analysis

10 SO strategies employ strengths to seize opportunities
ST strategies employ strengths to counter or avoid threats
WO strategies address weaknesses so as to be able to exploit opportunities
WT strategies are defensive, aiming to avoid threats and the impact of weaknesses

References

Aaker, D. & McLoughlin, D. (2007) Strategic Market Management, John Wiley, Chichester.

Ansoff, H.I. (1988) *Corporate Strategy*, (2nd revised edition), Penguin Books, London.

Drummond, G. Ensor, J. & Ashford, R. (2008) Strategic Marketing Planning and Control, (3rd edition), Elsevier Ltd, Oxford.

Johnson, G., Scholes, K., & Whittington, R. (2007) Exploring Corporate Strategy, (8th edition), FT Prentice Hall, London.

Kotler, P. (2001) Kotler on Marketing, New edition, Free Press, London.

Mortished, C. '*General Electric joins move downmarket in face of recession*' Times Online 8 May 2009.

BPP
LEARNING MEDIA

Chapter 7

Growth strategies

Topic list

Introduction

Organisations often seek to extend their reach without increasing their size by forming strategic alliances (closer working relationships) with other organisations. This involves partnerships and joint ventures as well as contracting out services to outside suppliers.

It results in improved access to information and technology, and quicker responses. However, alliances are vulnerable to management failures and so must be carefully selected; in addition they involve genuine moves away from bureaucracy and hierarchy.

You already know that the strategic choices available to an organisation can be classified and analysed using the Ansoff matrix. For example:

- Market penetration – increase market share; increase product usage (frequency,quantity, revitalise, new applications)
- Product development – line extensions; expand the product scope; develop new products
- Market development – expand geographically; target new segments
- Diversification – related and unrelated
- Vertical integration strategies – forward and backward

This chapter examines some areas where growth strategies can be pursued.

Syllabus-linked learning objectives

By the end of the chapter you will be able to:

Learning objectives	Syllabus link
1 Critically evaluate the nature of innovation and new product development (NPD) in marketing and the related factors impacting upon marketing decisions, including ongoing innovation management within an organisation	2.2.1
2 Assess the relevance to an organisation of mergers, acquisitions and strategic alliances in growing, expanding and maximising business potential	2.2.4
3 Critically evaluate a range of growth strategies for an organisation	2.2.5
4 Critically evaluate the concept of relationship marketing (CRM) as a means of achieving growth and profitability within an organisation	2.2.6
5 Critically evaluate the development of an organisation's brand and its contribution towards increasing the organisation's value and brand equity	2.2.7

1 Mergers, acquisitions and strategic alliances

"Strategic alliances play an important role in global strategies because it is common for a firm to lack a key success factor for a market. It may be distribution, a brand name, a sales organisation, technology, R & D capability or manufacturing capability." Aaker & McLoughlin (2007) p.218

1.1 Motives for strategic alliances

 KEY CONCEPT

concept

A **strategic alliance** is *"a collaboration leveraging the strengths of two or more organisations to achieve strategic goals. There is a long term commitment [of assets or competences] involved."* Aaker & McLoughlin *op. cit.* p.n 213

Alliances can take a number of forms.

- Agreements to co-operate on various issues
- Shared research and development
- Joint ventures, in which the partners create a separate business unit
- Supply chain rationalisation
- Licensing and franchising
- Purchase of minority stakes

Strategic alliances speed market penetration, normally by providing extra distribution effort. Many firms are expanding through alliances. For example, airlines have code sharing arrangements, which give them access to a larger base of assets. Such assets include:

- Market access
- Management skills
- Shared technology
- Exclusivity (eg shutting out competitors)

Strategic alliances can be motivated by the potential for

- Generating scale economies
- Gaining access to strategic markets
- Overcoming trade barriers

Or it may be needed (as hinted at in the opening quote) to compensate for a weakness:

- Filling out a product line (eg car manufacturers)
- Gaining access to technology
- Using excess capacity, such as spare or idle plant
- Gaining access to low cost manufacturing (eg consumer electronics)
- Access a particular customer relationship (eg via Japanese firms who prefer to do business with Japanese suppliers)

Hooley et al (2007) give an overview of some of the environmental factors that are stimulating the need for alliances.

- Scarce resources
- Increased competition
- Higher customer expectations
- Pressures from strong distributors
- Internationalisation of markets
- Changing markets and technologies
- Turbulent and unpredictable markets

Alliances have become a popular model for global expansion. Writers like Ohmae (1999) claim that globalisation has made them essential for successful strategies. According to Aaker (2007) the top 500 global companies have an average of 60 major alliances each. The participants tend to be competing firms from different countries, seeking to enhance their competences by combining resources, but without sacrificing autonomy. The strategic alliance is usually concerned with gaining market entry, remaining globally competitive and attaining economies of scale.

According to Hennessey (2004), they can be categorised as follows.

- **Production-based alliances** – improving manufacturing and production efficiency
- **Distribution-based alliances** – sharing distribution networks
- **Technology-based alliances** – pooling R & D costs

1.2 Alliances and networks

Many firms are growing by **alliances** with other firms, short of a full scale merger or acquisition. These are supposed to offer synergies and mutual benefits.

Growth can involve:

(a) **Building up new businesses** from scratch and developing them (sometimes called organic growth).

(b)   **Acquiring** already existing businesses from their current owners via the purchase of a controlling interest in another company.

(c)   A **merger** is the joining of two or more separate companies to form a single company.

(d)   Spreading the costs and risks (**joint ventures**, **alliances** or other forms of **co-operation**).

1.3 Acquisitions

The purpose of acquisitions

(a)   **Marketing advantages**

   (i)   Buy in a new product range

   (ii)   Buy a market presence (especially true if acquiring a company with overseas offices and contacts that can be utilised by the parent company)

   (iii)   Unify sales departments or to rationalise distribution and advertising

   (iv)   Eliminate competition or to protect an existing market

(b)   **Production advantages**

   (i)   Gain a higher utilisation of production facilities and reap economies of scale by larger machine runs
   (ii)   'Buy in' technology and skills
   (iii)   Obtain greater production capacity
   (iv)   Safeguard future supplies of raw materials
   (v)   Improve purchasing by buying in bulk

(c)   **Finance and management**

   (i)   Buy a high quality management team, which exists in the acquired company
   (ii)   Obtain cash resources where the acquired company is very liquid
   (iii)   Gain undervalued assets or surplus assets that can be sold off ('asset stripping')
   (iv)   Obtain tax advantages (eg purchase of a tax loss company)

(d)   **Risk-spreading**

(e)   **Independence**. A company threatened by a take-over might acquire another company, just to make itself bigger and so a more expensive 'target' for the predator company.

(f)   **Overcome barriers to entry**

 MARKETING AT WORK   application

Acquisitions research

Acquisitions are a financial disaster for shareholders, new research suggests.

A study of the performance of large takeovers completed between 1977 and 1994 has found that in the five years after a deal, the total return on investment underperformed by an average of 26%, compared with shares in companies of similar size.

The research, the University of Exeter's new Centre for Finance
and Investment, showed that the effect of acquisitions on share price and dividends varied according to whether the bids were hostile or non-hostile and whether they were equity–financed or cash backed.

The underperformance on share-based deals is 36% over five years, relative to unacquisitive companies.

Agreed bids also generated negative returns, with shareholders doing 27% less well. Agreed share-based deals led to underperformance of 37%.

Cash financing or bidder hostility were not enough on their own to make a profit likely, the report found. However, bids that are cash-backed and hostile have a better chance of creating, rather than destroying, shareholder value.

On a low sample, the academics found that a successful hostile cash bid generated an average 50% increase in the profitability of shares in the five years after the bid. Share-based bids perform poorly possibly because shares in the acquiring companies are overvalued in the first place.

The process of gaining co-operation from the target board might also increase the cost, as executives might have to be persuaded to agree only if the acquirer offers over-generous terms. Unnecessary cost may be incurred if executives in an acquired company retain their jobs after completion of deals.

The Times, 18 October 2004

1.4 Organic growth

Organic growth (sometimes referred to as **internal development**) is the primary method of growth for many organisations, for a number of reasons. Organic growth is achieved through the development of internal resources.

1.4.1 Reasons for pursuing organic growth

(a) **Learning**. The process of developing a new product gives the firm the best understanding of the market and the product.

(b) **Innovation**. It might be the only sensible way to pursue genuine technological innovations, and exploit them. (Compact disk technology was developed by Philips and Sony, which earn royalties from other manufacturers licensed to use it.)

(c) There is **no suitable target for acquisition**.

(d) Organic growth can be **planned more meticulously** and offers little disruption.

(e) It is often **more convenient** for managers, as organic growth can be financed easily from the company's current cash flows, without having to raise extra money on the stock market (eg to fund an acquisition).

(f) The **same style of management and corporate culture** can be maintained.

(g) **Hidden or unforeseen losses are less likely** with organic growth than with acquisitions.

(h) **Economies of scale** can be achieved from more **efficient use of central head office functions** such as finance, purchasing, personnel, management services and so on.

1.4.2 Problems with organic growth

(a) **Time** – sometimes it takes a long time to climb a **learning curve**.

(b) **Barriers to entry** (eg distribution networks) are harder to overcome: for example, a brand image may be built-up from scratch.

(c) The firm will have to **acquire the resources independently**.

(d) Organic growth may be **too slow for the dynamics of the market**.

 MARKETING AT WORK application

HDFC Bank

On 25 February 2008, the boards of HDFC Bank and Centurion Bank of Punjab (CBoP) agreed to the biggest merger in Indian banking history, valued at around Rs95.2 billion (US$2.4 billion) . . .
. . . regional strength is one of the benefits that HDFC Bank was looking for, but the merger will also offer several others. HDFC Bank says it was looking to supplement organic growth with a merger that would add scale, geographical reach and experienced staff, which are in short supply.

Economist Intelligence Unit ViewsWire, February 29th 2008

1.5 Alliances and synergy

KEY CONCEPT

concept

Synergy is achieved when combining resources results in a better rate of return than would be achieved by the same resources used independently in separate operations.

1.5.1 Obtaining synergy from alliances

(a) **Marketing synergy**: use of common marketing facilities such as distribution channels, sales staff and administration, and warehousing. Petrol stations can double as burger outlets.

(b) **Operating synergy**: arises from the better use of operational facilities and personnel, bulk purchasing, a greater spread of fixed costs whereby the firm's competence can be transferred to making new products.

(c) **Investment synergy**: the joint use of plant, common raw material stocks, transfer of research and development from one product to another – ie from the wider use of a common investment in fixed assets, working capital or research.

(d) **Management synergy**: the advantage to be gained where management skills concerning current operations are easily transferred to new operations because of the similarity of problems in the two industries.

1.5.2 Successful alliances

"The results of the collaboration should have strategic value and contribute to a viable venture that can withstand competitive attack and environmental change." Aaker & McLoughlin (2007) p.219

Factors for success:

* Choose partners with complementary skills, products, markets
* Understand the 'strategic intent' of the partnership
* Adopt the most appropriate partnership structure
* Resolve the leadership issue at the outset
* Define the benefits expected from the partnership
* Communicate the purpose and intent of the partnership internally
* Keep communicating with your partner and anticipate problems
* Define an exit strategy for failure at the outset
* Monitor the benefits the partnership delivers
* Recognise a company may need multiple partnerships in a global business market

1.5.3 Consortia

Consortia: organisations co-operate on specific business prospects. Airbus is an example, a consortium including British Aerospace, Dasa, Aerospatiale and Casa (of Spain). However, it does have an unusual financial structure, and it will soon turn into a normal company.

1.6 Joint ventures

Two firms (or more) join forces for manufacturing, financial and marketing purposes and each has a share in both the equity and the management of the business. A joint venture is a separate business unit set up for the reasons outlined below.

(a) **Share funding**. As the capital outlay is shared, joint ventures are especially attractive to smaller or risk-averse firms, or where very expensive new technologies are being researched and developed (such is the civil aerospace industry).

(b) **Cut risk**. A joint venture can reduce the risk of government intervention if a local firm is involved (eg Club Méditerranée pays much attention to this factor).

(c) Participating enterprises **benefit from all sources of profit**.

(d) **Close control** over marketing and other operations.

(e) Overseas, a joint venture with an indigenous firm provides **local knowledge, quickly**.

(f) **Synergies**. One firm's production expertise can be supplemented by the other's marketing and distribution facility.

(g) **Learning** can also be a 'learning' exercise in which each partner tries to learn as much as possible from the other.

(h) **Technology**. New technology offers many uncertainties and many opportunities. Such alliances provide funds for expensive research projects, spreading risk.

(i) **The joint venture itself can generate innovations**.

(j) The alliance can involve **'testing' the firm's core competence** in different conditions, which can suggest ways to improve it.

1.6.1 Disadvantages of joint ventures

(a) Conflicts of interest between the different parties.

(b) Disagreements may arise over profit shares, amounts invested, the management of the joint venture and the marketing strategy.

(c) One partner may wish to withdraw from the arrangement.

1.7 Licensing

A **licensing agreement** is a commercial contract whereby the licenser gives something of value to the licensee in exchange for certain performances and payments. The licenser may provide, in return for a royalty:

- Rights to produce a patented product or use a patented production process
- Manufacturing know-how (unpatented)
- Technical advice and assistance
- Marketing advice and assistance
- Rights to use a trademark, brand and so on

Subcontracting is also a type of alliance. Co-operative arrangements also feature in supply chain management, JIT and quality programmes.

1.8 Franchising

Franchising is a method of expanding the business on less capital than would otherwise be possible. For suitable businesses, it is an **alternative business strategy to raising extra capital** for growth. Franchisers include Budget Rent-a-car, Dyno-rod, Express Dairy, Holiday Inn, Kall-Kwik Printing, KFC, Prontaprint, Sketchley Cleaners, Body Shop and even McDonald's.

(a) The **franchiser** offers its:

    (i) Name, and any goodwill associated with it
    (ii) Systems and business methods
    (iii) Support services, such as advertising, training, help with site decoration etc

(b) The **franchisee**:

    (i) Provides capital, personal involvement and local market knowledge
    (ii) Pays the franchiser for being granted these rights and services
    (iii) Has responsibility for the running and profitability of his franchise

1.9 The virtual firm

An extreme example of an alliance is the so-called **virtual firm**. A virtual firm is created out of a **network of alliances** and subcontracting arrangements: it is as if most of the activities in a particular value chain are conducted by different firms, even though the process is loosely co-ordinated by one of them. It is outsourcing taken to its greatest extent.

For example, assume you manufacture small toys. You could in theory **outsource**:

- The design to a consultancy
- Manufacturing to a subcontractor in a low-cost country
- Delivery arrangements to a specialist logistics firm
- Debt collection to a bank (factoring)
- Filing, tax returns, bookkeeping to an accountancy firm

Virtual corporations effectively put market forces in all linkages of the value chain – this has the advantage of creating **incentives** for suppliers, perhaps to take risks to produce a better product, but can lead to a loss of control.

 ACTIVITY 1 _____ application

Summarise some of the features of strategic alliances

---

2 Innovation and new product development

"While many firms strive for innovation, not all achieve it. Success requires a true commitment to innovation that survives pressure for short term results. This commitment must be well-managed so that the right people are given the right environment. Further, the organisation must be competent at turning innovation ... into commercial products and must be willing to take chances and be wrong." Aaker & McLoughlin, *op.cit.*, p.197

2.1 The importance of innovation

 KEY CONCEPT _____ concept

Innovation "is about changing established products, processes and practices." Drummond *et al* (2008)

Innovation is a major responsibility of modern management, particularly in commercial organisations. This is because both technology and society are developing extremely rapidly; new products must be matched with new market opportunities if businesses are to survive and prosper. Innovation in marketing is particularly important, since marketing provides much of the interface between the organisation and its rapidly changing environment.

Since innovation is likely to be a major requirement for success in most commercial organisations, it will be an important part of the marketing manager's job: recognising innovative ideas when they appear and developing and managing the conditions and processes that support innovation.

It is important to remember that the need for innovation does not just relate to products and services: internal business processes are likely to be fertile ground for innovation and improvement. Innovation responses to the demands made of the marketing function will also be required and may prove to be particularly rewarding.

2.1.1 Innovation and the market orientation

A market orientation involves establishing customer needs and finding ways to satisfy them. Very obviously, innovation has a major role to play here. However, what of the kind of innovation that addresses no currently established need? Equally obviously, strategic management must take cognisance of such developments and investigate them carefully to see if they have the capacity to generate entirely new categories of demand. The Sony Walkman is the classic example of technical innovation of this type, but there are non-technological and service industry examples too. For example, before Starbucks, few people realised they needed a cup of coffee to take to work with them.

2.1.2 Innovation and control

One of the sources of innovation is increased delegation. In itself delegation has great value - morale and performance are improved, top management is freed for strategic planning and decisions are made by those closest to the problem concerned and therefore most informed about it. Most importantly, the organisation benefits from the imagination and thinking of its high flyers.

To encourage innovation the objective for management should be to create a more outward-looking organisation. People should be encouraged to use their initiative to look for new products, markets, processes, designs and ways to improve productivity.

Innovation thrives best in an organisation when it is supported by its culture.

- Ensure management and staff know what innovation is and how it happens
- Ensure that senior managers welcome, and are seen to welcome, changes for the better
- Stimulate and motivate management and staff to think and act innovatively
- Understand people in the organisation and their needs
- Recognise and encourage potential 'entrepreneurs'

2.2 Models of innovation

2.2.1 Small organisations and innovation

Research suggests that the following factors are crucial to the success of innovative small organisations.

(a) **Need orientation**. Lacking resources, successful small entrepreneurs soon find that it pays to approach potential customers early, test their solutions in the users' hands, learn from their reactions and adapt their designs rapidly.

(b) **Experts and fanatics**. Commitment allows the entrepreneur to persevere despite the frustrations, ambiguities and setbacks that always accompany major innovations.

(c) **Long time horizons**. Time horizons for radical innovations make them essentially 'irrational' from a present-value viewpoint - delays between invention and commercial production/success can range from three to 25 years.

(d) **Low early costs**. Innovators incur as few overheads as possible, their limited resources going directly into their projects. They borrow whatever they can and invent cheap equipment or processes, often improving on what is available in the marketplace.

(e) **Multiple approaches**. Committed entrepreneurs will tolerate the chaos of random advances in technology, adopting solutions where they can be found, unencumbered by formal plans that would limit the range of their imaginations.

(f) **Flexibility and quickness**. Undeterred by committees, the need for board approvals and other bureaucratic delays, the inventor/entrepreneur can experiment, recycle and try again, with little time lost. They quickly adjust their entry strategies to market feedback.

(g) **Incentives**. Tangible personal rewards are foreseen if success is achieved and the prospect of these rewards (which may not be principally of a monetary nature) is a powerful driver.

2.2.2 Large organisations and innovation

Within large organisations, by contrast, the following barriers to innovation and creativity may typically be encountered.

(a) **Top management isolation**. Financially-focused top managers are likely to perceive technological innovation as more problematic than, say, acquisitions or organic growth: although these options are just as risky, they may appear more familiar.

(b) **Intolerance of fanatics**. Big companies often view entrepreneurial fanatics as embarrassments or trouble-makers.

(c) **Short time horizons**. The perceived corporate need to report a continuous stream of upward-moving, quarterly profits conflicts with the long time-spans that major innovations normally require.

(d) **Accounting practices**. A project in a big company can quickly become an exposed political target and its potential net present value may sink unacceptably. Also there is a tendency to apply false logic to sunk costs: it is important to remember that costs incurred in the past are not relevant to decisions taken in the present about the future. It is, thus, equally erroneous to cancel a project on the grounds that its forecast revenues do not offer an adequate return on its total costs, as it is to persist with one on the grounds that a large amount has already been spent.

(e) **Excessive rationalism**. Managers in large organisations often seek orderly advance through early market research studies or systematic project planning.

(f) **Excessive bureaucracy**. Bureaucratic structures require many approvals that cause delays; the interactive feedback that fosters innovation is lost, important time windows can be missed and real costs and risks rise for the corporation.

(g) **Inappropriate incentives**. When control systems neither penalise opportunities missed nor reward risks taken, the results are predictable.

Successful large organisations have developed techniques that emulate or improve on the approaches used in small, fleet-of-foot companies.

(a) **Atmosphere and vision**. Continuous innovation occurs largely because top managers appreciate innovation and atmosphere in order to support it. They project clear long-term vision for the organisation that go beyond simple economic measures.

(b) **Orientation to the market**. Within innovative organisations, managers focus primarily on seeking to anticipate and solve customers' emerging problems.

(c) **Small, flat hierarchies**. Development teams in large organisations normally include only six to seven key people; operating divisions and total technical units are kept below 400 people.

(d) **Multiple approaches**. Where possible, several prototype programmes are encouraged to proceed in parallel. Such redundancy helps the organisation to cope with uncertainties in development, motivates people through competition and improves the amount and quality of information available for making final choices on scale-ups or new-product/service introductions.

(e) **Development shoot-outs**. The most difficult problem in the management of competing projects lies in re-integrating the members of the losing team. For the innovative system to work continuously, managers must create a climate that honours high-quality performance whether a project wins or loses, reinvolves people quickly in their technical specialities or in other projects and accepts rotation among tasks and groups.

(f) **Skunkworks**. This is the name given the system in which small teams of engineers, technicians, designers and model makers are placed together with no intervening organisational or physical barriers, to develop a new product from idea to commercial prototype stage. This approach eliminates bureaucratic controls; allows fast, unfettered communications; permits rapid turnround times for experiments; and instils a high level of group identity and commitment.

(g) **Interactive learning**. Recognising that the random, chaotic nature of technological change cuts across organisational and even institutional lines, the big company innovators tap into multiple sources of technology from outside as well as to their customers' capabilities.

With the complexities of balancing intellectual property management and the size and structure of research divisions, companies are looking outside of the boundaries of the firm for efficiency and value.

An example of a specific corporate strategy often found in discussions of open innovation is Procter & Gamble's 'Connect + Develop' strategy, by which P&G is shifting the source of innovation for new products from their internal research department and traditional suppliers to outside innovators. P&G's website reports more than 40% of their products now have a component of external collaboration.

2.3 Managing innovation

2.3.1 Identifying those innovations likely to succeed

Arguably, the new product development process can start with looking at how an innovation can benefit the customer. One way of doing so is by looking at customer benefits, or' buyer utility'.

Item	Comment
Customer productivity	Does the innovation save time and effort?
Simplicity	Does the innovation reduce the complexity a customer faces?
Convenience	Does innovation reduce the inconvenience the customer experiences? (eg speedier or automated check-ins)
Risk	Does the innovation reduce risk?
Fun image	Can the innovation be enjoyed?
Environmental friendliness	Is it responsible?

New products should only be taken to advanced development if there is evidence of:

*   **Adequate demand**
*   Compatibility with existing **marketing ability**
*   Compatibility with existing **production ability**

The stages of new product (or service) development are as follows.

New product development

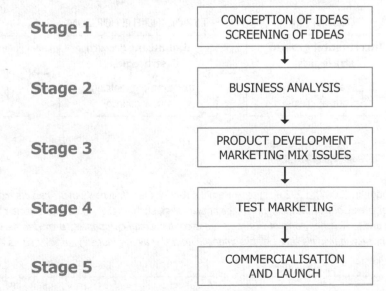

Stage 1 — CONCEPTION OF IDEAS / SCREENING OF IDEAS

Stage 2 — BUSINESS ANALYSIS

Stage 3 — PRODUCT DEVELOPMENT / MARKETING MIX ISSUES

Stage 4 — TEST MARKETING

Stage 5 — COMMERCIALISATION AND LAUNCH

The mortality rate of new products is very high. To reduce the risk of failure new product ideas must be screened. Only the best will make it to the next development stage.

2.3.2 Organising for innovation

Companies can be organised and run in a way that stimulates innovation. This depends in large part on practical measures.

An innovation strategy calls for a management policy of giving encouragement to innovative ideas. This will require positive action.

(a) Financial backing to innovation, by spending on R & D and market research and risking capital on new ideas.

(b) Giving employees the opportunity to work in an environment where the exchange of ideas for innovation can take place. Management style and organisation structure can help here. Management can actively encourage employees and customers to put forward new ideas. Participation by subordinates in development decisions might encourage employees to become more involved with development projects and committed to their success. Development teams can be set up and an organisation built up on project team-work.

(c) Where appropriate, recruitment policy should be directed towards appointing employees with the necessary skills for doing innovative work. Employees should be trained and kept up-to-date.

(d) Certain managers should be made responsible for obtaining information from outside the organisation about innovative ideas, and for communicating this information throughout the organisation.

(e) Strategic planning should result in targets being set for innovation, and successful achievements by employees should, if possible, be rewarded.

 EXAM TIP   application

Think about (a) why a company would wish to introduce new products and (b) the stages of the product development sequence. Do not forget that NPD can apply to a new service, such as a new route for an airline. Think about the stages that are involved – and be able to apply them to a specific product or market.

2.4 'Big ideas'

Aaker (2007) presents the following diagram on growth strategies.

Growth strategies

 MARKETING AT WORK   application

Aaker & McLoughlin (2007, p.273) refer to Hamel's theory that *"the real payoff results from development of revolutionary strategies that break out of industry norms or operations"* such as Dell, Ikea and Ryanair (the subject of the sample case study for this unit): *"Ryanair, one of Europe's most controversial companies, provided services at exceptionally low fares and challenged what Ryanair calls the 'establishment' within the airline industry, similar to its American counterpart, Southwest Airlines."*

3 Relationship marketing

"All organisations depend on establishing and developing relationships. In short, they must develop relationships with other organisations ... and ... with customers. Indeed, this latter relationship provides the fundamental basis of all marketing activity." Drummond *et al* (2008) p.231

In recent times emphasis has increased on building and maintaining good long-term **relationships** with customers. This is because such relationships are more profitable than constantly searching for new customers owing to repeat purchasing, ease of service and so on.

The **customer** is central to the marketing orientation, but so far we have not considered this important concept in detail. Customers make up one of the groups of stakeholders whose interests management should address. The **stakeholder concept** suggests a **wider concern** than the traditional marketing approach of supplying goods and services which satisfy immediate needs. The supplier-customer relationship extends beyond the basic transaction. The customer needs to remain satisfied with his purchase and positive about his supplier long after the transaction has taken place. If his satisfaction is muted or grudging, future purchases may be reluctant or non-existent and he may advise others of his discontent. Customer tolerance in the UK is fairly high, but should not be taken for granted.

In deciding strategic direction and formulating marketing strategy, any company needs to address issues of customer care, because of:

(a)   **Legal** constraints

(b)   Industry **codes of conduct**

(c)   The recognition that keeping existing customers happy is cheaper than acquiring new ones

(d)   The **value chain**. Customer care is part of after-sales service and offers an opportunity for differentiation. It is also a valuable source of information.

Not all customers are the same. Some appear for a single cash transaction and are never seen again. Others make frequent, regular purchases in large volumes, using credit facilities and building up a major relationship. Yet another type of customer purchases infrequently but in transactions of high value, as for instance in property markets. This variation will exist to a greater or lesser extent in all industries, though each will have a smaller typical range of behaviour. However, even within a single business, customers will vary significantly in the frequency and volume of their purchases, their reasons for buying, their sensitivity to price changes, their reaction to promotion and their overall attitude to the supplier and the product. **Segmentation** of the customer base can have a major impact on profitability, perhaps by simply tailoring promotion to suit the most attractive group of customers.

Many businesses sell to intermediaries rather than to the end consumer. Some sell to both categories; they have to recognise that **the intermediary is just as much a customer as the eventual consumer**. Examples are manufacturers who maintain their own sales organisation but appoint agents in geographically remote areas and companies who combine autonomous operations with franchising. While it is reasonable to give the highest priority to the needs of the ultimate consumer and insist on some control over the activities of the intermediary, it must be recognised that he will only perform well if his own needs are addressed. For instance, a selling agent who has invested heavily in stock after being given exclusive rights in an area should be consulted before further demands are made on his cash flow by the launch of a new product.

3.1 Customer retention

Variation in customer behaviour was mentioned above. The most important aspect of this variation is whether or not the customer comes back for more. Customers should be seen as potentially providing a lifetime of purchases so that **the turnover from a single individual over time might be very large indeed**. It is widely accepted that there is a non-linear relationship between customer retention and profitability in that **a fairly small amount of repeat purchasing generates significant profit**. This is because it is far more expensive in promotion and overhead costs to convert a non-buyer into an occasional buyer than to turn an occasional buyer into a frequent buyer. The repeat buyer does not have to be persuaded to give the product a try or be tempted by special deals; he needs less attention from sales staff and already has his credit account set up. New customers usually have to be won from competitors.

The process of retaining customers for a lifetime is an important one and one in which integrated marketing communications has an important role to play. Instead of one-way communication aimed solely at gaining a sale it is necessary to develop an effective two-way communication process to turn a **prospect into a lifetime advocate**. This is shown in the following ladder of customer loyalty.

Ladder of customer loyalty

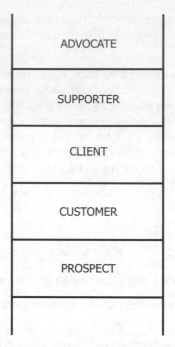

The purpose of relationship marketing is to establish, maintain and enhance relationships with customers and other parties so that the objectives of both parties involved are met.

(a)   Because **service and industrial companies** have direct, regular and often multiple contacts with their customers (for example, the regular hotel guest who interacts with reception), the importance of 'part-time' marketers is increased. Customer contact with all employees is vital.

(b)   **Trust and keeping promises**. To have an ongoing relationship, both parties need to trust each other and keep the promises they make. Marketing moves from one-off potentially manipulative exchanges towards co-operative relationships built on financial, social and structural benefits.

(c)   **Network of exchange partners**. Customer relationships are important but so too are the relationships which organisations have with other parties such as suppliers, distributors, professional bodies, banks and trade associations.

3.2 Customers as assets

You might already be familiar with the concept of the customer as a **current asset** in financial terms – except in cash businesses eg, a customer is a debtor. **Goodwill** – or a company's reputation – is also considered an asset.

However, it will sometimes help you in evaluating strategic marketing decisions and persuading sceptical management accountants of your case if you consider the customer base as an **asset worth investing in**. After all, if you are looking for repeat business, you will expect future benefits from customers.

Today's highly competitive business environment means that customers are only retained if they are **very satisfied** with their purchasing experience. **Any lesser degree of satisfaction is likely to result in the loss of the customer**. Companies must be active in monitoring customer satisfaction **because very few will actually complain. They will simply depart**. Businesses which use intermediaries must be particularly active, since research shows that even when complaints are made, the principals hear about only a very small proportion of them.

Customer care

In the increasingly competitive service sector, it is no longer enough to promise customer satisfaction. Today, customer 'delight' is the stated aim for companies battling to retain and increase market share.

Kwik-Fit, the car repair group, is another company that has included customer delight in its mission statement. Its forecourt promises to deliver '100 per cent customer delight' in the supply and fitting of vehicle brakes, tyres and exhausts leaves little margin for mistakes – and none at all for making any customer unhappy. Staff attend courses at company-run centres covering 'all practical aspects of their work, customer care and general management techniques'. Commitment is encouraged by 'job security', opportunities for promotion and a reward package that includes profit-related pay and shares in the company.

Customer satisfaction is monitored via reply-paid questionnaires distributed after work is carried out and through a freephone helpline that is open 24 hours a day. Kwik-Fit also says its customer survey unit '*allows us to make contact with 5,000 customers a day, within 72 hours of their visit to a Kwik-Fit Centre*'.

The most satisfactory way to retain customers is to offer them products which they perceive as providing **superior benefits** at any given price point. However, there are specific techniques which can increase customer retention. **Loyalty schemes** such as frequent flyer programmes, augment the product in the customer's eyes. The **club concept**, as used by Sainsbury and Tesco, offers small discounts on repeated purchases. The principal benefit of both these types of scheme, however, is the enhanced **knowledge of the customer** which they provide. Initial registration provides name, address and post code. Subsequent use of the loyalty card allows a detailed purchasing profile to be built up for individual customers. This enables highly targeted promotion and cross-selling later.

Research indicates that **the single largest reason why customers abandon a supplier is poor performance by front-line staff**. Any scheme for customer retention must address the need for careful selection and training of these staff. It is also a vital factor in **relationship marketing**.

3.3 Relationship marketing

There is a move away from 'transactions' to **relationship marketing**. Firms aim to build loyalty, especially where switching costs are high and a lost customer is probably lost for a long time.

 KEY CONCEPT   concept

Relationship marketing is defined very simply by Grönroos (2000) as the management of a firm's market relationships.

Much has been written in recent years on **relationship marketing**. Gummesson (2002) suggests it is a 'paradigm shift' requiring a **dramatic change** in marketing thinking and behaviour, not an add-on to traditional marketing.' H suggests that the core of marketing should no longer be the 4Ps, but 30Rs, which reflect the large number of complex relationships involved in business. Kotler (2001) says 'marketing can make promises but only the whole organisation can deliver satisfaction'.

Relationship marketing is thus as much about **attitudes and assumptions** as it is about techniques. The marketing function's task is to inculcate habits of behaviour at all levels and in all departments that will enhance and strengthen the alliance. It must be remembered, however, that the effort involved in long-term relationship building is more appropriate in some markets than in others. Where customers are purchasing intermittently and **switching costs are low**, there is always a chance of business. This tends to be the pattern in **commodity markets**. Here, it is reasonable to take a **transactions approach** to marketing and treat each sale as unique.

As stated earlier, **relationship marketing approach** is more appropriate where **switching costs are high** and a lost customer is thus probably lost for a long time. Switching costs are raised by such factors as the need for training on systems, the need for a large common installed base, high capital cost and the incorporation of purchased items into the customer's own designs.

The conceptual or philosophic nature of relationship marketing leads to a simple principle, that of **enhancing satisfaction by precision in meeting the needs of individual customers**. This depends on extensive **two-way communication** to establish and record the customer's characteristics and preferences and build a long-term relationship. *Adcock* mentions three important practical methods which contribute to this end.

- Building a customer database
- Developing customer-oriented service systems
- Extra direct contacts with customers

3.3.1 Databases

Modern **computer database systems** have enabled the rapid acquisition and retrieval of the individual customer's details, needs and preferences. Using this technology, relationship marketing enables telephone sales staff to greet the customer by name, know what he purchased last time, avoid taking his full delivery address, know what his credit status is and what he is likely to want. It enables new products to be developed that are precisely tailored to the customer's needs and new procedures to be established which enhance his satisfaction. It is the successor to **mass marketing**, which attempted to be customer-led but which could only supply a one-size-fits-all product. The end result of a relationship marketing approach is a mutually satisfactory relationship which continues indefinitely.

3.3.2 Customer care

Relationship marketing extends the principles of **customer care**. Customer care is about providing a product which is augmented by high quality of service, so that the customer is impressed during his transaction with the company. This can be done in ignorance of any detail of the customer other than those implicit in the immediate transaction. The customer is anonymous. **Relationship marketing is about having the customer come back for further transactions by ending the anonymity**.

It is inevitable that **problems** will arise. A positive way of dealing with errors must be designed into the customer relationship. Front line sales people cannot usually deal with the causes of mistakes as they **are built into the products**, **systems and organisation structure**. It is, therefore, necessary for management to promote vertical and horizontal interaction in order to spur changes to eliminate the **sources** of mistakes.

It is inevitable that there will be multiple contacts between customer and supplier organisations. Each contact is an opportunity to enhance or to prejudice the relationship, so staff throughout the supplier organisation must be aware of their marketing responsibilities. Two-way communication should be encouraged so that the relationship can grow and deepen. There is a link here to the database mentioned above: extra contacts provide more information. Confidential information must, of course, be treated with due respect.

 MARKETING AT WORK   application

Customer loyalty

The problem with profitable customers is retaining them, because they will attract the attention of your competitors. Building customer relationships may be the answer to both types of problem.

Relationship marketing is grounded in the idea of establishing a learning relationship with customers. At the lower end, building a relationship can create cross-selling opportunities that may make the overall relationship profitable. For example, some retail banks have tried selling credit cards to less profitable customers. With valuable customers, customer relationship management may make them more loyal and willing to invest additional funds. In banking, these high-end relationships are often managed through private bankers, whose goals are not only to increase customer satisfaction and retention, but also to cross-sell and bring in investment.

In determining which customers are worth the cost of long-term relationships, it is useful to consider their lifetime value. This depends on:

- Current profitability computed at the customer level
- The propensity of those customers to stay loyal
- Expected revenues and costs of servicing such customers over the lifetime of the relationship

Building relationships makes most sense for customers whose lifetime value to the company is the highest. Thus, building relationships should focus on customers who are currently the most profitable, likely to be the most profitable in the future, or likely to remain with the company for the foreseeable future and have acceptable levels of profitability.

The goal of relationship management is to increase customer satisfaction and to minimise any problems. By engaging in 'smarter' relationships, a company can learn customers' preferences and develop trust. Every contact point with the customer can be seen as a chance to record information and learn preferences. Complaints and errors must be recorded, not just fixed and forgotten. Contact with customers in every medium, whether over the Internet, through a call centre, or through personal contact, is recorded and centralised.

Many companies are beginning to achieve this goal by using customer relationship management (CRM) software. Data, once collected and centralised, can be used to customise service. In addition, the database can be analysed to detect patterns that can suggest better ways to serve customers in general. A key aspect of this dialogue is to learn and record preferences. There are two ways to determine customers' preferences: transparently and collaboratively.

Discovering preferences transparently means that the marketer learns the customers' needs without actually involving them. For example, the Ritz Carlton Hotel makes a point of observing the choices that guests make and recording them. If a guest requests extra pillows, then extra pillows will be provided every time that person visits. At upmarket retailers, personal shoppers will record customers' preferences in sizes, styles, brands, colours and price ranges and notify them when new merchandise appears or help them choose accessories.

3.3.3 Differences between transactional and relationship marketing

Transactional	Relationship
Importance of single sale	Importance of customer relation
Importance of product features	Importance of customer benefits
Short time scale	Longer time scale
Less emphasis on service	High customer service
Quality is concern of production	Quality is concern of all
Competitive commitment	High customer commitment
Persuasive communication	Regular communication

Adapted from Adcock *et al* (1998)

The most important issue in customer retention is focusing marketing effort on activities that promote a strong relationship rather than a single transaction.

3.3.4 The relationship marketing mix

By now you are familiar with the 4Ps of the basic marketing mix. Relationship marketing is highly dependent upon a fifth P: **people**. The features of the basic 4Ps must support the commitment to developing mutually beneficial customer relationships. The **behaviour of the people** involved in the customer relationship is even more important, because relationship marketing success depends on their motivation to achieve it. In turn, that motivation depends to a great extent upon the leadership exercised by marketing managers. It is not enough to expect self-motivation because *all* staff are involved, not just those with a sales role.

3.3.5 Implementing relationship marketing programmes

Kotler (2001) suggests five steps, suitable for business-to-business or service markets.

Step 1   Identify **key customers**

Step 2   Assign a **relationship manager** to each

Step 3   Develop clear **job descriptions**

Step 4   Appoint a manager to supervise the relationship managers

Step 5   Develop long-term plans for developing **relationships**

3.3.6 Sustaining the relationship

(a)   Offer **superior customer value** by personalising the interaction, involving two-way communication. This is essential for service industries such as life assurance. Hotels have systems that remember guests' preferences.

(b)   Be trustworthy and **reliable**, for example by offering a replacement.

(c)   **Tighten the connection**. Once the relationship is established, it must be nurtured to make it harder for the customer to defect.

(d)   **Co-ordinating capabilities**. The more successful the relationship, the greater the risk of imitation.

Kotler's approach is suitable for business-to-business markets or personal services such as financial advice. Some firms, however, have sought through data mining techniques to get a long-term view of the customer.

Loyalty cards are designed to reward customers for repeat purchase. They:

- Collect information about customer purchasing habits, enabling targeted marketing communication
- Reward customers for repeat purchase, to encourage sales volumes

Loyalty schemes vary in the benefit they offer.

(a)   Recent UK research indicates that owners of 'loyalty' cards spend more, but they are not necessarily loyal.

(b)   Furthermore, most customers still shop around and have one or more loyalty cards.

(c)   **Loyalty cards may prove to be an expensive failure**.

3.3.7 Key accounts

So far we have considered the retention of customers as an unquestionably desirable objective. **However, for many businesses a degree of discretion will be advisable**. 'Key' does not mean large. A customer's **potential** is very important. The definition of a key account depends on the circumstances. Key account management is about managing the future.

Customers can be assessed for desirability according to such criteria as the profitability of their accounts; the prestige they confer; the amount of non-value adding administrative work they generate; the cost of the selling effort they absorb; the rate of growth of their accounts and, for industrial customers, of the turnover of their own businesses; their willingness to adopt new products; and their credit history. Such analyses will almost certainly conform to a Pareto distribution and show, for instance that 80% of profit comes from 20% of the customers, while a different 20% generate most of the credit control or administrative problems. Some businesses will be very aggressive about getting rid of their problem customers, but a more positive technique would be to concentrate effort on the most desirable ones. These are the **key accounts** and the company's relationship with them can be built up by appointing **key account managers**.

Key account management is often seen as a high level selling task, but should in fact be a business wide team effort about relationships and customer retention. It can be seen as a form of co-operation with the customer's supply chain management function. The key account manager's role is to integrate the efforts of the various parts of the organisation in order to deliver an enhanced service. This idea has long been used by advertising agencies and was successfully introduced into aerospace manufacturing over 40 years ago. It will be the key account manager's role to maintain communication with the customer, note any developments in his circumstances, deal with any problems arising in the relationship and develop the long-term business relationship.

The key account relationship may progress through several stages.

(a) At first, there may be a typical **adversarial sales-purchasing relationship** with emphasis on price, delivery and so on. Attempts to widen contact with the customer organisation will be seen as a threat by its purchasing staff.

(b) Later, the sales staff may be able to foster **a mutual desire to increase understanding** by wider contacts. Trust may increase.

(c) A **mature partnership stage** may be reached in which there are contacts at all levels and information is shared. The key account manager becomes responsible for integrating the partnership business processes and contributing to the customer's supply chain management. High 'vendor ratings', stable quality, continuous improvement and fair pricing are taken for granted.

 MARKETING AT WORK application

"It is important to keep in mind that there are no complacent customers. Whether it is companies trying to survive, managers trying to hold on to their jobs, or families preparing to survive a layoff, customers everywhere are taking a new look at alternative suppliers that might offer better value or bring greater savings. This is true for existing customers who, therefore, need more loving attention, not less, and it is also true for competitors' customers."

Willem Burgers (2009)

4 Branding

"An important strategic option is to build brand equity ... Brands with high brand equity provide their owners with competitive and financial benefits." Aaker & McLoughlin (2007) p.181

4.1 What is a brand?

Much of the marketing mix activity goes to the development of **brands**, which are what the customers identify. Brands embody a set of expectations about the product. A brand image exists in the customer's mind.

 KEY CONCEPT concept

A **brand** is a collection of attributes which strongly influence purchase.

'A name, term, sign, symbol or design or combination of them, intended to identify the goods or services of one seller or group of sellers and to differentiate them from those of competitors.' (Kotler, 2001)

Branding and a firm's reputation are linked. The important thing to remember is that a brand is something **customers** value: it exists in the customer's mind. A brand is the link between a company's marketing activities and the customer's perception.

In suburban Philadelphia, not too many miles from Wharton's campus, is a retail establishment called Ed's Beer Store. It's a wonderfully prosaic name. Customers know what they can buy there, and if they have a complaint, they know whom to talk to.

But what about companies with names like Agere, Agilent or Altria? Or Diageo, Monday and Verizon? Or Accenture, Cingular and Protiviti?

Except for Monday, which may be a strange thing to call a company but it is nonetheless a real word, all these names are fabricated. What's more, none of them, even Monday, tells potential customers anything about the businesses they are in. Plus, they sound so contrived that you might conclude they will do nothing but elicit snickering and confusion in the market place.

According to marketing professors at Wharton, however, that is not necessarily the case. They say peculiar names, by themselves, may mean nothing to begin with. But if backed by a successful branding campaign, they will come to signify whatever the companies want them to mean.

Website: http://knowledge.wharton.upenn.edu

4.1.1 What makes up a brand?

- Effective product
- Distinctive identity
- Added values

supported by

Visible: Symbol, advertising, presentation (eg packaging)

Invisible: assets and competences, strong R&D, supply chain, effective selling, costs

4.1.2 Benefits of branding

Beneficiary	Benefit of branding
Customers	• Branding makes it easier to choose between competing products, if brands offer different benefits. Brands help consumers cope with information overload • Brands can support aspirations and self image • Branding can confer membership of reference groups
Marketers	• Enables extra value to be added to the product • Creates an impression in the consumer's mind; encourages re-purchase • Differentiates the product, especially if competing products are similar • Reduces the importance of price • Encourages a pull strategy • Other products/services can exploit the brand image (eg *Virgin*)

Shareholders	• A brand is an intangible asset; even though it is not on the financial statements, a strong brand promises to generate future cash inflows and profits. This is called **brand equity**.
	
	• Brands build market share, which can generate high profits through:
	   – Higher volume
	   – Higher value (higher prices)
	   – Higher control over distributors

Evolution of brands. Brands have evolved over time, to the extent that they satisfy customer needs.

(a) **Classic brands** (post World War II) were linked to a single goal (eg cleaner clothes).
(b) **Contemporary brands** meet functional needs but give associated benefits (eg Volvo and safety).
(c) **Post-modern brands**? Consumers use brands to attain a broad array of goals, as a result of 'time famine'.

Some marketers suggest that brands have an emotional content. Certainly, this might be the case for fashion items (eg trainers) where they confer status.

4.2 Brand strategies

There are several basic branding strategies: company, umbrella, range and individual product.

4.2.1 Different types of brand strategy

(a) **Company brand**. The company name is the most prominent feature of the branding (eg Mercedes).

(b) **The company brand combined with an individual brand name** (eg Kellogg's: Corn Flakes, Rice Krispies). This option both legitimises (because of the company name) and individualises (the individual product name). It allows **new names to be introduced quickly and relatively cheaply**. Sometimes known as **umbrella branding**, firms might use this approach as a short-term way to save money.

(c) **Range brand**. Firms group types of product under different brands

(d) **Individual name**. Each product has a unique name. This is the option chosen by Procter & Gamble for example, who even have different brand names within the same product line, eg Bold, Tide. The main advantage of individual product branding is that an unsuccessful brand does not adversely affect the firm's other products, nor the firm's reputation generally.

 MARKETING AT WORK   application

Penguin is one of the oldest brands in UK paperback publishing and over the years has introduced brand extensions (Puffin for children, Pelican for academic) and sub-brands (Penguin Classics, Penguin Modern Classics) and indeed other products (Penguin Classic CDs).

A key issue for publishing is to identify the core of the brand.

(a) The imprint or publisher?

(b) The author? It appears to go without saying that people will buy a book by a recognised author, and that the author is at the heart of the brand.

In contrast, people buy 'Mills & Boon' books – the core of the brand is the publisher, not the author.

The Folio Society publishes versions of classic literature, but markets its books partly as art objects, owing to the quality of the binding and paper, and the specially-commissioned illustrations.

4.2.2 Choice of brand strategy

(a) **Company and/or umbrella brand name**

Advantages	Disadvantages
• Cheap (only one marketing effort)	• Not ideal for segmentation
• Easy to launch new products under umbrella brand	• Harder to obtain distinct identity
• Good for internal marketing	• Risk that failure in one area can damage the brand
	• Variable quality

For example, Virgin is a company brand name, supported by advertising, PR and the celebrity status of Richard Branson.

(i)   Service industries use umbrella marketing as customer benefits can cross product categories. Marks & Spencer diversified from clothes, to food and to financial services. Tesco and Asda have followed suit.

(ii)   Communication media are more diffuse and fragmented.

(iii)   One brand is supported by integrated marketing communications.

(iv)   Umbrella branding supports **database marketing** across the whole product range.

(v)   Distributor/retailer brands are umbrella brands in their own right, so **brand owners** have to follow suit.

(b)   **Range brands** offer some of the advantages of an umbrella brand with more precise targeting.

(c)   **Individual brand** name

Advantages	Disadvantages
• Ideal for precise segmentation	• Expensive
• Crowds out competition by offering more choice	• Risky
• Damage limitation to company's reputation	

 MARKETING AT WORK

application

Factory equipment brands

MG Technologies industrial group, the company that owns the Tuchenhagen brand, promotes the name as part of a multi-brand philosophy. At Keyence, one of the world's biggest producers of sensors and vision systems for factory processes, the brand management is somewhat simpler; the Keyence name, rather than specialist 'sub-brands', is the brand most heavily promoted by the company.

Another leader in running different brands within the same business is Sandvik, the world's biggest manufacturer of machine-tool devices.

Sandvik's tooling division has about ten key brands. They include Coromant, which is associated with particularly hard cutting materials; Valenite, aimed at automotive applications; Walter (general machining); and Titex (drilling). Most of the company's advertising and marketing effort is aimed at establishing the value of these brands, rather than raising awareness of the Sandvik name itself.

Financial Times, 8 February 2005

4.3 Brand equity

The added value conferred by a brand is largely subjective. In blind testing many consumers cannot tell the difference between different products; however, they will exhibit a preference for a strong brand name when shown it. Apart from the quality and functionality of the product, brand equity is built on suggestion rather than substance.

 KEY CONCEPT

concept

Brand equity is the asset the marketer builds to ensure continuity of satisfaction for the customer and profit for the supplier.

Most consumer buying decisions, therefore, **do not depend on the functionality of the product**.

(a)   Products are bought for **emotional reasons**. For example, most sports trainers are fashion products.

(b)   Branding reduces the need for the intellectually challenging process of rational choice.

4.3.1 Sources of brand equity

Source	Comment
Experience	Customer's actual usage of a brand can give positive or negative associations.
User associations	Brands get an image from the type of people using them; brands might be associated with particular personalities.
Appearance	Design appeals to people's aesthetic sensibilities.
Manufacturer's name	The company reputation may support the brand.
Marketing communication	Building the brand by establishing its values is a major reason why marketing communication of all kinds is undertaken.

4.3.2 Brand identity

 KEY CONCEPTS

concept

Brand identity: the message sent out by the brand through its product form, name, visual signs, advertising. This is not the same as **brand image** which is how the target market perceives the brand.

 MARKETING AT WORK

application

"We are seeing more discounts, deeper discounts, more widespread discounts at Easter than we've seen for a very long time" (Richard Dodd of the British Retail Consortium).

While heavy price cuts may be great for consumers, there are fears that stores may be doing damage to their business – consumers feel no need to pay full price for anything any more, as one sale follows another in an effort to lure cash-strapped shoppers into stores.

Brands that are not generally seen as being discounters may see an erosion in brand value, as consumers learn to shop for discounts and bargains, and drive down prices even further.

BBC News, bbc.co.uk (2009)

4.3.3 Three aspects to a brand

Aspect	Comment
Core	Fundamental, unchanging aspect of a brand. (eg Cider is an alcoholic drink made from apples.)
Style	This is the brand's culture, personality, the identity it conveys and so on. Compare the: • Rustic personality of Scrumpy Jack • Almost club-oriented personality of Diamond White
Themes	These are how the brand communicates through physical appearance of the product.

Clearly, the **themes** are more easy to change than the **style**, which is more easy to change than the core.

Think about these three aspects in relation to Ryanair in the sample case study. One of the tasks on the sample question paper asks about the possibility of Ryanair repositioning itself, presumably in response to negative connotations associated with its brand: "the irresponsible face of capitalism" and so on.

4.4 How to build brands

Brand building is a logical process that can proceed gradually, step-by-step towards a position of strength.

The process for building the brand is similar to that of building a product (core product, an expected product, an augmented product and a potential product). However, a product is, in some respects, purely functional, whereas a brand offers more.

4.4.1 A step approach to designing brands

Step 1   **Have a quality product** – but remember quality means **fitness for use** not the **maximum specification**. Functionality is only a starting point.

Step 2   **Build the basic brand**. These are the marketing mix criteria.

- They should support product performance
- They should differentiate the brand
- They should be consistent with positioning
- The basic brand delivers the core product in an attractive way

Step 3   **Augmentations** include extra services, guarantees and so on. (Expensive guarantees provide evidence that the firm takes quality seriously.)

Step 4   **Reaching its potential**, so that customers will not easily accept substitutes.

Step 5   Maintain **brand value** by using the marketing mix to persuade customers to buy again.

Step 6   **Build brand loyalty**. Customers who buy again and are loyal are valuable because:

- Revenue from them is more predictable
- Existing customers are cheaper than new customers

Step 7   **Know where to stop in developing the brand**. (For example, an alcohol-free alcopop would be pointless.)

Brands that **reach their potential** have five key characteristics.

- A quality product underpinning the brand
- Being first to market, giving early-mover advantages
- Unique positioning concept: in other words they are precisely positioned
- Strong communications underpinning the brand
- Time and consistency

4.4.2 The brand planning process

Brand strategy is one of the steps in the brand planning process just as marketing strategy is one step in the marketing planning process. Arnold (1992) offers a five-stage brand planning process.

Stage	Description
Market analysis	An overview of trends in the macro- and micro-environment and so includes customer and competitor analysis and the identification of any PEST factors which may affect our brand.
Brand situation analysis	Analysis of the brand's personality and individual attributes. This represents the internal audit and questions such as, 'Is advertising projecting the right image?', 'Is the packaging too aggressive?', 'Does the product need updating?' need asking. This is a fundamental evaluation of the brand's character.
Targeting future positions	This is the core of brand strategy. Any brand strategy could incorporate what has been learnt in steps (1) and (2) into a view of how the market will evolve and what strategic response is most appropriate. Brand strategy can be considered under three headings. (1) Target markets (2) Brand positions (3) Brand scope
Testing new offers	Once the strategy has been decided the next step is to develop individual elements of the marketing mix and test the brand concept for clarity, credibility and competitiveness with the target market.
Planning and evaluating performance	The setting of the brand budget, establishing the type of support activity needed and measurement of results against objectives. Information on tracking of performance feeds into step (1) of the brand management process.

4.5 Brand extension

A brand can be used on a wide range of products and services if its values are appropriate.

 KEY CONCEPT

concept

Brand extension uses a brand name successfully established in one market or channel to enter other. It is often termed **brand stretching** when the markets are very different.

4.5.1 Examples of brand extension

- **Retailers** such as Dixons and Tesco launching themselves as **Internet Service Providers**

- Penguin Books launching its own brand of compact discs

- One of the greatest exponents of brand extension is Richard Branson. He has extended the Virgin brand, originally based on pop music, to cover mobile phones, trains, airlines and even financial services.

4.5.2 Conditions for brand extension

(a) The **core values** of the brand must be **relevant to the new market**. EasyJet has transferred to car rental and internet cafes.

(b) The new market area must not affect the core values of the brand by association. Failure in one activity can adversely affect brand equity.

Mark Ritson, assistant professor of marketing at the London Business School, wrote about two planned attempts at brand stretching. He did not expect either to succeed.

- Stelios Haji–Ioannou, founder of Easyjet has announced easy4men, a range of male grooming products. Ritson doubts this will succeed as easyGroup does not really have 'brand equity in the form of positive, valuable and extendable brand associations', it merely has *'an unusual business model built on a stripped-down product offering and dynamic pricing'*. Can cheap flights, cheap car rental, cheap cinema, cheap buses, cheap credit cards and other cheap stuff be joined by a cheap toiletries range? In the words of another commentator: *"Now I might boast about getting a cheap flight to Barcelona... but will anyone brag about how cheap their aftershave is?"*

- The Daily Telegraph launched a compact edition. Ritson expected this to fail because the Telegraph *'is tradition, it is conservatism, it is quality. It is all the things that a compact edition is not'*. He contrasts the Telegraph's prospects with the successful launch of a compact edition of The Independent, 'a younger, different and more contemporary newspaper brand.'

The single 'easy4men' product (a 'three-day travel pack') is still available. The compact edition of the Daily Telegraph seems to have disappeared without trace.

4.5.3 Advantages of brand extension

Advantage	Comment
Cheap	It is less costly to extend a brand then to establish a new one from scratch.
Customer-perception	Customer expectations of the brand have been built up, so this lower risk for the customer encourages 'trial'.
Less risky	Failure rate of completely new brands.

4.5.4 Disadvantages of brand extension

Disadvantage	Comment
Segments	The brand personality may not carry over successfully to the new segment. The brand values may not be relevant to the new market.
Strength	The brand needs to be strong already.
Perception	The brand still needs a differential advantage over competitors.
Over-dilution	Excessive extensions can dilute the values of the brand.

4.6 Revitalising and repositioning

At times, the performance of a brand will falter and managers will attempt to rectify the situation by enhancing sales volume and improving profits in other ways.

Revitalisation means increasing the sales volume through:

- New markets (eg overseas)
- New segments (eg personal computers are being sold for family, as opposed to business, use)
- Increased usage (encouraging people to eat breakfast cereals as a snack during the day)

Repositioning is more fundamental, in that it is a **competitive strategy** aimed to change position to increase market share.

Type of position	Comment
Real	Relates to actual product features and design
Psychological	Change the buyer's beliefs about the brand
Competitive	Alter beliefs about competing brands
Change emphasis	The emphasis in the advertising can change over time

4.6.1 Success criteria for branding

Beneficial qualities of a brand name

- Suggest **benefits**, eg Schweppes' Slimline tonic
- Suggest qualities such as **action** or **colour** (eg easyJet, with an orange colour)
- Be **easy to pronounce**, recognise and remember
- Be **acceptable in all markets**, both linguistically and culturally
- Be **distinctive**
- Be **meaningful**

 MARKETING AT WORK

 application

Compare the following mobile phone brands.

- Orange
- Vodafone
- Cellnet
- One-to-One

Orange appropriates the colour orange, whereas Vodafone and Cellnet suggest aspects of the product, and One-to-One suggests the actual consumer benefit.

4.7 Brands in the global market place

Brands, like most aspects of marketing practice, require a decision about standardisation or adaptation when taken into the global marketplace.

The most successful examples of worldwide branding occur where the brand has become **synonymous with the generic product** (eg Sellotape, Aspirin).

 MARKETING AT WORK

application

Brewing is an industry with significant economies of scale. Apart from Heineken and Guinness, it is only recently that big brewers have become 'international'. There are a variety of aspects of this development.

(a) Beers are branded across markets. Stella Artois is available in the UK as a premium product, whereas in Belgium it is 'a decent modestly priced lager'.

(b) Other firms are expanding by acquisition. Interbrew, the brewer of Stella Artois has purchased Labatt of Canada, to gain access to markets in North and South America.

(c) Big brewing companies see many European and American markets are stagnant: they are trying to revive them with imported or foreign brands.

(d) Firms co-operate in some markets but compete in others. (Guinness distributes Bass in the US, while competing with Bass in the UK.)

(e)   The greatest potential seems to be east Asia, where beer consumption is rising by 10% pa and South America, where growth is 4% pa.

Ultimately, even if the beer market eventually becomes truly global, it will remain fragmented for a long time to come.

4.7.1 Global or local brand?

The key differences between a standardised global brand approach and an approach based upon identifying and exploiting local marketing opportunities are as described below.

(a)   **Standardised global brand approach**

   (i)   A standardised product offering to market segments which have exactly similar needs across cultures

   (ii)   A common approach to the marketing mix and one that is as nearly standardised as may be, given language differences

(b)   **Local marketing opportunities**

   (i)   A recognition that the resources of the company may be adapted to fulfil marketing opportunities in different ways, taking into account local needs and preferences but on a global basis

   (ii)   A willingness to sub-optimise the benefits of having a single global brand (eg advertising synergy) in order to optimise the benefits of meeting specific needs more closely

 MARKETING AT WORK   application

It is possible to move from a local brand to a global brand approach as demonstrated by the Mars Corporation with their Snickers brand. In the UK market, the biggest 'candy market' in Europe, Mars had decided to use the brand name Marathon for the chocolate bar known as Snickers in the US and elsewhere around the world. Reportedly, this was done to avoid confusion with the word knickers. There was a very distinctive brand identity in the UK to the extent that the company would sponsor the London Marathon and other sporting events to tie in with the brand name. Competition from Nestlé in Europe persuaded the company that they needed to take up the potential benefits of a standardised global brand approach rather than merely relying on a global marketing approach. They, therefore, changed the name to Snickers in the UK market at very considerable cost of advertising support.

For the international company marketing products which can be branded there are two further policy decisions to be made.

*   The problem of deciding if and how to protect the company's brands
*   Whether there should be one global brand or different national brands for a product

The major argument in favour of a single global brand is the economies of scale that it produces, both in production and promotion. But whether a global brand is the best policy (or even possible) depends on a number of factors, which address the two basic policy decisions above.

4.7.2 Legal considerations

(a)   Legal constraints may limit the possibilities for a global brand, for instance, where the brand name has already been registered in a foreign country.

(b)   Protection of the brand name will often be needed, but internationally is hard to achieve.

   (i)   In some countries registration is difficult
   (ii)   Brand imitation and piracy are rife in certain parts of the world

   There are many examples of imitation in international branding, with products such as cigarettes, and denim jeans.

(c)   Worse still is the problem of piracy where a well known brand name is counterfeited. It is illegal in most parts of the world but in many countries there is little if any enforcement of the law. (Levis is one of the most pirated brand names.) Piracy is also a problem for intellectual property.

Even with trademark protection the impact of a market leader's branding may be weakened by consumers who perceive the brand name as a generic term. Can you think of some examples?

4.7.3 Cultural aspects

Even if a firm has no legal difficulties with branding globally, there may be cultural problems, eg unpronounceable names or names with other meanings, for example Maxwell House is Maxwell Kaffee in Germany, Legal in France and Monky in Spain. But sometimes a minor spelling change is all that is needed, such as Wrigley Speermint in Germany.

4.7.4 Other considerations

Many other influences affect the global branding decision.

(a) Differences between the firm's major brand and its secondary brands. The major brand is more likely to be branded globally than secondary brands.

(b) The importance of brand to the product sale. Where price, for example, is a more important factor, then it may not be worth the heavy expenditure needed to establish and maintain a global brand in each country; a series of national brands may be more effective.

(c) The problem of how to brand a product arising from acquisition or joint venture. Should the multinational company keep the name it has acquired?

Learning objectives	Covered
1 Critically evaluate the nature of innovation and new product development (NPD) in marketing and the related factors impacting upon marketing decisions, including ongoing innovation management within an organisation	☑ The importance of innovation (2.1) ☑ Models of innovation (2.2) ☑ Managing innovation (2.3) ☑ 'Big ideas' (2.4)
2 Assess the relevance to an organisation of mergers, acquisitions and strategic alliances in growing, expanding and maximising business potential	☑ Motives for strategic alliances (1.1) ☑ Alliances and networks (1.2) ☑ Acquisitions (1.3) ☑ Organic growth (1.4) ☑ Alliances and synergy (1.5) ☑ Joint ventures (1.6) ☑ Licensing (1.7) ☑ Franchising (1.8) ☑ The virtual firm (1.9)
3 Critically evaluate a range of growth strategies for an organisation	☑ Covered across the chapter content: mergers, acquisitions and strategic alliances; innovation and new product development; relationship marketing; branding
4 Critically evaluate the concept of relationship marketing (CRM) as a means of achieving growth and profitability within an organisation	☑ Customer retention (3.1) ☑ Customers as assets (3.2) ☑ Relationship marketing (3.3)
5 Critically evaluate the development of an organisation's brand and its contribution towards increasing the organisation's value and brand equity	☑ What is a brand? (4.1) ☑ Brand strategies (4.2) ☑ Brand equity (4.3) ☑ How to build brands (4.4) ☑ Brand extensions (4.5) ☑ Revitalising and repositioning (4.6) ☑ Brands in the global marketplace (4.7)

1   What constitutes a brand?

2   Who benefits from branding?

3   Identify two strategies for NPD.

4   What is relationship marketing?

5   What are some of the environmental factors stimulating the need for alliances?

6   List some purposes of acquisitions.

7   What is the biggest problem with relying upon organic growth?

8   Outline the process of new product development.

9   If a significant growth strategy is "expanding the horizon", what is a 'big idea'?

10   What is repositioning?

11   Give some of the differences between transactional and relationship marketing.

12   What is brand equity?

1   (a)   They are collaborations between two or more competing companies of similar strength, generally from industrialised countries.

    (b)   The relative contributions by the companies are balanced.

    (c)   The motivation for the alliance is generally broadly strategic or competitive, rather than purely for market access or economies of scale.

    (d)   The relationships are reciprocal and provide the opportunity for learning.

    (e)   They have a strategic and global focus, and seek to enhance global competitiveness via gaining access to a whole series of resources and skills.

2   The classic example in the UK is Hoover, which is now a generic term for any vacuum cleaner and is even used as a verb meaning 'to clean with a vacuum cleaner'. Words you may be surprised to know were once brand names include nylon, aspirin, cellophane and escalator: all have lost trade mark legal status. Kleenex and Xerox almost went the same way.

1   A branded product has a distinctive identity and added values that exist in the consumer's mind

2   All parties to the transaction: the customers and the management and owners of the supplying company

3   Leader and follower

4   The management of the company's marketing relationships

5   Scarce resources
    Increased competition
    Higher customer expectations
    Pressures from strong distributors
    Internationalisation of markets
    Changing markets and technologies
    Turbulent and unpredictable markets

6   Marketing advantages
    Production advantages
    Finance and management
    Risk-spreading
    Independence
    Overcome barriers to entry

7   It takes a very long time

8   **Stage 1**

CONCEPTION OF IDEAS SCREENING OF IDEAS

↓

Stage 2

BUSINESS ANALYSIS

↓

Stage 3

PRODUCT DEVELOPMENT MARKETING MIX ISSUES

↓

Stage 4

TEST MARKETING

↓

Stage 5

COMMERCIALISATION AND LAUNCH

9   A 'breakthrough"

10 Brand repositioning is a competitive strategy aimed at changing position to increase market share.

11

Transaction	**Relationship**
Importance of single sale	Importance of customer relation
Importance of product features	Importance of customer benefits
Short time scale	Longer time scale
Less emphasis on service	High customer service
Quality is concern of production	Quality is concern of all
Competitive commitment	High customer commitment
Persuasive communication	Regular communication

12 Brand equity is the asset the marketer builds to ensure continuity of satisfaction for the customer and profit for the supplier.

Aaker, D. & McLoughlin, D. (2007) <u>Strategic Market Management</u>, John Wiley, Chichester.

Adcock, D., Halborg, A., Ross, C. & Bradfield, R (1998) <u>Marketing: Principles and Practice</u>, (3rd edition), FT Prentice Hall, Harlow.

Ansoff, H.I. (1988) <u>Corporate Strategy</u>, 2nd revised edition, Penguin Books, London.

Arnold, D. (1993) <u>The Handbook of Brand Management</u>, Perseus Books, US.

Burgers, W. '*Marketing during economic downturns*' FT.com Special Reports, 5 February 2009.

Drummond, G. Ensor, J. & Ashford, R. (2008) <u>Strategic Marketing Planning and Control</u>, (3rd edition), Elsevier, Oxford.

Grönroos, C (2000) <u>Service Management and Marketing</u>, Wiley, Chichester.

Gummesson, E. (2002) <u>Total Relationship Marketing: Rethinking Marketing Management</u>, (2nd edition), Butterworth Heinemann, Oxford.

Hamel, G. (1996) '*Strategy as revolution*', Harvard Business Review, July-August, pp. 69-81.

Hooley, G., Saunders, J., Piercy, N., & Nicoulaud, B., (2007) <u>Marketing Strategy and Competitive Positioning</u>, (4th edition), FT Prentice Hall, Oxford.

Jeannet, J-P. & Hennessey, H. (2004) <u>Global Marketing Strategy,</u> (6th edition), Houghton Mifflin (Academic).

Johnson, G., Scholes, K., & Whittington, R. (2007) <u>Exploring Corporate Strategy</u>, (8th edition), FT Prentice Hall, Harlow

Kotler, P. (2001) <u>Kotler on Marketing</u>, (new edition), Free Press, NY.

Moshiri, M. (2009) '*Easter sales 'may harm retailers*' BBC News, bbc.co.uk, 11 April 2009.

Ohmae, K. (1999) <u>The Borderless World: Power and Strategy in the Interlinked Economy</u>, (revised edition), Harper Business, London.

Chapter 8

International marketing strategy

Topic list

Introduction

This chapter deals with the complexities faced in competing internationally. These topics are relevant to all commercial organisations, including those that might feel they are not active internationally. This is because all companies are likely to have suppliers, customers or competitors who are themselves involved in international business operations.

In Section 1, we offer an overview of some of the issues a firm faces when competing overseas. A huge variety of factors have to be dealt with.

In Section 2 we examine specific issues related to new countries and markets. For example, the importance of new technology is without doubt – but technology is influential in different ways, depending on the economic development of each market. Cultural issues also feature very significantly in the difficulties facing firms seeking to do international business.

Syllabus-linked learning objectives

By the end of the chapter you will be able to:

Learning objectives	Syllabus link
1 Critically evaluate the appropriateness of developing an international marketing strategy for an organisation investing in international markets	2.2.2
2 Critically evaluate a range of issues that impact on an organisation when entering new countries and markets and consider how they may be managed to achieve the organisation's objectives	2.2.3
3 Assess an organisation's readiness for developing a global strategy	3.1.2

1   Marketing internationally

"Businesses are increasingly able, or indeed compelled, to compete on a world scale." Drummond *et al* (2008)

1.1 Globalisation

Globalisation of business has a number of aspects. It has attracted a great deal of criticism.

Globalisation can mean many things.

(a) Relaxation of trade barriers for goods and services
(b) Free flow of investment capital
(c) International co-operation and standardisation
(d) Growth of international business organisations

For companies and marketers, globalisation offers the opportunity to enter new markets. Sound marketing principles still apply but there is no doubt that global marketing is more complex (and risky) than marketing at home.

Conversely, globalisation offers increased competitors to domestic producers.

Key issues for marketers

(a) Characteristics of overseas markets
(b) Can the same segmentation and positioning strategies be adopted?
(c) Is there a global market, or equivalent segments within each country market?
(d) Impact of culture and regulation on resourcing, distribution, advertising and promotion
(e) Management and structure of overseas operations

MARKETING AT WORK

Global finance

Traders cannot resist a bet, even on their own fate. Amid a bidding war over Chicago's derivatives exchanges, the US Futures Exchange, also based in the Windy City, has launched a "binary" contract which allows speculators to take a punt on whether the Intercontinental Exchange (ICE) can snatch the Chicago Board of Trade, America's oldest derivatives exchange, from the grasp of the biggest, the Chicago Mercantile Exchange (CME). Until recently ICE, a fast-growing electronic upstart from Atlanta, had the edge. Then the CME upped its offer to $9.8 billion and its chances of success – as measured by the binary contracts – leapt to over 70%.

The shoot-out in Chicago is part of a pattern of bold deals that are reshaping financial exchanges. In April the New York Stock Exchange (NYSE) completed its merger with Euronext, itself formed from the union of the Paris, Amsterdam, Brussels and Lisbon bourses. Germany's Deutsche Börse, which had wanted Euronext, has consoled itself by agreeing to buy ISE, an American options market, for $2.8 billion. And having failed to conquer the London Stock Exchange (LSE), NASDAQ is now eyeing up other exchanges on both sides of the Atlantic.

Financial exchanges are a booming business. This reflects the growth of capital markets, which expanded at twice the rate of global GDP from 1993 to 2004, according to McKinsey, a firm of consultants.

The Economist, 24 May 2007

1.2 Should the strategy be global?

KEY CONCEPT

A **global strategy** is representative of *"a worldwide perspective in which the interrelationship between country markets are drawn on to create synergies, economies of scale, strategic flexibility and opportunities to leverage insights, programmes, and production economies".* (Aaker & McLoughlin)

In contrast, a **multinational strategy** is one in which separate strategies are developed for a series of country markets, and implemented autonomously.

Motivations for a global strategy

Obtain scale economies	Product, marketing, operations
Create global associations	A global presence symbolises strength
Access low cost labour and materials	Such access can be a source of competitive advantage, but flexibility is needed. See also the 'Marketing at Work' example below, on the dangers
Access to investment incentives	Countries use these to attract investment in targeted/depressed areas
Cross subsidisation	A global strategy allows resources generated in one area to back up efforts in another
Dodge trade barriers	Strategic location of assembly plant can help gain access to markets and foster goodwill
Access to strategically important markets	Important because of size of market resources, trends and developments, and technology

Aaker & McLoughlin (2007, p.209) give the following indicators that a company strategy needs to be a global one.

- Its major competitors have a presence in several countries
- Standardisation provides opportunities for scale economies
- Costs can be reduced, and effectiveness increased, by locating value-adding activities in different countries
- The company can use sales volumes and profits from one market to help invest and gain position in another
- A global name is available
- The brand's positioning and advertising will work across countries
- Local markets do not necessarily require a local operation

The following issues need to be addressed:

- Should the firm become global by entering new countries?
- What countries, and in what sequence?
- Should the product/service be standardised?
- Should the brand/marketing activities be standardised?
- How do you manage a global brand?
- Should strategic alliances be used to enter new countries?

 ACTIVITY 1   application

Give reasons why a company might want to implement its global strategy on a gradual, country-by-country basis.

Why might a 'full frontal' assault on several countries at once have its advantages?

1.3 Hostility to globalisation

A number of pressure groups have emerged, linked in their hostility to global capitalism. Thanks, possibly, to better communications and the Internet, they are able to co-ordinate their activities on a worldwide scale. Indeed, the anti-globalisation brigade has spawned its own anti-marketing literature. Naomi Klein's book, No Logo (2001), is a key text on the anti-capitalist reading list. In particular she attacks **brands**. Perhaps marketers need to go back to fundamentals as to what brands actually promise.

Globalisation is blamed for environmental degradation and global inequality, standardisation and the destruction of local cultures – all under the control of multinational firms which, it is said, are greedy, exploitative and are not democratically accountable.

Successful global brands such as McDonald's or Starbucks are subjects of particular hostility.

 MARKETING AT WORK   application

A Bangladeshi teenager who died in a factory that supplies cheap jeans for the European market was "overworked to death", a rights group said. Fatema Akter, 18, died during her shift in December last year, the US-based National Labor Committee said.

"Forced to work 13 to 15 hours a day, seven days a week, Fatema was sick and exhausted, with pains in her chest and arms", the report said. Her job was to clean 90 to 100 pairs of finished jeans an hour.

The committee said an investigation showed that 14-hour shifts with few breaks were common at the factory, overtime was compulsory and workers were regularly beaten by their superiors. The report, released this week, said 80 per cent of garments produced at the factory were supplied to German-based retail giant Metro Group.

A statement issued by Metro Group said the company was "deeply saddened" by the death and had immediately terminated its contract with the Bangladeshi supplier that used the factory.

Rights groups have long questioned the working conditions in Bangladesh's thousands of garment "sweatshops", which provide some of the cheapest labour in the world.

Last year Spanish fashion firm Zara forced the closure of a supplier's factory in the capital Dhaka after workers said they were being abused.

www.smh.com.au

2 Understanding international markets

2.1 PEST factors

PEST factors are all key issues in a firm's **domestic** environment. The same factors apply when we are discussing a firm's international exposure – they just become more complex.

An organisation is subject to the following international influences.

(a) In times of increasing free trade, firms can expect **incoming competition**. That said, the possibility of competing abroad is also available.

(b) A firm can **attract investment** from overseas institutions. Competing firms from overseas can receive investments from domestic institutions. For example, non-UK banks paid large sums to acquire UK stock brokers and investment firms.

(c) The **barrier** between the domestic and international environment is relatively **permeable**.

(d) **Political factors** and **legal factors** include the following.

   (i)   **Political conditions** in individual foreign markets (eg package tour firms and Egypt after terrorist shootings of tourists) or sources of supply (eg risk of nationalisation)

   (ii) **Relationships between governments** (eg UK exporters and investors were worried that Anglo-Chinese disputes over Hong Kong would damage their trade with China)

   (iii) Activities of **supranational** institutions (eg EU regulations on packaging / recycling)

   (iv) **Laws and regulations** (eg California's new tough emission standards for cars)

(e) **Economic factors**

   (i)   The overall level of **economic activity**
   (ii) The relative levels of **inflation** in the domestic and overseas market
   (iii) The **exchange rate**
   (iv) The **relative prosperity** of individual overseas markets
   (v)   **Economic growth** in newly industrialised countries
   (vi) A shift towards **market economies**

The environment of international trade may be analysed in the same way as the domestic environment, though it has its own special features, including international political relationships, supranational institutions, a variety of currencies and a wider range of social and economic influences.

(f) **Social and cultural factors**

   (i)   The **cultures and practices** of customers and consumers in individual markets
   (ii) The **media and distribution** systems in overseas markets
   (iii) The differences of **ways of doing business**
   (iv) The degree to which **national** cultural differences matter
   (v)   The degree to which a firm can use its own **national culture as a selling point**

(g) **Technological factors**

   (i)   The degree to which a firm can **imitate** the technology of its competitors
   (ii) A firm's access to domestic and overseas **patents**
   (iii) **Intellectual property** protection
   (iv) **Technology transfer** requirements
   (v)   The relative **cost** of technology compared to labour
   (vi) The **competence of potential service contractors** in the target country

In almost any question in this syllabus, SLEPT (PEST or PESTLE) factors can be brought in, but be very careful to make them relevant to the context of the question.

When deciding which country to enter, there are several initial questions to be asked:

- Is the market attractive in terms of size and growth?
- How intense is the competition?
- Can the firm add value?
- Do operational or cultural barriers exist?
- Can a critical mass be achieved?

Aaker & McLoughlin (2007) describe four kinds of 'distance' between countries.

- **Geographic** (affecting distance, access, borders, climate)
- **Administrative** (government policies, taxes, politics, exchange rates, trade barriers)
- **Cultural** (language, religions, social norms)
- **Economic** (income levels, infrastructure, costs)

2.2 The political and legal framework

At some time, most companies engaged in international marketing suffer because of the political or legal structure of a country.

2.2.1 Political risk

Political factors offer extra risks to the exporter, in terms of the stability of the country, the attitude of the government to trade generally and to the company in particular.

 KEY CONCEPT

concept

Political risk is the possibility of turbulence (eg civil war, revolution, changes in government policy) in the political environment.

The **level of risk** involved will depend on several factors.

- The attitudes of the country's **government**
- The **product** being traded
- The **company** wishing to trade

2.2.2 Government

The development of plans for international marketing will depend on the following factors.

(a) **The stability of the government**. Rapid changes or political unrest make it difficult to estimate reactions to an importer or a foreign business.

(b) **International relations**. The government's attitude to the firm's home government or country may affect trading relations.

(c) The **ideology** of the government and its **role in the economy** will affect the way in which the company may be allowed to trade, and this might be embodied in legislation.

(d) **Informal relations** between government officials and businesses are important in some countries. Cultivation of the right political contacts may be essential for decisions to be made in your favour.

In early 2005 American politicians objected to IBM's plan to sell its PC business to Lenovo, China's biggest maker of PCs. The proposed deal was said to be a threat to the security of the USA.

However, by the time of the 2008 banking crisis, sovereign wealth funds such as the Abu Dhabi Investment Authority and the Government of Singapore Investment Corporation had bought major shareholdings in banks such as UBS, Citigroup, Barclays and Standard Chartered.

2.2.3 The product

The nature of the goods or services being offered may affect the **degree of interest which a government takes** in a particular trading deal. Generally the more important the goods to the economy or the government, the more interest will be taken.

2.2.4 The company wishing to trade

The previous relations of the company (and its home country) with the host country can affect the risk to the company. **Factors influencing the company's acceptability** include the following.

- Relations between the company's home government and the overseas government
- Size of company
- The past relations and reputation of the company in dealing with foreign governments
- The degree of local employment and autonomy of operations generated by the activity

2.2.5 Expropriation and other dangers

Political risk is still relevant with regard to overseas investment, especially in large infrastructure projects overseas. History contains dismal tales of investment projects that went wrong, and were **expropriated** (nationalised) by the local government.

(a)   **Suspicion** of foreign ownership is still rife, especially when prices are raised.

(b)   Opposition politicians can appeal to **nationalism** by claiming the government sold out to foreigners.

(c)   Governments might want to **renegotiate** a deal to get a better bargain, at a later date, thereby affecting return on investment.

In addition to expropriation, there are other dangers.

- Restrictions on **profit repatriation** (eg for currency reasons)
- **Cronyism** and **corruption** leading to unfair favouring of some companies over others
- Arbitrary changes in **taxation**
- **Pressure group** activity

There are many sources of data. The Economist Intelligence Unit offers assessment of risk. Management consultants can also be contacted. Companies should ask the following six questions (according to Hennessey, 2004).

1	How stable is the host country's political system?
2	How strong is the host government's commitment to specific rules of the game, such as ownership or contractual rights, given its ideology and power position?
3	How long is the government likely to remain in power?
4	If the present government is succeeded, how would the specific rules of the game change?
5	What would be the effects of any expected changes in the specific rules of the game?
6	In light of those effects, what decisions and actions should be taken now?

2.2.6 Coping with political risk

The approach taken depends on the **degree of risk** and the **level of involvement**.

Level of involvement

	Low	High
High	• Keep low profile • Communicate via third parties • High level contacts • Short-term deals • Export credit insurance	• Contingency plans • Disinvest? • Act for stability?
Low	No need to worry	No need to worry – but monitor for increasing riskiness

Level of risk

Measures to **reduce political risk** are as follows.

- Use **local partners** with good contacts
- **Vertical integration** of activities over a number of different countries
- **Local borrowing** (although not a good idea in high inflation countries)
- **Leasing** rather than outright purchase of facilities in overseas markets
- Take out **insurance**

2.3 Legal factors

Legal factors in individual markets include product regulations and control over the marketing mix generally. Human resource usage is also determined by legal factors.

In international markets we are interested in legislation which may affect a firm's trade with a particular country.

- Domestic legal system
- Structure of company law
- Local laws

Legal implications extend far beyond the marketing mix. Each country may legislate on issue, and these may affect the marketer to a greater or lesser degree. Here are some examples.

(a) **Export and import controls** for political, environmental, or health and safety reasons. Such controls may not be overt but instead take the form of bureaucratic procedures designed to discourage international trade or protect home producers.

(b) **Law of ownership**. Especially in developing countries, there may be legislation requiring local majority ownership of a firm or its subsidiary in that country.

(c) **Acceptance of international trademark, copyright and patent conventions**. Not all countries recognise such international conventions.

2.4 Protectionism in international trade

Although trade has benefits, many countries have sought to limit its effects in order to **protect** local producers. In the long-term this serves to harm economic welfare as resources are not allocated where they are most productive.

KEY CONCEPT

concept

Protectionism is the discouraging of imports by raising tariff barriers, imposing quotas etc in order to favour local producers.

Some governments seek to prevent the influence of international trade by making it harder to import from overseas.

- **Tariffs**
- Import **quotas and embargoes**
- **Subsidies** for domestic producers
- Exchange **controls**
- Exchange rate policy
- Non-tariff **barriers**

2.4.1 Tariffs

A **tariff** is a **tax on imports**. The government **raises revenue** and domestic producers may expand sales, but **consumers** pay higher prices if they buy imported goods. They may have to buy domestic goods of a lesser quality.

2.4.2 Import quotas

Import quotas are **restrictions** on the quantity of product allowed to be imported into a country. The restrictions can be imposed by **import licences** (in which case the government gets additional revenue) or simply by granting the right to import only to certain producers.

2.4.3 Minimum local content rules

Related to quotas is a requirement that, to avoid tariffs or other restrictions, products should be made **in** the country or region in which they are sold. In the EU the product must be of a specified **minimum local content** (80% in the EU) to qualify as being 'home' or 'EU-made'. This is one of the reasons Japanese and Korean manufacturers have set up factories in Europe.

2.4.4 Minimum prices and anti-dumping action

Dumping is the sale of a product in an overseas market at a price lower than charged in the domestic market. **Anti-dumping measures** include establishing quotas, minimum prices or extra excise duties.

2.4.5 Embargoes

An embargo on imports from one particular country is a **total ban**, a zero quota. An embargo may have a political motive, and may deprive consumers at home of the supply of an important product.

2.4.6 Subsidies for domestic producers

An enormous range of government **subsidies** and assistance for exporters is offered, such as **export credit guarantees** (insurance against bad debts for overseas sales), financial help and assistance from government departments in promoting and selling products. The effect of these grants is to make unit production costs lower. These may give the domestic producer a **cost advantage** over foreign producers in export as well as domestic markets.

2.4.7 Exchange controls and exchange rate policy

Many countries have **exchange control regulations** designed to make it difficult for importers to obtain the currency they need to buy foreign goods.

If a government allows its currency to depreciate, imports will become more expensive. Importers may cut their profit margins and keep prices at their original levels for a while, but sooner or later prices of imports will rise. A policy of exchange rate depreciation in this context is referred to as a **competitive devaluation**.

2.4.8 Unofficial non-tariff barriers

Some countries are accused of having **unofficial barriers to trade**, perpetrated by government. Here are some examples.

(a) **Quality and inspection procedures** for imported products, adding to time and cost for the companies selling them.

(b) **Packaging and labelling** requirements may be rigorous, **safety and performance** standards difficult to satisfy and **documentation procedures** very laborious.

(c) Standards which are much easier for domestic manufacturers to adhere to.

(d) Restrictions over **physical distribution**.

(e) Toleration of **anti-competitive practices** at home.

 MARKETING AT WORK

 application

In 2003 the EU was the world's leading exporter of textiles and the second largest exporter of clothing, employing 2.7 million people in the textile industry. However, EU imports of Chinese textiles increased by almost 100% between 2001 and 2003. From 1 January 2005 all restrictions had been lifted from the world textiles trade and by February 2008, China was the world's largest clothing exporter, though the expanded EU remained the largest exporter of textiles.

The run up to deregulation destroyed one-third of the jobs in the French textile industry between 1993 and 2003.

 ACTIVITY 2

 application

Why might a US car manufacturer support protectionist policies, despite the effects of restraining trade, and a Swedish manufacturer choose to oppose protectionist measures?

2.5 Economic structure and development

Economic factors include the overall level of growth and stage of development, frequently measured by GDP. The balance of payments is an influence on government policy.

Economic factors affect the demand for, and the ability to acquire, goods and services. Even in **lesser developed countries** (see below) there often exists a wealthy elite who provide a significant demand for sophisticated consumer goods.

Countries generally have larger agricultural sectors in the early stages of economic development (for example India and Africa). As the economy develops, the manufacturing sector increases.

2.5.1 Level of economic development

GDP on a **per capita** basis, suitably adjusted for purchasing power, is probably the **best single indicator of economic development**.

A danger in using GDP is that it considers only the **average**. The **distribution of wealth** is critical in poor countries, where a market may exist amongst above average sections of the population.

2.5.2 Classification of economic development

Generally each country can be classified under one of five headings.

KEY CONCEPTS

concept

Lesser developed country (LDC). Relies heavily on primary industries (mining, agriculture, forestry, fishing) with low GDP per capita, and poorly developed infrastructure.

Early developed country (EDC). Largely primary industry based, but with developing secondary (manufacturing) industrial sector. Low but growing GDP, developing infrastructure.

Semi-developed country (SDC). Significant secondary sector still growing. Rising affluence and education with the emergence of a 'middle class'. Developed infrastructure.

Fully developed country (FDC). Primary sector accounts for little of the economy. Secondary sector still dominates, but major growth in tertiary (service) sector. Sophisticated infrastructure.

Former Eastern Bloc country (EBC). May be any of the above, but the 'command economy' under communism has left a legacy that defies straightforward classification. For example, Russia, has most of the features of an SDC but lacks a developed infrastructure though it has a well educated middle class.

2.5.3 Measuring levels of economic development

Measures that may be used by the international marketer include the following.

- **GDP** per head
- **Source of GDP** (primary, secondary or tertiary sector based economy)
- **Living standards** (ownership of key durables may be used as a surrogate measure)
- **Energy** availability and usage
- **Education** levels

MARKETING AT WORK

application

The Department for International Development (DFID) was created by the UK Government in 1997. Its job is *"to make sure every pound of British aid works its hardest to help the world's poor"*, through working with overseas governments, charities, businesses and international bodies including the World Bank and the United Nations. Working in 150 countries with 2,600 staff, the department spent £5.3bn on aid to poorer countries in 2007/08.

Under the International Development Act of 2002, British aid cannot be tied to British goods and services: governments receiving UK aid are free to use suppliers who compete on price, quality and service.

Areas of activity for DFID:

- Fighting AIDS, tuberculosis and malaria
- Aid to Africa
- Funding for children (UNICEF)
- Funding on global health
- Fighting crime (eg corruption and money laundering)
- Reconstruction of Afghanistan
- Peacebuilding and humanitarian efforts

2.5.4 Identifying market size

The economic worth of a consumer market is based on some general factors.

*   The **number of people** in the market
*   Their **desire to own** the goods
*   Their **ability to purchase** the goods

Thus in measuring a market, the marketer will obtain information on the following, although they are often crude measures.

(a)   **Population**. Its size, growth and age structure, household composition, urban v rural distribution. Household size and spatial distribution affect demand for many consumer goods.

(b)   **Income**. GDP per head is a crude measure of wealth and account should also be taken of distribution of GDP among various social groups, and their purchasing power.

(c)   **Consumption patterns**. The ownership of various goods and the consumption of consumables are indicators of potential demand.

(d)   **Debt and inflation**. A high level of debt in a country may indicate import controls (or their possible introduction) or weak currency and currency controls. Inflation may affect purchasing power. In either case ability to pay will be reduced.

(e)   **Physical environment**. Physical distance, climate and topography will affect demand in various ways. The availability of natural resources can directly affect demand for equipment and so on to exploit these resources.

(f)   **Foreign trade**. The trade relations of a country will affect the attitude towards foreign goods. Factors include economic relations (for example, a member of same economic group such as the EU) and balance of trade.

2.6 Regional trading groups

Regional trading blocs promote trade between countries in groups. The environment of world trade is becoming freer, globally, with the influence of the World Trade Organisation.

Currently, a number of **regional trading arrangements** exist, as well as global trading arrangements. These regional trading groups take three forms.

*   Free trade areas
*   Customs unions
*   Common markets

2.6.1 Free trade areas

Members in these arrangements agree to lower barriers to trade amongst themselves. They enable free movement of **goods** and **services**, but not always the factors of production.

 MARKETING AT WORK   application

In the context of the sample case study for this unit, a new 'Open Skies' agreement was signed in March 2008 between the EU and the United States – this agreement allows any European or American airline to fly from anywhere in Europe to anywhere in the US. Following decades of regulation of such flights, it opens up the routes for those airlines that can afford the investment.

2.6.2 Customs unions

Customs unions provide the advantages of free trade areas and agree a common policy on tariff and non-tariff barriers to **external countries**. Internally they attempt to harmonise tariffs, taxes and duties amongst members.

2.6.3 Economic unions/common markets

In effect the members become one for economic purposes. There is free movement of the factors of production. The EU has economic union as an aim, although not all members, including the UK, necessarily see this goal as desirable. The EU has a 'rich' market of over 300 million people and could provide a counterweight to countries such as the USA and Japan.

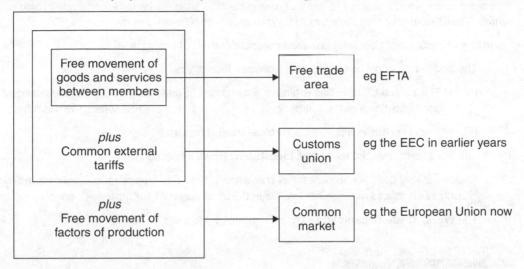

The major regional trade organisations are as follows.

(a)   North American Free Trade Agreement (**NAFTA**) – US, Canada and Mexico.

(b)   European Free Trade Association (**EFTA**) – Norway, Switzerland, Iceland, Liechtenstein.

(c)   European Union (**EU**) – Ireland, United Kingdom, France, Germany, Italy, Spain, Portugal, Finland, Sweden, Denmark, Luxembourg, Belgium, the Netherlands, Austria, Greece, Bulgaria, Cyprus, Czech Republic, Estonia, Hungary, Latvia, Lithuania, Malta, Poland, Romania, Slovakia, Slovenia.

(d)   Asean Free Trade Area (**AFTA**) – Brunei, Indonesia, Malaysia, the Philippines, Singapore, Thailand.

(e)   Asia-Pacific Economic Co-operation (**APEC**) – Australia, Brunei, Malaysia, Singapore, Thailand, New Zealand, Papua New Guinea, Indonesia, the Philippines, Taiwan, Hong Kong, Japan, South Korea, China, Canada, US, Mexico, Chile.

(f)   **Mercosur** – Brazil, Argentina, Paraguay and Uruguay (Chile is an associate).

(g)   Southern African Development Community (**SADC**); Angola, Botswana, Lesotho, Malawi, Mozambique, Mauritius, Namibia, South Africa, Swaziland, Tanzania, Swaziland, Zimbabwe.

(h)   West African Economic and Monetary Union (**UEMOA**) – Ivory Cost, Burkina Faso, Niger, Togo, Senegal, Benin and Mali.

(i)   South Asian Association for Regional Co-operation (**SAARC**) – India, Pakistan, Sri Lanka, Bangladesh, the Maldives, Bhutan and Nepal.

(j)   **Andean Pact** – Venezuela, Colombia, Ecuador, Peru and Bolivia.

(k)   Association of Southeast Asian Nations (**ASEAN**) – Indonesia, Malaysia, Philippines, Singapore and Thailand.

2.6.4 Regional trading agreements and the global market

Regional trading blocs only extend the benefits of free trade to their members. They may distort **global** trading patterns.

There is a widely held idea that the industrial world is falling into **three trading blocs**, each led by a lead country. (This is called the 'Triad' theory.)

• The EU (led by Germany)
• The Americas (led by the USA) and particularly NAFTA
• The Far East and Pacific Rim (led by Japan)

Trading within the blocs would be relatively **liberalised** but there would be **barriers to competition** from outside. The blocs would trade with each other, but this would be more restricted. Countries would have to try to attach themselves to one of the blocs.

Non-bloc countries were not seen as terribly important. Given that some non-bloc countries (eg India and China) are likely to be some of the world's largest and fastest growing markets, suggestions to restrict trade to bloc countries are short-sighted. The Chinese economy, for example is growing at over 10% per annum.

The theory of trading blocs does not provide a complete analysis of world trade.

(a) The bloc theory works better for some industries than others.

   (i) The EU and US have had extensive programmes to protect agriculture, to the outrage of more efficient producers (such as the Cairns Group representing Australia and some other countries).

   (ii) Even in sensitive industries aerospace, there is free trade.

(b) The bloc theory does not really take **investment flows** into account.

(c) The bloc theory does not account for all **trade** flows. The US is Japan's most significant **individual** export market, although East Asia as a region has overtaken the US as a market for Japanese's goods.

(d) The **World Trade Organisation** (WTO) regulates world trade.

 MARKETING AT WORK

application

Opposing free trade

When it comes to the US economy, trade has replaced the devil as the reason things go bad. A Fortune magazine poll conducted this January asked Americans what was the most important reason for the recent economic slowdown. The largest number – 28% – answered "losing jobs to economies where labour is cheaper" and an additional 7% mentioned "foreign competition". Fully 78% of the respondents said that trade has made things worse for American workers.

Given these perceptions, the Democratic candidates seeking votes in Ohio found it impossible to resist joining those who blame trade agreements such as the North America Free Trade Agreement (NAFTA) for the traumatic loss of manufacturing jobs in the US over the past six years. In the primary campaign, Hillary Clinton and Barack Obama competed vociferously for the title of champion NAFTA-hater. Both said they would withdraw from NAFTA unless Canada and Mexico came back to the negotiating table.

Both insisted that the labour and environmental provisions, currently in side agreements, should be strengthened, included in the agreement itself and enforced in the same way as the agreement's other provisions. Clinton went even further in expressing her scepticism about US trade agreements generally and called for a time-out so they can all be reviewed.

Robert Lawrence, Guardian Unlimited, 6 March 2008

(e) **Knowledge-based industries** (which many writers believe are the motors of future economic growth) are hard to evaluate and control. **Technology** might make ideas as to trading blocs obsolete.

(f) All trading blocs have extensive economic interactions with **third world countries**. They will have a growing relationship with countries in the former Soviet Union which have recently entered the global market.

A significant effect of regional trade blocs has been the rush to qualify for **local status** by multinational firms. This has been achieved by the multinationals setting up within one or more member states. Thus France, Germany and the UK have seen considerable inward investment from US and Japanese firms.

2.7 Social issues

Social factors include overall global population growth, and the disparity between the ageing and stable (in numbers) populations of the developed world, with the young and growing populations of lesser developed countries. In individual markets, **culture** can be a determining factor of marketing success.

The higher rate of population growth in **less-developed countries** compared with developed countries has arisen due to a continuing high birth rate and a declining death rate although some populations are being threatened by the HIV virus (for example, in South Africa). Social changes (eg attitudes to large families) have not accompanied medical advances imported from developed societies. People are living longer.

(a)   **Growing populations**

    (i)   Require fast economic growth just to maintain living standards

    (ii)   Result in overcrowding on land and/or cities and a decline in the quality of life

    (iii)   Require more resources for capital investment

    (iv)   Stimulate investment (as the market size is increasing)

    (v)   Lead to enhanced labour mobility

(b)   **Falling populations**

    (i)   Require more productive techniques to maintain output

    (ii)   Make some scale economies harder to achieve

    (iii)   Put a greater burden on a decreasing number of young people

    (iv)   Exhibit changing consumption patterns

2.7.1 Buying patterns

Buying behaviour is an important aspect of marketing. Many factors influence the buying decisions of individuals and households. Demography and the **class structure** (the distribution of wealth and power in a society) are relevant in that they can be both **behavioural determinants** and **inhibitors**.

(a)   **Behavioural determinants** encourage people to buy a product or service. The individual's personality, culture, social class, and the importance of the purchase decision (eg a necessity such as food or water, or a luxury) can predispose a person to purchase something.

(b)   **Inhibitors** are factors, such as the individual's income, which will make the person less likely to purchase something.

Socio-economic status can be related to buying patterns in a number of ways, both in the amount people have to spend and what they spend it on. It affects both the quantity of goods and services supplied, and the proportion of their income that households spend on goods and services.

 MARKETING AT WORK   application

Retailing in India

India tops the AT Kearney's annual Global Retail Development Index (GRDI) for the third consecutive year, maintaining its position as the most attractive market for retail investment.

The Indian retail market, which is the fifth largest retail destination globally, according to industry estimates, is estimated to grow from the US$ 330 billion in 2007 to US$ 427 billion by 2010 and $637 billion by 2015. Simultaneously, modern retail which presently accounts for 4% of the total market is likely to increase its share to 22% by 2010.

India has one of the largest number of retail outlets in the world. Of the 12 million retail outlets present in the country, nearly 5 million sell food and related products. Even with this large number of outlets, organised retail accounts for only 4% of the total market, opening huge growth potential in this segment.

Driven by changing lifestyles, strong income growth and favourable demographic patterns, Indian retail is expanding at a rapid pace. Mall space, from a meagre one million square feet in 2002, is expected to touch 40 million square feet by end-2007 and an estimated 60 million square feet by end-2008, says Jones Lang LaSalle's third annual Retailer Sentiment Survey-Asia.

India Brand Equity Foundation, 7 March 2008

2.8 Technology

Technology creates new products and industries, and enhances productivity and growth. It also influences the marketing mix.

The history of the past 200 years has been one of enormous economic growth. Many countries are able to support populations which in the early 19th century would have been inconceivable.

Material advances have promoted a large complex of economic, social, political and cultural changes. These changes have included the following.

(a)   **Industrialisation** (eg movement of labour and resources from agriculture to industry) which has been a feature of many overseas markets.

(b)   **Modernisation** (urbanisation, reduction in death rates, centralising government and so forth).

2.8.1 Technological development and the marketing mix: a cautionary perspective

Technology, or investment in it, in the narrow sense, cannot on its own promote economic growth. The first use of **steam** power was discovered, not in 18th century England, but almost 2,000 years before: there was, however, no 'use' for it. Societies with large pools of slave labour had little need for 'labour-saving' inventions.

Modern apparatus and techniques have had very uneven success in 'modernising' underdeveloped countries.

(a)   The **environmental consequences** of introducing western technology to underdeveloped countries have been ill thought out.

(b)   The **economic consequences** have not been as beneficial as might at first be supposed. 'The prestigious new production technologies have not worked optimally or even satisfactorily.' The problems are two-fold.

   (i)   **Technological dependency** leading to a heavy foreign currency payments burden. The country has to import **spare parts**, and even raw materials, to run machinery. It might have to pay for **expatriate technicians**. This is expensive, and so the costs of the technology might be greater than anticipated, thus reducing any economic benefit.

   (ii)   The inappropriateness of Western technology. **Climatic** conditions can affect performance. **Infrastructural** deficiencies such as naturally poor roads affect, for example, the 'good design' of a car. The **labour/capital** mix means that in poor countries, with surplus labour, labour intensive industries rather than labour saving capital equipment might be a better use of resources.

 ACTIVITY 3

application

The Republic of Rukwa is a largely agricultural society. For foreign exchange, it is dependent on the exports of kwat. Kwat is a grain which can only be grown in Rukwa's climate. It is, however, widely in demand in Western markets as a 'health' food. Kwat is grown by peasant farmers on small plots of land on banks of the River Ru. At present, the harvested Kwat is transported by ox-drawn barges down the River Ru to Port Ruk for export. The process is slow, owing to bottlenecks on the river. The government is thinking of several alternatives to ease this situation. Rukwa has no other natural resources.

1   Build a high speed road, and use foreign loans to buy lorries and four-wheel drive vehicles for farmers.
2   Build a railway, with imported steel and engines.
3   Widen the River Ru at key points, and purchase outboard motors for the barges.

What do you think is right or wrong with all these alternatives?

The relevance of this to international marketers is as follows.

(a)   **How do you define customer needs?** Elite groups sometimes 'need' products which are not economically beneficial for society.

(b)   To what extent do you apply the societal marketing concept to overseas markets?

(c)   The marketing mix may presuppose a level of **technological development** which is in fact non-existent for large parts of the population.

2.8.2 Level of technological development

The level of technological development in a country is important in the marketing of many products.

* **Understanding how the product is used**: Many products are technically sophisticated and require a level of **technological awareness** that may not be widely available. Technologically aware cultures recognise switches and buttons and instructions almost instinctively.

* **The provision of support services for the product**: Many products require maintenance and spare parts which may be unavailable outside the most technologically advanced economies. The classic solution is known as the **'backward invention'** in which the product is simplified to either the level of support available or, ultimately, the point at which the owner can support the product himself.

* **The existence of an appropriate distribution network**: Certain products require an **infrastructure for their distribution** and use. Thus a TV requires both electricity and a TV transmission service. Telephones require a carrier network. Distribution of medicines and foodstuffs require careful handling and temperature conditions in transit, necessitating specialised and sophisticated transport.

* **Communication with the customer**

 ACTIVITY 4

application

A firm has developed a drug which can cure Alzheimer's disease. What factors do you think would distinguish its export marketing efforts to a country in the EU from its export marketing efforts to a country in the Third World?

3 Standardisation versus customisation

Entry into foreign markets mandates decisions about whether or not to adopt the marketing mix to local conditions. The choice is between standardising the product in all markets to reap the advantages of scale economies in manufacture and, on the other hand, adaptation which gives the advantages of flexible response to local market conditions.

 MARKETING AT WORK

application

The Rolex watch is the same all over the world. Its positioning as the watch for the high achiever is the same across the globe. It is an upmarket product and will be found in upmarket outlets.

Unilever's Lifebuoy soap is positioned identically in India and East Africa, despite having different ingredients. It is promoted as an inexpensive soap that protects health.

Complete global standardisation would greatly increase the profitability of a company's products and simplify the task of the international marketing manager. The extent to which standardisation is possible is controversial in marketing. Much of the decision-making in an international marketing manager's role is concerned with taking a view on the necessity, or lack of it, of adapting the product, price and communications to individual markets.

3.1 Factors encouraging standardisation

(a) Economies of scale

    (i) Production
    (ii) Marketing/communications
    (iii) Research and development
    (iv) Stock holding

(b) Easier management and control.

(c) Homogeneity of markets, in other words world markets available without adaptation (eg denim jeans).

(d) Cultural insensitivity, eg industrial components and agricultural products.

(e) Consumer mobility means that standardisation is expected in certain products.

    (i) Camera film
    (ii) Hotel chains

(f) Where 'made in' image is important to a product's perceived value (eg France for perfume, Sheffield for stainless steel).

(g) For a firm selling a small proportion of its output overseas, the incremental adaptation costs may exceed the incremental sales value.

(h) Products that are positioned at the high end of the spectrum in terms of price, prestige and scarcity are more likely to have a standardised mix.

Adaptation may be mandatory or discretionary.

Mandatory product modification normally involves either adaptation to comply with government requirements or unavoidable technical changes. An example of the former would be enhanced safety requirements, while the requirements imposed by different climatic conditions would be an example of the latter.

Discretionary modification is called for only to make the product more appealing in different markets. It results from differing customer needs, preferences and tastes. These differences become apparent from market research and analysis; and intermediary and customer feedback.

(a) Levels of customer purchasing power. Low incomes may make a cheap version of the product more attractive in some less developed economies.

(b) Levels of education and technical sophistication. Ease of use may be a crucial factor in decision-making.

(c) Standards of maintenance and repair facilities. Simpler, more robust versions may be needed.

(d) 'Culture-bound' products such as clothing, food and home decoration are more likely to have an adapted marketing mix.

These strategies can be exercised at global and national level, depending on the type of product. Not all products are suitable for standardisation.

 MARKETING AT WORK   application

Take the example of Cadbury-Schweppes which deals with chocolate and soft drinks.

(a) The UK consumer's taste in chocolate is not shared by most European consumers, who prefer a higher proportion of cocoa-butter in the final product. Marketing Cadbury's UK brands of chocolate on a Europe-wide basis would not seem to be appropriate: instead the acquisition of a European company would be the best way to expand into this market. The UK is thus a segment of a global market with its unique needs.

(b) The market for soft drinks on the other hand is different, with Schweppes tonic water well established as a brand across Europe.

3.2 Global brand management

Global brands were first discussed in the previous chapter in the context of branding and growth strategies. A global, standardised brand may be sought after by many companies, but it is unlikely to work in the following circumstances:

- Different market share positions in different countries will necessitate different positioning
- Different brand images in different countries will mitigate against a standardised strategy
- Names and symbols may not be appropriate everywhere
- Customers will have different motivations in different cultures
- A competitor may have already occupied the chosen position with their own product

Successful global brand management depends upon excellent cross-country communications, common planning systems across the various business branches and an organisation structure that supports the operation of a "global brand team" with the necessary authority to manage the brand fully.

ACTIVITY 5

application

"The key to a standardised brand is to find a position that will work in all markets."

Give three examples of true worldwide brands, and note their positions.

3.3 International competitive strategy

Standard strategic models may be applied to international business, but must be applied in a suitable way.

As we have already established, competitive strategies are the strategies an organisation will pursue for competitive advantage. They determine how you compete. Competitive advantage is anything which gives one organisation an edge over its rivals in the products it sells or the services it offers. This is equally applicable to global strategic decisions.

Porter's generic strategies may be applied in global operations, but they must be managed in a way that takes account of the international business environment.

(a) **Cost leadership** means being the lowest cost producer in the industry as a whole.

(b) **Differentiation** is the offer of a product or service which is unique or in some way different from other products.

(c) **Focus** involves a restriction of activities to a segment through:

   (i) Providing goods and or services at lower cost to that segment (a cost-focus)
   (ii) Providing a differentiated product or service for that segment (differentiation-focus)

Cost leadership and differentiation are industry-wide strategies. Focus involves market segmentation, but involves pursuing, within the segment only, a strategy of cost leadership or differentiation.

Although there is a risk with any of the generic strategies, *Porter* argues that a firm must pursue one of them. A stuck-in-the-middle strategy is almost certain to make only low profits, he says. Recent research has indicated that this is too simplistic. Being the lowest cost producer does not mean you have to compete on price.

It is, of course, fairly easy to see how such competitive strategy decisions can be taken in a large domestic market, such as the US, where many economies of scale are readily available. But international marketing involves recognising differences between country markets, the barriers to entry caused by national and cultural borders, and the global market.

It is hard to achieve overall **cost leadership**. In terms of international and global marketing it perhaps only applies to a few companies, and even they might face restrictions on market entry.

(a) Only a few companies are available to take advantage of global sourcing and the economies this offers.

(b) Cost leadership is a dangerous strategy, as companies from developing countries might, for a short time, benefit from those countries' comparative advantages in lower labour costs. (Generally speaking higher productivity in advanced economies neutralises many of the gains from cheap labour. Thus, the NAFTA agreement has not led to a collapse in US employment. US workers are far more productive than Mexican ones.)

(c)   Domestic producers might have substantial cost advantages owing to their proximity to the local markets.

(d)   A firm's ability to compete as the lowest cost producer in certain markets will be hampered.

    (i)   Tariffs raise the price of your goods in relation to competitors (eg producers of Scotch whisky trying to export to Japan)

    (ii)   Exchange fluctuations can render your efficiently-made products more expensive than a those of local producers

(e)   Many of the costs of goods can be increased by factors outside management control, such as intricacies of the distribution system.

Clearly, then, a strategy of **differentiation** or **focus** can be more realistic.

(a)   Products can be differentiated for the international market, while keeping the same brand name (eg coffee).

(b)   The fact that, despite trade liberalisation, there are real differences between markets might suggest that focus is appropriate. Use national boundaries as a means of segmentation, or, as has been suggested, concentrate on those consumers in the international market who share characteristics across national segments.

 MARKETING AT WORK   application

An example of having the right 'product' for emerging markets is provided by the Bangladeshi firm, Beximco Pharmaceuticals, which pursues a differentiation-focus strategy.

Western firms, such as Glaxo, invest heavily in research and development, producing sophisticated but expensive products. Beximco, which sells to poorer markets, makes simple products cheaply.

In developing countries, such as Vietnam and Iran, and even in Russia, a good supply of basic drugs is what is required. There will be less emphasis on vertical expansion, which involves growing sales of sophisticated products to a small section of the population at ever-increasing prices.

Beximco has low wages and low research. In addition, Western drugs may go out of patent and can then be copied.

Models such as the Ansoff matrix, described in earlier chapters, can also be applied, although its application might be more complex than in the single domestic market.

How can it be applied to international marketing strategy? Unfortunately the categories tend to shift.

(a)   It is easy to suggest what the new market might be: another country.

(b)   What, however, do we mean by 'new product'? Is the product new to the company? Has it only been developed? Is the company still on a learning curve in its domestic market? In this case there might be a choice.

    (i)   Introduce the new product simultaneously in domestic and overseas markets.

    (ii)   Have a continuing rolling programme.

        Year 1: the domestic market is dealt with first
        Year 2: existing overseas markets are serviced
        Year 3: genuinely new overseas markets are addressed

    By year 3, the decision to introduce new products into new markets has effectively become one of market development, on the grounds that product has already been on sale at home and in existing overseas markets.

(c)   It would appear unlikely that a company would set up abroad in a completely unfamiliar market with a completely new product, when there are easy opportunities to minimise the risk.

The Ansoff matrix can be applied equally to a company looking for new international development or to an established global player. Many strategic developments are concerned with building on where the organisation currently sits in the global market, via current products and competences and stretching them to improve competitive position.

Note that other strategic models such as the BCG matrix may also be applied to global operations.

Learning objectives	Covered
1 Critically evaluate the appropriateness of developing an international marketing strategy for an organisation investing in international markets	☑ Globalisation (1.1) ☑ Should the strategy be global? (1.2) ☑ Hostility to globalisation (1.3) ☑ Factors encouraging standardisation (3.1) ☑ Global brand management (3.2) ☑ International competitive strategy (3.3)
2 Critically evaluate a range of issues that impact on an organisation when entering new countries and markets and consider how they may be managed to achieve the organisation's objectives	☑ PEST factors (2.1) ☑ The political and legal framework (2.2) ☑ Legal factors (2.3) ☑ Protectionism in international trade (2.4) ☑ Economic structure and development (2.5) ☑ Regional trading groups (2.6) ☑ Social issues (2.7) ☑ Technology (2.8)
3 Assess an organisation's readiness for developing a global strategy	☑ Should strategy be global? (1.2)

1   On what factors does the level of political risk depend?

2   Draw up a checklist for companies to consider when dealing with the political environment.

3   List some protectionist measures.

4   What is meant by LDC, EDC, SDC?

5   How do you measure economic development?

6   Contrast a global and a multinational strategy.

7   What questions should be asked when deciding upon which country market to enter?

8   What is 'administrative' distance?

9   What is the DFID?

10 What is an 'inhibitor' in the context of buyer behaviour?

11 How might a marketer measure the level of technological development in a target country?

12 What is a 'differentiation' strategy?

1   A 'gradual' strategy has the advantage of reduced initial commitment, which can be tested and improved as a regional presence is built up.

A 'full frontal' strategy can bring economies of scale and 'first mover' advantages

2   Protectionism is about the relative benefits and drawbacks to countries of restraining trade. For commercial organisations, however, protectionism has some short run advantages. The USA is the largest market for automobiles. US car manufacturers produce overseas for foreign markets, generally speaking, as opposed to exporting from the US itself. Free trade in motor vehicles automatically means a great deal of competition at home (particularly from Japan).

A closed market would allow them to raise prices. On the other hand, Swedish car manufacturers, such as Volvo, depend on successful exports since the home market is too small to support them. The benefits of protection would be exceeded by the disadvantages.

3   There is often no right answer, but here are some ideas.

(a) Will the foreign exchange earnings from Kwat justify the infrastructural investment at all? After all, the government will have to use the foreign exchange earnings to pay interest on loans. Option (3) might be the least risky here.

(b) Does the country have an educational and technical infrastructure to support the technology? Road vehicles need spare parts and trained service personnel. Spare parts might be an additional drain on foreign exchange. Again option (3) might be the least risky.

4   You could write reams here, but there are a few preliminary ideas.

Western countries

(a) Attitudes to elderly.

(b) Distribution: over the counter? Prescribed by doctors?

(c) Current health care of elderly.

(d) Demographic trends: is the age structure of the country becoming more heavily weighted towards older people?

(e) Drug testing and certification regime.

Third World country

(a) Is Alzheimer's seen as a major problem, compared to other medical conditions (eg diseases from poor sanitation)?

(b) Would the drug be affordable?

(c) Attitudes to elderly.

(d) Age structure of the country (fewer old people than in the West).

You will doubtless think of more.

5 Aaker & McLoughlin (2007) pp. 212-213 give several examples.

You may have thought of examples such as Disney (family entertainment); Mercedes (high-end); Levi's (American classic).

---

1   Government attitudes; the nature of the product; the company involved.

2   • How stable is the country politically?
     • Are the local rules of the game known and enforced?
     • How long is the government likely to be in power?
     • How would a new government change the rules?
     • What would be the effects of expected changes to the rules?
     • What decisions and actions should be taken now?

3   Tariffs; barriers; import quotas and embargoes; domestic subsidies; exchange controls; exchange rate policy.

4   Lesser developed country; early developed country; semi-developed country.

5   Several measures are used including: GDP/head; sector source of GDP; living standards; energy usage; education level.

6   A global strategy is representative of a worldwide perspective which is used to create economies of scale and other advantages through an integrated global approach.

     In contrast, a multinational strategy is one in which separate strategies are developed for a series of country markets, and implemented autonomously.

7   Is the market attractive in terms of size and growth?

     • How intense is the competition?
     • Can the firm add value?
     • Do operational or cultural barriers exist?
     • Can a critical mass be achieved?

8   Differences between countries created by factors such as government policies, taxes, politics, exchange rates and trade barriers

9   The Department for International Development (DFID), which oversees the application of British aid in needy areas throughout the world.

10   Inhibitors are factors (such as the individual's income) which will make the person less likely to purchase

11   Level of understanding of how the product is used

     • The provision of support services for the product
     • The existence of an appropriate distribution network
     • Level of communication with the customer

12   **Differentiation** is the offer of a product or service which is unique or in some way different from other products.

References

Aaker, D. & McLoughlin, D. (2007) <u>Strategic Market Management</u>, John Wiley, Chichester.

Anon (2009) *'Teen 'overworked to death' in jeans factory'* http://www.smh.com.au/action/printArticle?id=517789, May 14 2009.

Ansoff, H.I. (1988) <u>Corporate Strategy</u>, (2nd revised edition), Penguin Books, NY.

Drummond, G. Ensor, J. & Ashford, R. (2008) <u>Strategic Marketing Planning and Control</u>, (3rd edition), Elsevier, Oxford.

Jeannet, J-P. & Hennessey, H. (2004) <u>Global Marketing Strategy</u>, (6th edition), Houghton Mifflin (Academic), London.

Klein, N. (2001) <u>No Logo</u>, New edition, Flamingo, London.

Porter, M.E (2004) <u>Competitive Strategy: Techniques for Analyzing Industries and Competitors</u>, (New edition), Free Press, NY.

Chapter 9

Financial assessment of marketing opportunities

Topic list

1   Financial tools
2   Sources of funds
3   Shareholder value
4   Value drivers

Introduction

Those developing marketing strategy should:

(a) Understand the impact of their decisions on the finances of the business

(b) Be able to work effectively with the finance professionals in the business

(c) Be competent in the use of financial techniques necessary in day-to-day management and planning for their own departments

Financial comparisons can aid decision-making.

(a) **Past comparisons and trends**. Looking back at the organisation's financial history and records can identify similar situations and help draw conclusions and trends from the information.

(b) **Competitor analysis**. Examining published information of other organisations, such as competitors, for financial indicators may aid decision-making.

(c) **Forecasting the future** is based in part on financial assumptions.

(d) **Modelling**. Financial data may be used to model the effect of decisions.

The interpretation of financial data is the therefore a key part of understanding any business, either in a practical application or during your studies. This chapter looks at financial tools that can be used by the marketer, the sources of funds that are available to a business, and the important concepts of shareholder value and economic value.

You will not be required to undertake lengthy and complicated numerical analysis in the exam, but it is worth noting the words of the syllabus guidance for this unit:

"Students will be expected to apply a range of financial and risk models to support their assessments ... ultimately, students should be able to prepare a business case or investment appraisal to support the strategic marketing decision making process."

Syllabus-linked learning objectives

By the end of the chapter you will be able to:

Learning objectives	Syllabus link
1 Utilising a range of financial tools, assess the financial benefits and risks for an organisation when selecting from its strategic options	3.2.1
2 Critically evaluate the source of funds appropriate to the strategic marketing choice and the long-term sustainability and impact of their utilisation	3.2.2
3 Assess the impact of the strategic choice upon the shareholder value of organisations in different contexts	3.2.3
4 Assess the impact on the economic value of an organisation arising from specific decisions on expenditures/cash flows	3.2.4
5 Critically assess strategic alternatives against pre-determined criteria for an organisation	3.1.1

1 Financial tools

1.1 Ratios

Large companies have been effectively managed for many years simply by ensuring that the ratios relevant to their businesses were kept within acceptable limits. These are the important lessons to be learned.

- **Ratios** are a useful measure when in comparison with something else: either the company's history, or a competitor or an industry norm.

- **Consistency in calculation** and in the base data is important otherwise we could end up comparing apples and oranges.

- **Return on capital employed** is the product of two other ratios.

  ROCE = profit margin × asset turnover

- **Gearing** is a measure of how funds have been generated to buy assets.

- Proper control of cash is vital to the continued financial strength of any company. Marketing managers should be aware of the **debt collection periods** (also known as the debtor turnover or day sales outstanding) and other tests of liquidity such as stock turnover.

The financial statements provide sources of useful information about the condition of a business. They are in the **public domain** and can be an important feature in a **competitor analysis**. A company which is losing money and has borrowed heavily may behave quite differently in marketing terms than one which has many sources of cash.

The analysis and interpretation of these statements can be carried out by calculating certain ratios and then **using the ratios for comparison**.

(a) Comparison between **one year and the next**, for a particular business, is used to identify any trends, or significantly better or worse results.

(b) Comparison between **one business and another**, is used to establish which business has performed better, and in what ways. You should be very careful, when comparing two different businesses, to ensure that the accounts have been prepared in a similar way.

Below we identify some typical ratios used.

1.2 Profitability and performance ratios

1.2.1 Profit margin

Profit margin is the ratio of **profit before interest and tax to sales turnover**. For example, in 20X0, ARC's profit margin was 17.6% (hence costs as a percentage of sales were 82.4%). Profit before interest and tax (PBIT), is also known as the **operating profit**. In the accounts of ARC Ltd, the PBIT for 20X1 is £20,640,000 and for 20X0, £9,400,000. The profit margins for the two years are:

20X0	*20X1*
$\dfrac{9,400}{53,470} = 17.6\%$	$\dfrac{20,640}{98,455} = 21\%$

If the ratio of costs to sales goes down, the profit margin will automatically go up. For example, if the cost: sales ratio changes from 80% to 75%, the profit margin will go up from 20% to 25%. What does this mean?

- A **high margin** indicates costs are controlled and/or sales prices are high.
- A **low margin** can mean **high costs** or **low prices**.

Reebok and Adidas

Adidas, the world's second-largest sporting goods company, yesterday installed one of its own managers as head of Reebok as the struggling US brand it bought for $3.8 billion continued to drag on the group's performance.

Uli Becker, who worked at Adidas for 16 years before becoming head of marketing at Reebok two years ago, will replace Paul Harrington as chief executive of the US brand next month. Reebok is doing particularly badly in the US where its order backlog – a central measure that predicts future sales – declined 20% against an 8% drop for the brand as a whole.

Reebok's woes continued to overshadow a strong performance by the Adidas brand, which increased its operating margin by one percentage point to 12.9%. Reebok itself also lifted its margin to 4.7% from 3.5% as it grew strongly outside the US but it is still well below the profitability for which Adidas is aiming.

Richard Milne, *Financial Times,* 6 March 2008

1.2.2 Asset turnover

Asset turnover is the ratio of **sales turnover** in a year to the amount of **net assets**, which should equate to the amount invested in the business. In the accounts of ARC Ltd, the asset turnover for 20X1 and 20X0 is:

$$20X0 \qquad\qquad 20X1$$

$$\frac{53,470}{9,000} = 5.9 \text{ times} \qquad\qquad \frac{98,455}{16,100} = 6.1 \text{ times}$$

This means that for every £1 of assets employed in 20X0, the company generated sales turnover of £5.90 per annum. To utilise assets more efficiently, managers should try to create a higher volume of sales and a higher asset turnover ratio.

1.2.3 Return on capital employed (ROCE)

Return on capital employed (ROCE) is the **amount of profit** as a **percentage** of **capital employed** (net assets). If a company makes a profit of £30,000, we do not know how good or bad the result is until we look at the amount of capital which has been invested to achieve the profit. £30,000 might be a good sized profit for a small firm, but this would not be satisfactory for a 'giant' firm such as Marks & Spencer. For this reason, it is helpful to measure performance by relating profits to capital employed. The ROCE of ARC Ltd for 20X1 and 20X1 is:

$$20X0 \qquad\qquad 20X1$$

$$\frac{9,400}{9,000} = 104.4\% \qquad\qquad \frac{20,640}{16,100} = 128\%$$

You may already have realised that there is a mathematical connection between return on capital employed, profit margin and asset turnover:

$$\frac{\text{Profit}}{\text{Capital employed}} = \frac{\text{Profit}}{\text{Sales}} \times \frac{\text{Sales}}{\text{Capital employed}}$$

$$\text{ie ROCE} = \text{Profit margin} \times \text{Asset turnover}$$

This is important. If we accept that ROCE is the single most important measure of business performance, comparing profit with the amount of capital invested, we can go on to say that business performance is dependent on two separate 'subsidiary' factors, each of which contributes to ROCE, **profit margin** and **asset turnover**. We can improve ROCE by increasing profit from the same assets, or by matching the same profit with a lower level of assets.

Example

Company A and Company B both sell electrical goods. Both have £100,000 capital employed (net assets) and both want to achieve a target ROCE of 20%. Company A is a specialist retailer and Company B is a discount warehouse.

(a) **Specialist Company A** might decide to sell its products at a fairly high price and make a profit margin on sales of 10%. It would require an asset turnover of 2.0 times to achieve a ROCE of 20%. It would, therefore, need annual sales of £200,000.

(b) **Discount warehouse Company B** might decide to cut its prices so that its profit margin is only 2½%. Provided that it can achieve an asset turnover of eight times a year, attracting more customers with its lower prices, it will **still make a ROCE of 2½% × 8 = 20%**. It would need annual sales of £800,000.

ACTIVITY 1

application

What might be the implications for marketing mix decisions of the two approaches to achieving a target ROCE in the example above?

ACTIVITY 2

application

Suppose that Swings and Roundabouts Ltd achieved the following results in 20X6:

	£
Sales	100,000
Profit	5,000
Capital employed	20,000

The company's management wish to decide whether to raise its selling prices. They think that if they do so, they can raise the profit margin to 10% and by introducing extra capital of £55,000, sales turnover could be increased to £150,000.

You are required to evaluate the decision in terms of effect on ROCE, profit margin and asset turnover.

A single ratio is nearly meaningless. What is important is the movement in that ratio over time and the comparison of that ratio with other companies in a similar business.

1.2.4 Investment ratios

Earnings per share (EPS) shows the return due to the ordinary shareholders. This simply divides profit after tax by the average number of ordinary shares in issue while the profit was generated.

The **price/earnings (P/E) number** (also known as the P/E ratio and the P/E multiple) reflects the investors' view of the **future prospects** of a share. Share prices depend on expectations of future earnings.

$$P/E = \frac{\text{The market price of a share (in pence)}}{\text{Earnings per share}}$$

In effect, the P/E number calculates the payback period for money invested in a share.

Dividend per share is important to investors who seek a regular income from their investment.

Dividend cover is also important, since it indicates the company's ability to pay dividends and still retain some profit for purpose of investment.

$$\text{Dividend cover} = \frac{\text{EPS}}{\text{Dividend per share}}$$

1.3 Gearing

Gearing is a method of comparing how much of the long-term capital of a business is provided by **equity** (ordinary shares and reserves) and how much is provided by long-term **loan capital**.

Why is gearing important?

(a) If a company's gearing is too high (say over 50%), we might find that it is difficult to raise more loans.

(b) Loan capital is cheaper, because the interest cost diminishes in real terms if secured on company assets and attracts tax benefits.

(c) Interest must be paid, whereas the directors of a company can decide not to pay a dividend.

(d) High gearing might be considered risky for lenders in that the more loan capital a business has, the bigger becomes the size of profit before interest and tax (PBIT) which is necessary to meet demands for interest payments.

1.4 Operational ratios

Operational ratios relate to the **cash cycle** of a business.

(a) A business which cannot pay its debts as they fall due is insolvent. **Liquidity** is a critical and urgent issue, which is why working capital is monitored thoroughly. A company facing crises in liquidity has few options.

(b) Often external parties, such as banks, will provide extra funds, but in extreme cases **marketing strategies** must be devised to raise as much cash as possible.

Consequently, the finance function will monitor **turnover periods**. These ratios, usually expressed in days, measure how long or how many times the business is exchanging cash over a period of time.

Debtors' (receivables) turnover period, or **debt collection period**: the length of the credit period taken by customers or the time between the sale of an item and the receipt of cash for the sale from the customer.

(a) This describes the level of debtors compared with the sales turnover. So the ratio for ARC Ltd is:

	20X0	20X1
$\dfrac{\text{Debtors}}{\text{Sales}}$	$\dfrac{8,900}{53,470} = 17\%$	$\dfrac{27,100}{98,455} = 28\%$

(b) This can be expressed in days. By multiplying our ratio by 365 we recognise that the debtors are on average:

20X0	20X1
$\dfrac{8,900}{53,470} \times 365 = 61 \text{ days}$	$\dfrac{27,100}{98,455} \times 365 = 100 \text{ days}$

We can, of course, do similar turnover calculations for **stock turnover period**. This is the length of time an item stays in stores before use.

$$\frac{\text{Average finished goods stocks (use closing stock)}}{\text{Total cost of goods sold in the period}} \times 365 \text{ days}$$

	20X0	20X1
Stock (inventory) turnover period	$\dfrac{5,000}{40,653} \times 365 = 45 \text{ days}$	$\dfrac{15,000}{70,728} \times 365 = 77 \text{ days}$

Similarly, the **creditors' (payables) turnover period**, or period of credit taken from suppliers, is the length of time between the purchase of materials and the payment to suppliers.

$$\frac{\text{Average trade creditors (use closing creditors)}}{\text{Total purchases in the period} *} \times 365 \text{ days}$$

	20X0	20X1
Creditors' payment period	$\dfrac{6,000}{40,653} \times 365 = 54$ days	$\dfrac{10,000}{70,728} \times 365 = 52$ days

* Cost of sales can be substituted as an approximation

Again these can be expressed in days or months.

The **importance** of turnover ratios is their impact on **cash requirements**. An increase in the **stock turnover ratio** or in the **debtor turnover ratio** means that more money is being tied up in funding **working capital** and this may not be desirable.

1.5 Liquidity ratios

Liquidity, as we have seen, is an organisation's ability to convert its assets into cash to meet all the demands for payments when they fall due. They are particularly important for **credit control**.

Current liabilities are items which must be paid for in the near future. When payment becomes due, enough cash must be available to make the payment.

Let us see how some ratios apply.

Ratio	Current ratio $\dfrac{\text{Current assets}}{\text{Current liabilities}}$	Quick ratio $\dfrac{\text{Current assets less stock}}{\text{Current liabilities}}$
ARC 20X0	$\dfrac{14,500}{13,000} = 1.1\!:\!1$	$\dfrac{14,500 - 5,000}{13,000} = 0.7\!:\!1$
ARC 20X1	$\dfrac{42,100}{38,400} = 1.1\!:\!1$	$\dfrac{42,100 - 15,000}{38,400} = 0.7\!:\!1$

The best way to judge liquidity would be to look at the current ratio at different dates over a period of time. If the trend is towards a **lower current ratio**, we would judge that the **liquidity position is getting steadily worse**.

 ACTIVITY 3   application

Calculate liquidity and working capital ratios from these accounts of a manufacturer of products for the construction industry.

	20X3 £m	20X2 £m
Turnover	2,065.0	1,788.7
Cost of sales	1,478.6	1,304.0
Gross profit	586.4	484.7
Current assets		
Stocks	119.0	109.0
Debtors (note 1)	400.9	347.4
Short-term investments	4.2	18.8
Cash at bank and in hand	48.2	48.0
	572.3	523.2
Creditors: amounts falling due within one year		
Loans and overdrafts	49.1	35.3
Corporation taxes	62.0	46.7
Dividend	19.2	14.3
Creditors (note 2)	370.7	324.0
	501.0	420.3
Net current assets	71.3	102.9

Notes

1	Trade debtors	329.8	285.4
2	Trade creditors	236.2	210.8

1.6 Investment appraisal techniques

The best project appraisal method is net present value, but payback period is also useful. Note that all investment appraisal methods depend for their use on having reasonably accurate estimates of the cash flows associated with the proposal, both the immediate cost and the costs and revenues expected in the future. In this context remember that profit is not the same thing as positive cash flow, since profit is affected by non-cash flow items such as depreciation.

We will look first at the payback method.

1.6.1 Payback

 ## KEY CONCEPT

concept

Payback is the time it takes the cash inflows from a capital investment project to equal the cash outflows, expressed in years.

Payback is often used as a 'first screening method'. By this, we mean that when a capital investment project is being considered, the first question to ask is: 'How long will it take to pay back its cost?' The organisation might have a target payback, and so it would reject a capital project unless its payback period was less than a certain number of years.

However, a project should not be evaluated on the basis of payback alone. If a project passes the payback test, it ought then to be evaluated with a more sophisticated investment appraisal technique.

 ## MARKETING AT WORK

application

Almost as soon as the "Gorilla" television commercial for Dairy Milk chocolate first aired on August 31, the questions began. What role did the extraordinary take-up of the gorilla ad on the internet play in Dairy Milk's success? . . .

Analysts – and the company itself – will struggle to put a value on this internet-generated exposure. This contrasts with the more easily measured £6 million that Cadbury spent mostly on television airtime for Dairy Milk.

According to Thomson Intermedia, the media measurement group, Cadbury's expenditure on media advertising for Dairy Milk is up almost 90% year-on-year in 2007. Any bounce in chocolate sales is also compared with a weak performance in 2006.

But few would deny Dairy Milk has enjoyed some commercial benefit from its internet exposure and that this could lift the return that Cadbury can claim on its marketing investment.

Martin Deboo, Investec analyst, said: "What the Gorilla campaign has shown is that viral advertising can give you a pretty big 'leverage' effect on the investment you have already made in traditional media advertising. On the sales figures Cadbury has disclosed, I would estimate it is already enjoying a positive return on its Dairy Milk marketing spend, which is unusual. You would expect the payback to be longer."

Carlos Grande, FT.com, 11 December 2007

The reason why payback should not be used on its own to evaluate capital investments should seem fairly obvious if you look at the figures below for two mutually exclusive projects (this means that only one of them can be undertaken).

	Project P £	Project Q £
Capital asset	60,000	60,000
Profits before depreciation (a rough approximation of cash flows)		
Year 1	20,000	50,000
Year 2	30,000	20,000
Year 3	40,000	5,000
Year 4	50,000	5,000
Year 5	60,000	5,000

Project P pays back in year 3 (about one-quarter of the way through year 3). Project Q pays back half-way through year 2. Using payback alone to judge capital investments, project Q would be preferred. However the returns from project P over its life are much higher than the returns from project Q. Project P will earn total profits before depreciation of £140,000 on an investment of £60,000. Project Q will earn total profits before depreciation of only £25,000 on an investment of £60,000.

There are a number of serious drawbacks to the payback method.

(a) It ignores the timing of cash flows within the payback period, the cash flows after the end of payback period and therefore, the total project return.

(b) It ignores the time value of money (a concept incorporated into more sophisticated appraisal methods). This means that it does not take account of the fact that £1 today is worth more than £1 in one year's time. An investor who has £1 today can either consume it immediately or alternatively can invest it at the prevailing interest rate, say 10%, to get a return of £1.10 in a year's time.

(c) Payback is unable to distinguish between projects with the same payback period.

(d) The choice of any cut-off payback period by an organisation is arbitrary.

(e) It may lead to excessive investment in short-term projects.

(f) It takes account of the risk of the timing of cash flows but not the variability of those cash flows.

Advantages of the payback method

In spite of its limitations, the payback method continues to be popular, and the following points can be made in its favour.

(a) It is simple to calculate and simple to understand. This may be important when management resources are limited. It is similarly helpful in communicating information about minimum requirements to managers responsible for submitting projects.

(b) It uses cash flows rather than accounting profits.

(c) It can be used as a screening device as a first stage in eliminating obviously inappropriate projects prior to more detailed evaluation.

(d) The fact that it tends to bias in favour of short-term projects means that it tends to minimise both financial and business risk.

(e) It can be used when there is a capital rationing situation to identify those projects which generate additional cash for investment quickly.

1.6.2 Discounted cash flows (DCF)

Discounting is a numerical process that determines the **present value** of a future cash flow.

In the next section we will discuss shareholder value analysis (SVA). This technique depends on the **discounting** of cash flows, both current and in the future. Discounting is a basic tool of financial analysis that is also widely used in other business techniques, so we will start off by showing you how it works.

The **basic principle of compounding** is that if we invest £X now for n years at r% interest per annum, we should obtain £S in n years' time, where £S = £X$(1+r^n)$.

Thus if we invest £10,000 now for four years at 10% interest per annum, we will have a total investment worth £10,000 × 1.10^4 = £14,641 at the end of four years (that is, at Year 4 if it is now Year 0).

 KEY CONCEPT concept

The basic principle of **discounting** is that if we wish to have £S in n years' time, we need to invest a certain sum now (Year 0) at an interest rate of r% in order to obtain the required sum of money in the future.

For example, if we wish to have £14,641 in four years' time, how much money would we need to invest now at 10% interest per annum? This is the reverse of the situation described above and, fairly obviously, the answer is £10,000. We can prove this.

Using our formula, $S = X(1 + r)^n$

where
X = the original sum invested
r = 10%
n = 4
S = £14,641

$£14,641 = X(1 + 0.1)^4$

$£14,641 = X \times 1.4641$

Therefore, $X = \dfrac{£14,641}{1.4641} = £10,000$

£10,000 now, with the capacity to earn a return of 10% per annum, is the equivalent in value of £14,641 after four years. We can, therefore, say that £10,000 is the **present value** of £14,641 at Year 4, at an interest rate of 10%.

KEY CONCEPT

concept

The **present value** of a future sum is obtained by discounting that future sum at an appropriate discount rate.

The discounting formula is:

$$X = S \times \frac{1}{(1+r)^n}$$

where
S is the sum to be received after n time periods
X is the present value (PV) of that sum
r is the rate of return, expressed as a proportion
n is the number of time periods (usually years)

The rate r is sometimes called the cost of capital.

Example: Discounting

(a) Calculate the present value of £60,000 at Year 6, if a return of 15% per annum is obtainable.

(b) Calculate the present value of £100,000 at Year 5, if a return of 6% per annum is obtainable.

(c) How much would a person need to invest now at 12% to earn £4,000 at Year 2 and £4,000 at Year 3?

Solution

The discounting formula, $X = S \times \dfrac{1}{(1+r)^n}$ is required.

(a)
S = £60,000
n = 6
r = 0.15

$PV = 60,000 \times \dfrac{1}{1.15^6}$

$= 60,000 \times 0.432$

$= £25,920$

(b)   S = £100,000

      n = 5

      r = 0.06

      PV = $100,000 \times \dfrac{1}{1.06^5}$

            = $100,000 \times 0.747$

            = £74,700

(c)   S = £4,000

      n = 2 or 3

      r = 0.12

      PV = $(4,000 \times \dfrac{1}{1.12^2}) + (4,000 \times \dfrac{1}{1.12^3})$

            = $4,000 \times (0.797 + 0.712)$

            = £6,036

This calculation can be checked as follows.

	£
Year 0	6,036.00
Interest for the first year (12%)	724.32
	6,760.32
Interest for the second year (12%)	811.24
	7,571.56
Less withdrawal	(4,000.00)
	3,571.56
Interest for the third year (12%)	428.59
	4,000.15
Less withdrawal	(4,000.00)
Rounding error	0.15

ACTIVITY 4

application

The present value at 7% interest of £16,000 at Year 12 is £?

Discounted cash flow techniques can be used to evaluate expenditure proposals such as marketing budgets or plans to purchase equipment.

KEY CONCEPT

concept

Discounted cash flow (DCF) involves the application of discounting arithmetic to the estimated future cash flows (receipts and expenditures) from a project in order to decide whether the project is expected to earn a satisfactory rate of return.

BPP
LEARNING MEDIA

1.6.3 The net present value (NPV) method

The **net present value** of a project is the sum of the present values of all the future cash flows associated with it.

KEY CONCEPT

concept

The **net present value (NPV) method** works out the present values of all items of income and expenditure related to an investment at a given rate of return, and then works out a net total. If it is positive, the investment is considered to be acceptable. If it is negative, the investment is considered to be unacceptable.

Example: The net present value of a project

Dog Ltd is considering whether to spend £5,000 on an item of equipment. The excess of income over cash expenditure from the project would be £3,000 in the first year and £4,000 in the second year.

The company will not invest in any project unless it offers a return in excess of 15% per annum.

Required

Assess whether the investment is worthwhile.

Solution

In this example, an outlay of £5,000 now promises a return of £3,000 **during** the first year and £4,000 **during** the second year. It is a convention in DCF, however, that cash flows spread over a year are assumed to occur **at the end of the year**, so that the cash flows of the project are as follows.

	£
Year 0 (now)	(5,000)
Year 1 (at the end of the year)	3,000
Year 2 (at the end of the year)	4,000

The NPV method takes the following approach.

(a)   The project offers £3,000 at Year 1 and £4,000 at Year 2, for an outlay of £5,000 now.

(b)   The company might invest elsewhere to earn a return of 15% per annum.

(c)   If the company did invest at exactly 15% per annum, how much would it need to invest now to earn £3,000 at the end of Year 1 plus £4,000 at the end of Year 2?

(d)   Is it cheaper to invest £5,000 in the project, or to invest elsewhere at 15%, in order to obtain these future cash flows?

If the company did invest elsewhere at 15% per annum, the amount required to earn £3,000 in Year 1 and £4,000 in Year 2 would be as follows.

Year	Cash flow £	Discount factor 15%	Present value £
1	3,000	$\frac{1}{1.15} = 0.870$	2,610
2	4,000	$\frac{1}{(1.15)^2} = 0.756$	3,024
			5,634

The choice is to invest £5,000 in the project, or £5,634 elsewhere at 15%, in order to obtain these future cash flows. We can therefore reach the following conclusion.

- It is cheaper to invest in the project, by £634.
- The project offers a return of over 15% per annum.

The net present value is the difference between the present value of cash inflows from the project (£5,634) and the present value of future cash outflows (in this example, £5,000 × 1/1.15^0 = £5,000).

An NPV statement could be drawn up as follows.

Year	Cash flow £	Discount factor 15%	Present value £
0	(5,000)	1.000	(5,000)
1	3,000	$\frac{1}{1.15} = 0.870$	2,610
2	4,000	$\frac{1}{(1.15)^2} = 0.756$	3,024
Net present value			+634

The project has a **positive net present value, so it is acceptable**.

Notes

(1) $\dfrac{1}{1.15} = 0.870$

(2) $\dfrac{1}{(1.15)^2} = 0.756$

  ACTIVITY 5 application

A company is wondering whether to spend £18,000 on an item of equipment, in order to obtain cash profits as follows.

Year	£
1	6,000
2	8,000
3	5,000
4	1,000

The company requires a return of 10% per annum.

Required

Use the NPV method to assess whether the project is viable.

Discount tables

Assuming that money earns, say, 10% per annum:

(a) The PV (present value) of £1 at Year 1 is £1 × $\dfrac{1}{1.10}$ = £1 × 0.909

(b) Similarly, the PV of £1 at Year 2 is £1 × $\dfrac{1}{(1.10)^2}$ = £1 × 0.826

(c) The PV of £1 at Year 3 is £1 × $\dfrac{1}{(1.10)^3}$ = £1 × 0.751

Discount tables show the value of $1/(1 + r)^n$ for different values of r and n. Note, however, that in practice NPV calculations will usually be done using a spreadsheet.

Limitations of using the NPV method

There are a number of problems associated with using the NPV method in practice.

(a)   **The future discount factors** (or interest rates) which are used in calculating NPVs can only be **estimated** and are not known with certainty. Discount rates that are estimated for time periods far into the future are therefore less likely to be accurate, thereby leading to less accurate NPV values.

(b)   Similarly, NPV calculations make use of estimated **future cash flows**. As with future discount factors, cash flows which are estimated for several years into the future cannot be predicted with any real certainty.

(c)   When using the NPV method it is common to assume that all cash flows occur **at the end of the year**. However, this assumption is also likely to give rise to less accurate NPV values.

There are a number of computer programs available these days which enable a range of NPVs to be calculated for different circumstances (best-case and worst-case situations and so on). Such programs allow some of the limitations mentioned above to be alleviated.

2   Sources of funds

2.1 The cost of capital

Many groups of companies have a corporate treasury function within the holding company, which controls the use of the group's internally generated funds by means of a central banking system.

The holding company will loan capital to subsidiary operating units and charge out the funds at the corporate **cost of capital**. The target DCF rate of return selected by an organisation might be based on the following:

(a)   The **weighted average cost of capital (WACC) is the average of the cost of equity and the cost of debt. If the cost of equity for a company is 10% and its cost of debt is 6%, the cost of capital will be 8% (assuming that the amounts of debt and equity are equal).**

(b)   The **marginal cost of capital** – ie the cost of the extra capital required to finance a specific project

(c)   The **opportunity cost** of the capital required to finance the project (ie what is lost by not investing somewhere else, such as putting the money into the bank and earning interest on it)

(d)   A cost of capital that is adjusted to allow for the **risk element** in the particular capital investment

(e)   A return based upon the **capital asset pricing model (CAPM)**.   This is expressed in the formula below:

$$\bar{r}_a = r_f + \beta_a \left(\bar{r}_m - r_f \right)$$

Where: $\bar{r}_a$ = expected return on the security

r_f = risk free rate

β_a = Beta of the security

$\bar{r}_m$ = Expected market return

The general idea behind CAPM is that investors need to be compensated in two ways: for the time value of money, and for risk. The time value of money is represented by the risk-free (r_f) rate in the formula and compensates the investor for placing money in an investment over a period of time. The other half of the formula represents risk, and calculates the amount of compensation the investor needs for taking on that risk. This is calculated by taking a risk measure (beta) that compares the returns of the investment with those of the market over a period of time and to the market premium ($\bar{r}_m - r_f$).

The CAPM says that the expected return of an investment equals the rate on a risk-free investment, plus a risk premium. If this expected return does not meet or beat the required return, then the investment should not be undertaken.

Using the CAPM model and the following assumptions, we can compute the expected return of a project: if the risk-free rate is 3%, the beta (risk measure) of the project is 2 and the expected market return over the period is 10%, the investment will be expected to return 17% (3% + 2 (10% – 3%)).

Calculating an accurate cost of capital is very difficult and the subject of much debate and research by financial management professionals. While the level of loan interest is clearly easily available, it can vary from loan to loan and in the case of overdraft finance may vary from time to time. The cost of share capital is much more difficult to compute since it is really only accessible through an examination of stock market behaviour and that is extremely complex. A further complication is the issue of risk premium. To some extent this is built into the cost of loan and share capital, but where money is allocated internally, management must make up their own minds. All these factors mean that choice of discount rate is very much a matter of judgement and the 'correct' rate may be unknowable to an accuracy of better than plus or minus several percentage points.

2.2 Optimal capital structure

In determining what is the appropriate level of debt to be held by a business, one useful ratio is the debt-to-equity ratio. The higher this ratio is, the larger the interest payment burden and the lower the ability of the business to generate additional funds via debt (or loans) in the future or in an emergency.

The optimal level of debt/equity is influenced by a number of factors (Aaker & McLoughlin 2007).

- The ability to carry added interest payments
- The policy of the firm towards debt
- The return expected on investments
- The debt/equity ratio of competitors

3 Shareholder value analysis

Shareholder value analysis may be used to measure corporate (and hence management) performance in terms of benefit created for shareholders. **Economic value added** is a simple measure but backward looking. The cash flow approach is a better method for assessing future prospects.

Shareholder value analysis (SVA) is a method of approaching the problem of business control by focusing on the **creation of value for shareholders**. Independent financial analysts measure the **value offered by a company's shares** by considering the **market value** of all the shares in existence (the **market capitalisation**), in the light of the **company's prospects** for generating both cash and capital growth in the future. If the current market capitalisation is less than the estimate of actual value, then the shares are undervalued. Investment is necessary to produce either assets that grow in value or actual cash surpluses, so the process of shareholder value analysis is essentially one of estimating the likely effectiveness of the company's **current investment decisions**. It is thus both a system for judging the worth of current investment proposals and for judging the performance of the managers who are responsible for the company's performance.

In the past, marketing managers have tended to pursue purely **marketing objectives**, such as sales growth, market share, customer satisfaction and brand recognition. None of these marketing objectives *necessarily* translates into increased shareholder value, and as a result, marketing has suffered from a lack of perceived relevance to true business value. An emphasis on profitability as a measure of success has led to a certain amount of **short-termism** in strategic management, with an emphasis on **containing and reducing current costs** in order to boost current profits. Unfortunately, this approach tends to underestimate the longer-term effect of such action and can lead to corporate decline. Investment in **intangible assets** such as brands can make a positive contribution to long-term shareholder value.

3.1 Computing value

According to Doyle (2008), the extent of a company's success may be measured in two ways. The first is by using the concept of **economic profit** (trademarked by Stern, Stewart and Company as **Economic Value Added®**). The expression economic profit is used to distinguish the measure from accounting profit, which is computed according to the strict rules of accountancy. These feature, in particular, the principle of **prudence**. This makes it impossible for **accounting profit** to recognise spending on pure research, for instance, as an investment in an asset, since there is no guarantee that it will ever produce anything worth having; the same would be true of much marketing spending on building long-term effectiveness.

Economic profit is created when the return on a company's capital employed exceeds the cost of that capital.

Economic profit = NOPAT − (capital employed × cost of capital)

where NOPAT is net operating profit after tax.

The cost of capital is, effectively, the return that has to be made to providers of capital in the form of interest on loans and dividends on shares. It may be calculated as a **weighted average**, which takes account of both the expectations of shareholders and lenders. (Buying shares generally entails greater risk than making a loan, so shareholders generally demand higher returns than lenders. This is why a weighted average figure must be used.)

Economic profit is related to capital employed by **return on capital employed** (ROCE). This is a percentage and may thus be compared directly with cost of capital. When ROCE exceeds the cost of capital (r), economic value is created: under these circumstances (ROCE > r), the company is offering a greater return on capital than is available elsewhere.

3.1.1 The cash flow approach

Economic profit is useful for examining the company's **current and past performance**, but is less useful for **assessing future prospects**. Doyle suggests that it is more appropriate to use the second of the methods he discusses, the **cash flow approach** for this purpose. Be aware that both the **economic profit** method and the **cash flow method** should produce the same result when applied to a particular company.

The **cash flow approach** may be used to estimate the degree of economic value a company may be expected to create in the future. It is based on an estimation of likely future **cash flows**, both positive and negative, as indicated in the corporate plans. (A cash flow is simply a sum of money paid or received by the company.) This is easier to compute than future NOPAT, because it is far less complex and depends on far fewer variables.

3.2 Discounting cash flows

Because the SVA technique depends very much on the estimation of future cash flows arising from current investments, it is necessary to use **discounting arithmetic** in order to make the necessary judgements.

3.2.1 Business risk

Some businesses are inherently **riskier** than others: the degree of risk can be measured by the degree of predictability that attaches to its expected cash flows. A low risk business will have steady income from period to period, without any unexpected highs and lows. A high-risk business will have returns that vary wildly and unexpectedly from period to period, though its total long-term return may be as great or greater than the low risk operation. Generally, **investors are risk averse** and, as a result, they demand higher returns from high-risk businesses than from low risk ones. The high-risk business must therefore use a **higher cost of capital** in its shareholder value analysis than the low risk business.

3.3 Value-based management

Value-based management is about maximising shareholder returns by developing competitive advantage in segments where profits can be made.

Doyle (2003), tells us that business success should be measured by shareholder value analysis because of the property rights of shareholders and the 'pressures to oust management that does not deliver competitive returns'. Purely marketing objectives are no longer acceptable to investors or the analysts whose reports they rely on. What Doyle calls **value-based management** is based on three elements.

(a)   A **belief** that maximising shareholder returns is the objective of the firm.

(b)   The **principles**, or strategic foundations of value are first, to target those market segments where profits can be made and second, to develop competitive advantage 'that enables both the customer and the firm to create value'.

(c)   The **processes** 'concern how strategies should be developed, resources allocated and performance measured'.

SVA is particularly appropriate for judging strategic investment decisions and applies the same principles that have long been used for appraising investment in such tangible assets as premises and plant. It is necessary to consider both the **cash costs** of the strategic investment to be made, and the **positive cash flows** that are expected to be produced by it. These may then be discounted to a net present value (NPV) using an appropriate cost of capital, and a judgement made on the basis of the NPV. Any specific marketing proposal, such as an enhanced advertising spend or a new discount structure may be assessed in this way, though it will almost certainly be necessary to take advice from the finance function on the process.

Estimating the value of such investments forms one part of basic shareholder value analysis. Doyle also recommends that when considering the total value of a business, it is also necessary to consider the probable **residual value** of the business. This is the present value of cash flows in the more distant future, outside the normal planning horizon, which Doyle suggests is five years. This assumes no special competitive advantage from current investments and simply uses the cost of capital as an estimate of the rate of return on investment.

3.3.1 Marketing assets

Value-based management means that purely marketing investment proposals will be judged as detailed above. It will be necessary for marketing managers to justify their spending requests in such terms, on the basis that such spending is not a cost burden to be minimised but an investment in intangible assets such as the four that Doyle suggests.

- Marketing knowledge
- Brands
- Customer loyalty
- Strategic relationships with channel partners

The obstacle that lies in the path of this approach to marketing use of SVA is the common perception that marketing spending is merely a cost to be controlled and minimised. The onus is on marketing managers to demonstrate that their budgets do in fact create assets that provide competitive advantage for the business and that the benefits exceed the costs.

4 Value drivers

Doyle (2003) suggests that it is possible to identify the factors that are critical to the creation of shareholder value. These he calls **value drivers**; he divides them into three categories.

- Financial
- Marketing
- Organisational

It is important to remember that **the financial drivers should not be targeted directly**: they are objectives, not the components of strategy. The company influences them by the proper management of the **marketing** and **organisational** drivers.

4.1 Financial value drivers

There are four drivers of **financial value**.

- Cash flow volume
- Cash flow timing
- Cash flow risk
- Cash flow sustainability

4.1.1 Cash flow volume

Clearly, the higher that positive cash flows are and the lower negative cash flows are, the greater the potential for creating value.

Profitability. In the most simple terms, profit margin is measured by net operating profit after tax (NOPAT). NOPAT can be increased in three ways.

(a) **Higher prices**. Marketing strategies such as building strong brands can enable the charging of premium prices. A particularly powerful route to higher prices is **innovation**, since desirable new products will normally justify increased prices.

(b) **Reduced costs**. Cost reduction depends on increased efficiency in all aspects of the business operation.

(c) **Volume increases**. Other things being equal, volume growth increases the absolute profit margin and may increase the profit rate as well.

Sales growth. If increases in sales volume can be achieved without disproportionate increases in costs or, in particular, excessive discounting, positive cash flows will naturally increase. Increased sales can also bring increased **economies of scale**, which will take the form of reduced costs of all types. Overheads are spread over greater volumes and purchasing discounts reduce the cost of sales.

Investment. Investment provides the resources necessary to do business. These include premises, equipment, stocks, transport and well-trained, experienced staff. However, ill-advised investment can destroy value faster than profitable investment can create it, so any proposal for investment must be judged on its potential for generating acceptable returns. The **net present value** (NPV) approach is the investment appraisal method best suited to the shareholder value principle, in that any project that has a NPV greater than zero provides a return greater than the cost of capital used in the discounting arithmetic.

4.1.2 Cash flow timing

The further into the future a cash flow occurs, the lower its present value. If positive cash flows can be achieved in the near future and negative ones delayed, the company benefits. This is why companies and individuals put off paying their bills for as long as possible. Buying on credit and selling for cash is another approach.

Doyle gives five examples of ways that marketing managers can accelerate cash flows.

(a) **Faster new product development** processes, including the use of cross-functional teams and conducting projects concurrently rather than consecutively.

(b) **Accelerated market penetration** through pre-marketing campaigns, early trial promotions and word-of-mouth campaigns using early adopters.

(c) **Network effects**: that is, achieving market status as the industry standard. This is a self-reinforcing, feedback effect in which success leads to even greater success. Aggressive marketing measures to build the installed base are required.

(d) **Strategic alliances** speed market penetration, normally by providing extra distribution effort.

(e) **Exploiting brand assets**: new products launched under a suitable, established brand are likely to be more successful than others.

4.1.3 Cash flow risk

The higher the degree of **risk** associated with future cash flows, the greater the proportion of them that will not actually come to pass. High risk can produce low returns as easily as high ones. Apart from this overall averaging effect, there is the disadvantage associated with **infrequent large cash flows**: failure of such a cash flow to occur can have catastrophic consequences. Risk is also associated with timing: the further into the future that a cash flow is expected to occur, the greater the risk associated with it, since there is a greater likelihood of **changed conditions** affecting its eventual value and even whether or not it actually occurs.

Doyle suggests that the most effective marketing route to reduced cash flow risk is 'to increase customer satisfaction, loyalty and retention' by deploying such techniques as loyalty programmes and measures to increase satisfaction. Building **good channel relationships** also helps, both by building an element of loyalty based on good service and by sharing information on demand patterns to smooth stock fluctuations.

4.1.4 Cash flow sustainability

A single positive cash flow is useful. A positive cash flow that is repeated at regular intervals is much more useful. Quite apart from the extra cash involved, sustainable cash flows make it easier to plan for the future. Positive cash flows derive from the creation of competitive advantage and a sustainable advantage will lead to sustainable cash flows.

There are many **threats to sustainable profits**, including aggressive competition from copies and substitutes and, particularly in B2B markets, the bargaining power of customers. Part of the role of marketing management is to counter such threats using techniques, such as those outlined above, in connection with reducing risk.

Sustainable advantage also offers a benefit in the form of **enhanced options** for future development. Just as financial options to buy and sell securities and currency have their own value, so a strategy that creates **real options** for future activity has a value over and above any immediate competitive advantage it may offer. A simple example is the development of a completely new product for a given market that can also be made viable in other markets at low incremental cost.

Richard Branson's ability to use his brand Virgin with almost any consumer product is another example. There are network effects here too, in that as more and more dissimilar Virgin products become available, the brand's suitability for use with even more types of product grows.

4.2 Marketing value drivers

Doyle analyses four **marketing value drivers**. The first, choice of markets, is only applicable to the large, diversified organisation, but the remaining three apply to all companies.

4.2.1 Choice of markets

A large organisation operating a number of strategic business units (SBUs) must apply a continuing **portfolio analysis** to them. You will be familiar with such portfolio analysis tools as the BCG matrix and the GE business screen from your earlier studies, but you may only have considered their use at **the product level**. Nevertheless, it is both feasible and proper to apply the concept at **the SBU level** in order to determine priorities for investment and policies for exploitation. Doyle suggests a very simple, one-dimensional classification of SBUs.

(a)   **Today's businesses** generate the bulk of current profits and cash, but probably have only modest growth potential. If successful, they attract modest investment for incremental developments; if performing badly they are put right rapidly or sold off.

(b)   **Tomorrow's businesses** have high potential and require major investment.

(c)   **Options for growth** are the seeds of more distant businesses; such as research projects, market trials and stakes in new, small businesses that are a long way from success. Recognising the worth of such ventures is a difficult task; in the world of venture capital, it is recognised that many good ideas will come to nothing in the end.

A large company needs a suitable mix of the three types of SBU each with its own appropriate strategic objectives, though there may be opportunities for **synergy**, such as the use of common brand names. SBUs that do not fit into one of the categories should be divested.

4.2.2 Target markets

Most customers are not worth selling to. The loyal, long-term customer that pays full price and requires little special service attention is the ideal – but very few fall into this category. Nevertheless, it is appropriate to target this class of customer specifically rather than simply to aim for a large customer base. Desirable customers display four important characteristics.

*   They are **strategic** in that their needs match the company's core capabilities.
*   They are **significant** in terms of their size or potential for growth.
*   They are **profitable**.
*   They are **loyal**.

4.2.3 Differential advantage

For other than convenience purchases, customers must have a reason for buying from a particular supplier. **Differential advantage** is created when target customers decide to buy and to remain loyal. Doyle proposes four types of customer, each of which is suited by a particular strategic approach to creating differential advantage.

A strategy of **product leadership** is based on innovation and speed to market. It is the differential advantage that enables a company to sell to **customers who want the latest, most fashionable products**. A good example is Sony, with its continuing development of well-designed, expensive customer electronics.

Operational excellence is needed to offer a combination of **customer convenience** and the **lowest prices**. Wal-Mart and Toyota are good examples of this approach.

Brand superiority is based on careful marketing research and strong and consistent marketing communication. This approach works with customers who identify with the **brand's values** or seek the **reassurance** that brands provide.

A growing segment is made up of customers seeking customised solutions to their specific wants. The appropriate strategy here is **customer intimacy**. This approach is becoming more feasible as information technology developments improve the ability of companies to store and access details of customer habits, needs and preferences.

Note that concentration on one particular strategy does not mean that the others can be neglected. A level of **threshold competence** must be achieved in all four, with one being established as the field of **core competence**.

4.2.4 Marketing mix

Marketing mix decisions derive from, and should support, policies established for the other three marketing value drivers. For example, the chosen market segment will have characteristics and usage patterns that govern decisions about promotion and distribution, while differential advantage derived from brand superiority will lead to, and be supported by, a policy of premium pricing.

4.3 Organisational value drivers

Organisational capabilities and culture will have great influence on success and failure. The McKinsey 7S model illustrates the interplay of the factors involved.

Doyle declares that 'in most situations organisational capabilities and culture are more important than strategy', and goes on to make several comparisons between pairs of companies that use similar strategies in the same industries but with markedly differing degrees of success. The differences arise from the extent to which the companies involved are able to develop and deploy appropriate **core competences** and this in turn is highly conditional upon the **culture** of the organisation and the **attitudes** of the people working in it.

An important variable is **organisational structure**. In the days of mass marketing, a vertically organised hierarchical form was appropriate for achieving economies of scale and expertise. Companies now seeking to cut overheads, achieve fast response to changing markets and competition and exploit the advantages of a mass customisation approach need something better. Increasingly, advances in IT are producing organisations based on **networks**.

(a) **Internal networks** take the form of horizontally-oriented, cross-functional teams with responsibility for processes that deliver customer satisfactions. Communication flows freely, making the best use of resources whatever their functional label. This style of working reduces costs, speeds response and improves motivation.

(b) **External networks** are created when companies withdraw from activities that are not fundamental to their specific value-creating strategy and **concentrate on their core competences**. They buy in the services they no longer perform for themselves, using the core competences of other companies to support their own. This type of organisation arises under the pressure of new technologies, new markets and new processes that make it difficult for any organisation to do everything well.

Learning objectives	Covered
1 Utilising a range of financial tools, assess the financial benefits and risks for an organisation when selecting from its strategic options	☑ Ratios (1.1)
	☑ Profitability and performance ratios (1.2)
	☑ Gearing (1.3)
	☑ Operational ratios (1.4)
	☑ Liquidity ratios (1.5)
	☑ Investment appraisal techniques (1.6)
2 Critically evaluate the source of funds appropriate to the strategic marketing choice and the long-term sustainability and impact of their utilisation	☑ The cost of capital (2.1)
	☑ Optimal capital structure (2.2)
3 Assess the impact of the strategic choice upon the shareholder value of organisations in different contexts	☑ Computing value (3.1)
	☑ Discounting cash flows (3.2)
	☑ Value-based management (3.3)
4 Assess the impact on the economic value of an organisation arising from specific decisions on expenditures/cash flows	☑ Financial value drivers (4.1)
	☑ Marketing value drivers (4.2)
	☑ Organisational value drivers (4.3)
5 Critically assess strategic alternatives against pre-determined criteria for an organisation	☑ The techniques presented in this chapter can provide criteria against which strategic alternatives can be assessed.

1   How is liquidity defined?

2   How can ratios be used?

3   If I expect to receive a payment of £10.50 in 6 months' time and I can earn 10% by putting money on deposit, what is the payment worth today?

4   A marketing project costing £10,000 is assessed as having a net present value of £147. Should the project go ahead?

5   What, in the context of SVA, are value drivers?

6   In simple terms, what is the formula for EVA?

7   Define ROCE.

8   Why is gearing important?

9   What is the WACC of a company?

10   "The CAPM says that the expected return of an investment equals the rate on a .... investment, plus a .... premium." Fill in the blanks.

11   What is 'economic profit'?

12   What are Doyle's three value drivers?

13   How can cash flow risk be reduced?

14   What factors will influence the optimal capital structure for a company?

15   "The further into the future a cash flow occurs, the .... its present value." Fill in the blank.

1 (a) Company A – low volume of sales, but high margin on each unit sold. To justify the high profit margin, the firm might have to differentiate its offer in some way, for example, by superior service or another differentiating factor, or by effective segmentation.

   (b) Company B – high volume, low margin. This might be similar to the 'Every Day Low Pricing' policy adopted by B&Q. Its explicit aim was to increase sales volume by lowering prices. It is unlikely that A or B would sell exactly the same product/service. Of course, they might sell the same equipment, but augmentation to the product might be made.

   Furthermore, Company A and Company B may have little option but to pursue their different strategies, because of the characteristics of the industry and their existing position within it. This is relevant to strategic group analysis.

2 Is the increased profit figure necessarily a good thing?

   (a) At present, ratios are:

Profit margin	5%
Asset turnover	5 times
ROCE (5/20)	25%

   (b) With the proposed changes, the profit would be 10% × £150,000 = £15,000, and the asset turnover would be:

   $$\frac{£150,000}{£75,000} = 2 \text{ times}, \text{ so that the ratios might be:}$$

Profit margin	×	Asset turnover =		ROCE	
10%	×	2 times =	20%	ie	$\frac{15,000}{75,000}$

   (c) In spite of increasing the profit margin and raising the total volume of sales, the extra assets required (£55,000) only raise total profits by £(15,000 – 5,000) = £10,000. The return on capital employed **falls** from 25% to 20% because of the sharp fall in asset turnover from 5 times to 2 times. In other words, the new investment is not used efficiently.

   (d) This does not mean that the management of the company would not raise its prices. However, the financial analysis has provided them with another piece of the decision-making jigsaw. It may be that this is a weakness because the owners of the business, although very happy with the increased profitability, may not be happy with the reduced ROCE. The management must judge which aspect is most acceptable.

3

	20X3	20X2
Current ratio	$\frac{572.3}{501.0} = 1.14$	$\frac{523.2}{420.3} = 1.24$
Quick ratio	$\frac{453.3}{501.0} = 0.90$	$\frac{414.2}{420.3} = 0.99$
Debtors payment period	$\frac{329.8 \times 365}{2,065.0} = 58 \text{ days}$	$\frac{285.4 \times 365}{1,788.7} = 58 \text{ days}$
Stock turnover period	$\frac{119.0 \times 365}{1,478.6} = 29 \text{ days}$	$\frac{109.0 \times 365}{1,304.0} = 31 \text{ days}$
Creditors turnover period	$\frac{236.2 \times 365}{1,478.6} = 58 \text{ days}$	$\frac{210.8 \times 365}{1,304.0} = 59 \text{ days}$

4    $\boxed{£7,104}$

Working

Using the discounting formula, $X = S \times \dfrac{1}{(1 + r)^n}$

where $S = £16,000$

$n = 12$

$r = 0.07$

$X = PV$

$PV = £16,000 \times \dfrac{1}{1.07^{12}} = £7,104$

5

Year	Cash flow £	Discount factor 10%	Present value £
0		1.000	(18,000)
1	6,000	$\dfrac{1}{1.10} = 0.909$	5,454
2	8,000	$\dfrac{1}{1.10^2} = 0.826$	6,608
3	5,000	$\dfrac{1}{1.10^3} = 0.751$	3,755
4	1,000	$\dfrac{1}{1.10^4} = 0.683$	683
Net present value			(1,500)

The NPV is negative. We can therefore draw the following conclusions.

(a)   It is cheaper to invest elsewhere at 10% than to invest in the project.

(b)   The project would earn a return of less than 10%.

(c)   The project is not viable (since the PV of the costs is greater than the PV of the benefits).

1   Liquid assets can be converted quickly into cash. Liquidity is an organisation's ability to convert its assets into cash to meet all the demands for payments when they fall due.

2   Generally, ratios are used for making comparisons. The same ratio can be compared year on year to see if progress is being made and different ratios can be compared to give clues to problem solutions.

3   £10

4   Yes, in theory. Any NPV greater than zero means that wealth is being increased. However, a more robust NPV might be required to allow for the uncertainty of future cash flows.

5   The factors having significant impact on shareholder value. Management attention is focused upon them.

6   Profit minus a charge for the use of capital.

7   Return on capital employed (ROCE) is the amount of profit as a percentage of capital employed (net assets).

8   (a)   If a company's gearing is too high (say over 50%), it might become difficult to raise more loans.

    (b)   Loan capital is cheaper, because the interest cost diminishes in real terms if secured on company assets and it attracts tax benefits.

    (c)   Interest must be paid, whereas the directors of a company can decide not to pay a dividend.

    (d)   High gearing might be considered risky for lenders in that the more loan capital a business has, the larger the interest payments.

9   The weighted average cost of capital (WACC) is the average of the cost of equity and the cost of debt.

10 Risk free; risk.

11 Economic profit is created when the return on a company's capital employed exceeds the cost of that capital.

12 • Financial
    • Marketing
    • Organisational

13 Doyle suggests that increasing customer satisfaction, loyalty and retention by deploying such techniques as loyalty programmes and measures to increase satisfaction will reduce the risk. Building good channel relationships also helps, by building an element of loyalty based on good service and by using information on demand patterns to smooth fluctuations in demand.

14 The ability to carry added interest payments
    The policy of the firm towards debt
    The return expected on investments
    The debt/equity ratio of competitors

15 Lower

Aaker, D. & McLoughlin, D. (2007) <u>Strategic Market Management</u>, John Wiley, Chichester.

Doyle, P. (2008) Value-Based Marketing: <u>Marketing Strategies for Corporate Growth and Shareholder Value</u>, (2nd Edition) John Wiley & Sons, Chichester.

Doyle, P. (2003), <u>Strategy as Marketing in Images of Marketing</u>, eds Cummings S and Wilson D, Blackwell Publishing Limited, London.

References

Chapter 10

Corporate and reputational risk

Topic list

Introduction

Some businesses are inherently riskier than others: the degree of risk can be measured by the degree of predictability that attaches to its expected cash flows. A low risk business will have steady income from period to period, without any unexpected highs and lows. A high-risk business will have returns that vary wildly and unexpectedly from period to period, though its total long-term return may be as great or greater than the low risk operation. Generally, investors are risk averse and, as a result, they demand higher returns from high-risk businesses than from low risk ones. The high-risk business must therefore use a higher cost of capital in its shareholder value analysis than the low risk business.

Syllabus-linked learning objectives

By the end of the chapter you will be able to:

Learning objectives	Syllabus link
1 Utilising a range of risk analysis tools, assess the strategic risks facing an organisation in the selection of strategic alternatives leading to strategic choice	3.3.1
2 Assess the potential for organisational constraints to limit an organisation's success in using any given strategic choice	3.3.2
3 Assess the risk to an organisation of hostile or declining markets and recommend mitigation strategies	3.3.3
4 Recommend a range of mitigation strategies designed to reduce risks, so as to enhance an organisation's selection of a strategic option	3.3.4
5 Critically analyse the impact of the priority decisions on an organisation	3.4.1

1 Strategic risks

"The conventional wisdom that the strategist should seek out growth areas often overlooks a substantial set of associated risks." Aaker & McLoughlin (2007 p.89)

Risks of high growth markets (Aaker & McLoughlin, 2007)

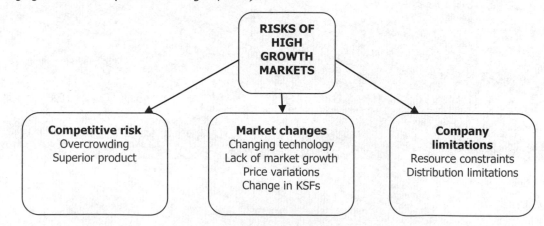

Risk must be managed and to do this, it must be quantified and its implications considered.

Strategic uncertainties focus on specific unknown factors that will impact a strategic decision. For example, for a holiday firm thinking of extending its market from budget to luxury accommodation and tours to more unusual destinations, a key strategic uncertainty might be "What is the likely future demand for luxury travel to the Yemen?"

The impact of strategic uncertainties was discussed in section 3 of Chapter 1 in the context of the external environment.

1.1 Types of risk

KEY CONCEPT

concept

Risk relates to uncertainty about the future. Any forward looking strategy is risky, because events might not turn out as anticipated.

(a)   **Physical risk**, such as fire, earthquakes, computer failure.

(b)   **Economic risk**. The strategy might be based on assumptions as to the economy which might turn out to be wrong.

(c)   **Financial risk** relates to the type of financial arrangement in the decision, and the quality of the cash flows. The potential for erosion of shareholder value (see below)

(d)   **Business risk**. These risks relate to commercial and industry factors. In other words, there is the possibility that the strategy will fail because of new technology, competitors, customer reaction, operational failures. Diverting from the core business carries with it another type of business risk, ie that the business does not have the resources or expertise to carry out the strategy.

(e)   **Political or country risk** includes nationalisation, sanctions, civil war and political instability, if these have an impact on the business.

(f)   **Exchange risk**. Changes in exchange rates affect the value of a transaction in a foreign currency.

(g)   **Information risk**. The data may not be reliable.

1.2 Risk appraisal in strategy evaluation

Some strategies will be more risky than others. One of the problems arising when evaluating alternative strategies is the reliability of the data used. Since the figures are compiled on estimates of the future, there must be considerable uncertainty about the final accuracy of the figures. Business planners frequently use the following.

*   **Operational research** techniques to measure the degree of uncertainty involved
*   **Probability theory** to express the likelihood of a forecast result occurring

1.2.1 Risk and evaluating strategies

(a)   If an individual strategy involves an **unacceptable amount of risk** it should be eliminated from further consideration in the planning process.

(b)   However, the risk of an **individual strategy** should also be considered in the context of the **overall 'portfolio' of investment strategies** and products adopted by the company.

Risk can be quantified in statistical terms. In decision trees, a variety of possible outcomes are developed. Each is given an **expected value (EV),** based on probabilities. The EVs at each decision point are then aggregated to produce an EV for the decision as a whole. However, the EVs do not deal in the relative riskiness of each project.

(a) Project A might offer **profits** of £1,000,000 and **losses** of £500,000. If the probability of each is 50:50, the EV is (£1,000,000 × 50%) – (£500,000 × 50%) = £250,000.

(b) Project B offers a 75% probability of a £300,000 profit and a 25% probability of a loss of £100,000. The EV is thus £200,000 ie (£300,000 × 0.75%) – (£100,000 × 25%)

Project A would be favoured, on a basis of EV **alone**, which is £250,000. There is a much higher prospect of **large** profits or **large** losses compared to project B. However, A is much more **risky** as the spread of outcomes is diverse.

Sensitivity analysis involves asking 'what if?' questions. By changing the value of different variables in the model, a number of different **scenarios** for the future will be produced. Price rises can be altered to 10% from 5%, demand for a product can be reduced from 100,000 to 80,000, the introduction of new processing equipment can be deferred by six months, on the revised assumption that there will be delays, and so on. Sensitivity analysis can be formalised by identifying **key variables** in the model and then changing the value of each, perhaps in progressive steps. For example, prices might be increased in steps by 5%, 7½%, 10%, 12½% and 15% and the effect on demand, profits and cash flows under each of these assumptions can be tested.

Sensitivity analysis would show which were the **key variables**.

1.2.2 Example

A company is producing a new product and a key variable is time to market. If it launches on time, it will sell 1,000 units at £10 each. If it is a month late, demand will fall by 50%. Each unit costs £5 to make. The company has learned that a material supplier has gone out of business. It can get the material for the same price, at the expense of being a month late, or it can pay £1 per unit more for the material and keep to the original deadline.

	Original plan £	Month delay £	Pay more for material £
Revenue	10,000	5,000	10,000
Cost	5,000	2,500	6,000
Profit	5,000	2,000	4,000

In this example we can see that profits are more sensitive to **demand** than to costs, so the firm would pay more for the new material.

A firm has a choice.

- Apply the most stringent controls to the most critical variables
- Alter the plans so that the most critical variables are no longer as critical
- When different planning options are available, choose a lower-risk plan

2 Organisational constraints

"Consideration of organisational components [structure, systems, people and culture] can help a business identify actual and potential implementation problems, as well as determine how its organisation would adapt to a new strategy." Aaker & McLoughlin (2007) p.322

 EXAM TIP

application

Chapter 4 is specifically devoted to organiasational capability. Note that the syllabus lists the following organisational constraints:

- **Regulation** – legal influences on a business should be familiar to you from your studies of PEST factors

- **Structure and competencies** – see Chapter 3 on the internal marketing environment, which includes organisational performance.

- **Capital and investment capability** – see Chapter 9 on financial assessment of marketing opportunities

- **Stakeholder/shareholder** engagement and involvement – see Chapter 5 for a discussion of stakeholder analysis and relationships
- **Competitor activity** – Chapter 1 discusses the competitive environment

3 Hostile and declining markets

"A declining market involves a fall in demand, often caused by an external event such as the creation of a competing technology, a change in customer needs or tastes, or a shift in government policy." Aaker & McLoughlin (2007) p.296

Markets decline because of **environmental factors**. Some can be revitalised. In others, a firm has to choose whether it wants to stay in the market or withdraw.

Many of the portfolio models assume that markets are growing. However, this is certainly not the case in many markets and firms within them still have to survive.

3.1 Declining markets

3.1.1 Why do markets decline?

- Obsolete technology
- Change in customer needs, leading to fall in demand
- Alternative satisfactions

Strategic alternatives include:

- Revitalising the market
- Becoming a profitable survivor
- Milk, harvest and withdraw

3.1.2 Revitalising the market

- Identify new market segments or submarkets
- Introduce new products
- Introduce new applications of existing products
- Change the market

Aaker & McLoughlin (2007) offer the following summary of routes to revitalising a stagnant market:

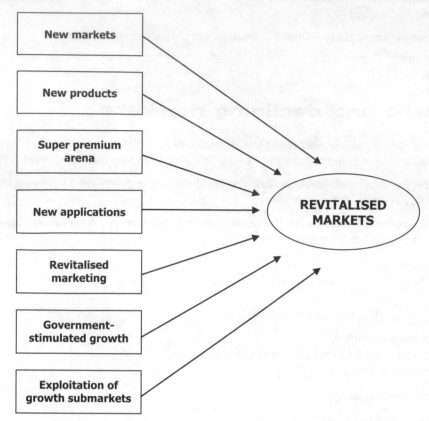

 MARKETING AT WORK

application

When Tim Richards decided to leave his job as a high-flying executive at Warner Brothers in 1998 to create a UK cinema business, there were those who had their doubts.

After all, cinema attendance at that time was stagnating and, after a period of aggressive expansion, even Warner Brothers had ceased the development of new circuits. This, plus the rise and proliferation of new forms of home entertainment such as video games and DVDs, appeared almost to sound the death knell for the industry.

Yet eight years on, Vue Entertainment has grown from strength to strength. From a garage-based start-up operating one cinema, Vue is now the third biggest cinema chain in the UK, with 55 multiplex theatres across the country and in Ireland. There are plans to build another 20 before the end of 2008.

That Vue is a success comes as no surprise to Mr Richards . . .

'No matter how big TVs get. No matter how sophisticated surround sound systems get, people are always going to want to get out and see a movie . . .

'We are inherently social beings who enjoy a laugh collectively. We enjoy being scared and frightened together. There will always be a demand for that. You just have to give spectators a really good reason to go back to the theatres.'

In particular, Mr Richards wanted to break away from the 'nightclub feel' of UK cinemas in the 1990s, which he felt alienated a very large segment of the cinema going audience.

'We wanted to make cinemas more accessible and accommodating to a broader group of people, especially greying baby boomers,' he says. *'These are the people with higher disposable income and more leisure time, yet their needs are not being catered to . . .*

'We invested fairly heavily to give the cinemas a new and more upmarket look,' he says. *'It's no longer the horrible old flea pit or the loud flashing discotheque that made families and older people stop going to the cinemas so many years ago'*

Kwan Yuk Pan, *Financial Times,* 14 November 2006

The latest news:

"Vue is to upgrade 200 cinema screens to the 3D format, in a multi-million pound investment with Real D." 23ʳᵈ Feb 2009

"Vue Entertainment is to set up a ten-screen cinema in the £300m extension of the Buchanan Galleries shopping mall in Glasgow." 10ᵗʰ Nov 2008

"Vue Entertainment is to invest £4m in a new multiplex cinema in Thanet, Kent, and £2.5m at a new site in Stirling." 29ᵗʰ Oct 2007

www.ukbusinesspark.co.uk – accessed 25 June 2009

3.1.3 Becoming a profitable survivor

(a)   Make a visible commitment to the market, as a signal to other competitors.

(b)   Encourage competitors to leave by aggressive competition or by making it easier for them to quit.

(c)   Purchase the competitor's capacity, close it down and carry on in a smaller niche.

3.1.4 Milk, harvest and withdraw

This strategy involves reducing investment and operating resources in order to make a graceful and orderly exit, the underlying assumption being that funds can be better employed elsewhere.

Profits may still be made. However employees and customers may fear the lack of commitment and go elsewhere. A milking or harvesting strategy can be reversed, as the firm still has a market presence.

Conditions favouring a **milking strategy** (Aaker & McLoughlin, 2007):

- The decline rate is pronounced and 'set in', but some demand still exists to ensure that the decline rate is not too steep

- The price level is stable and still profitable

- There is enough customer loyalty to generate some profits during the 'milking' mode

- The business is not central to the current strategic direction

- There are resources to ensure that the milking strategy can be successfully managed

By contrast, the following conditions would suggest that an exit decision would be the most appropriate:

- The decline is rapid and accelerating
- Price pressures are extreme (through competition and lack of brand loyalty)
- Business position is weak against competitors
- Strategic direction has changed, and the role of the business is superfluous
- Exit barriers can be overcome

3.2 Hostile environments

Aaker and McLoughlin (2007) write on the conditions for hostile markets to exist. These include overcapacity, low margins, intense competition and management in turmoil. They continue to remark that most industries are hostile or likely to become so.

 KEY CONCEPT

concept

Hostility arises from a decline in demand and/or competitive expansion.

One approach is to describe a six-phase cycle for hostile markets.

Phase 1: **Margin pressure.** Overcapacity leads to predatory pricing, benefiting large customers

Phase 2: **Share shift.** Each year, up to 5% of market share will shift under price pressure, and is difficult to regain

Phase 3: **Product proliferation.** Firms create excess value by adding new lines

Phase 4: **Self-defeating cost reduction.** Firms cut costs but, in doing so, weaken themselves

Phase 5: **Shakeout.** Closures, mergers

Phase 6: **Rescue.** Some markets recover with fewer companies competing

3.2.1 Winning in hostile markets

- Focus on **large customers**, to benefit from economies of scale
- **Differentiate on intangible factors** such as reliability and relationships
- Offer a broad **array of products** at a variety of prices
- Turn price into a commodity by **removing price from the customer's buying criteria**
- **Control cost** structures

3.3 Wear-out and renewal

 KEY CONCEPT

concept

Strategic wear-out occurs when firms continue with old strategies that are no longer viable.

Strategic and tactical **wear-out** is the problem that any organisation will face if it retains its current strategies and tactics without any review or consideration of changed circumstances.

The following factors give rise to wear-out.

(a) Market changes

    (i) Customer requirements
    (ii) Distribution requirements

(b) Competitor innovations

(c) Internal factors

    (i) Poor cost control
    (ii) Lack of consistent investment
    (iii) Ill-advised tinkering with successful strategies

Some organisations still continue to pursue marketing programmes long after their effectiveness has diminished. Many reasons can be put forward to explain this.

(a) **Fear of change.** Most people are afraid of change, preferring to stay in their own comfort zone.

(b) **Change is becoming harder to forecast.** Many organisations opt to stay with what is familiar.

(c) **'If it ain't broke, don't fix it!'** Market leaders, having developed a successful strategy, are understandably reluctant to change it.

(d) **Change too late.** The need for change often only becomes apparent when the gap between what a company is doing and what it should be doing increases to a point at which performance suffers in an obvious way.

(e) **Failure to learn**. Companies fail because managers' **theory of the business** no longer works. A theory of the business contains the assumptions (about markets, technology etc) that shape any organisation's behaviour.

(f) **The wrong customers**. Keeping too close to existing customers, rather than thinking about future customers, can also result in strategic wearout: 'an industry's leaders are rarely in the forefront of commercialising new technologies that do not initially meet the functional demands of mainstream customers'.

(g) **New technologies** are developed and take industry leaders unawares.

(h) **Failure to look**. Some organisations do not have environmental monitoring and strategic review procedures embedded within their marketing planning systems.

Four interlinked avenues of action are required to overcome the danger of strategic wear-out.

(a) **Regular and detailed reviews** of each of the significant elements of the external environment

(b) **Identification** of the ways these elements are changing

(c) **Evaluation** of the implications of these changes on the organisation

(d) **Internal audit** to establish the appropriateness of actions both currently and for the future

In order to avoid strategic wear-out a multi-functional perspective is required. A combination of strategic, organisational and cultural change is required. Companies are likely to be unsuccessful in maintaining change unless five demanding criteria are met.

* **Coherence** of direction, actions and timing
* **Environmental** assessment of competitors, customers and regulatory climate
* **Leading** change by creating the correct climate
* **Linking** strategic with operational change (communication and reward systems)
* Treating **people as assets** and investments rather than costs

 EXAM TIP application

A past examination question at this level was based on a manufacturing company suffering from strategic wear-out. The requirement was to say how the firm should reassess its capabilities and use them to exploit a new opportunity. The value chain is the obvious model to use when answering this question.

This illustrates an important point about examinations at this level: it is easy to think of each exam as a separate and distinct entity, but this is not the case. You must be prepared to treat the entire level as an integrated whole and, as in this example, be prepared to apply knowledge you have gained from studying for a particular paper to the other exams if appropriate.

4 Impact analysis

Aaker & McLoughlin (2007) define impact analysis in terms of assessing the relative importance of strategic uncertainties.

In the context of the syllabus, impact analysis involves an assessment of the impact of these uncertainties (and the decisions made following an assessment of them) upon the organisation.

 EXAM TIP application

Aaker gives the example of a beer firm thinking about the future prospects of the microbrewery market. It has a proposed entry into the microbrewery market, but it already has an imported beer positioned in the same area.

An impact analysis based upon the syllabus criteria could look like this:

(a) **Strategic vision and direction** – is a microbrewery compatible with the existing position?

(b) **Value proposition** – the company might adopt a position along the lines of "quality beers for discerning customers"

(c) **Key success factors** – quality, availability, innovation

(d) **Assets and competencies** – can they run the new business?

(e) **Positioning, segmentation and targeting** – this is a niche market, requiring specialist expertise to deliver to demanding and expert customers

(f) **Distribution** – dependent upon pubs and retailers; packaging considerations (bottles, cans etc)

(g) **Branding** – should the company use its existing brand, or design a new one?

(h) **Investment** – resources may be overstretched. What is the payback?

(i) **Innovation and manufacturing** – developing the capability and capacity to deliver the new product

(j) **Increased opportunities and threats** – this is a new market, with other players already established; does the company have the resources to support market growth?

Learning objectives	Covered
1 Utilising a range of risk analysis tools, assess the strategic risks facing an organisation in the selection of strategic alternatives leading to strategic choice	☑ Types of risk (1.1) ☑ Risk appraisal in strategy evaluation (1.2)
2 Assess the potential for organisational constraints to limit an organisation's success in using any given strategic choice	☑ Regulation (2) ☑ Structure and competencies (2) ☑ Capital investment capability (2) ☑ Stakeholder engagement (2) ☑ Competitor activity (2) ☑ See chapter 4 for more comprehensive coverage
3 Assess the risk to an organisation of hostile or declining markets and recommend mitigation strategies	☑ Declining markets (3.1) ☑ Hostile environments (3.2) ☑ Wear out and renewal (3.3)
4 Recommend a range of mitigation strategies designed to reduce risks, so as to enhance an organisation's selection of a strategic option	☑ See Chapter 1 on scenario planning and forecasting techniques in the overall context of understanding the external environment
5 Critically analyse the impact of the priority decisions on an organisation	☑ Impact analysis (4)

1   What are the three risks in high growth markets as identified by Aaker and McLoughlin?

2   What is 'business risk'?

3   What are the potential organisational constraints identified by the syllabus?

4   What is the application of probability theory to risk appraisal?

5   Why do markets decline?

6   How does a company become a profitable survivor?

7   How does a company win in a hostile market?

8   Why would a company 'milk' a market, rather than exit?

1   Competitive risk, market changes and company limitations

2   Business risk relates to commercial and industry factors: the possibility that the strategy will fail because of new technology, competitors, customer reaction or operational failures. Diverting from the core business carries with it another type of business risk, ie that the business does not have the resources or expertise to carry out the strategy.

3   Regulation
     Structure and competencies.
     Capital and investment capability
     Stakeholder/shareholder engagement and involvement
     Competitor activity

4   Probability theory can be used to assess the likelihood of a forecast event occurring, and this will help to assess the level of risk

5   • Obsolete technology
     • Change in customer needs, leading to fall in demand
     • Alternative satisfactions

6   (a)   Make a visible commitment to the market, as a signal to other competitors.
     (b)   Encourage competitors to leave by aggressive competition or by making it easier for them to quit.
     (c)   Purchase the competitor's capacity, close it down and carry on in a smaller niche.

7   • Focus on **large customers**, to benefit from economies of scale
     • **Differentiate on intangible factors** such as reliability and relationships
     • Offer a broad **array of products** at a variety of prices
     • Turn price into a commodity by **removing price from the customer's buying criteria**
     • **Control cost** structures

8   • The decline rate is pronounced and 'set in', but some demand still exists to ensure that the decline rate is not too steep

     • The price level is stable and still profitable

     • There is enough customer loyalty to generate some profits during the 'milking' mode

     • The business is not central to the current strategic direction

     • There are resources to ensure that the milking strategy can be successfully managed

     When less favourable conditions exist (eg prices are under pressure, or the decline rate is steep, or there has been a change in strategic direction) then an exit strategy may be preferred

Aaker, D. & McLoughlin, D. (2007) Strategic Market Management, John Wiley, Chichester.

Key concepts

Assets, 36, 82

Benchmarking, 63
Brand, 157
Brand equity, 160
Brand extension, 163
Brand identity, 161
Brand image, 161
Business strategy, 129

Competences, 48
Competitive advantage, 9
Corporate appraisal, 118
Corporate strategy, 99, 129
Customer profitability analysis, 39

Direct distribution, 8
Discounted cash flow (DCF), 209
Discounting, 207

Early developed country (EDC), 183
Economy of scale, 64
Emergent strategies, 105
Extrapolation, 26

Forecasting, 26
Former Eastern Bloc country (EBC), 183
Fully developed country (FDC), 183
Functional and operational strategy, 130

Global strategy, 175

Hostility, 231

Indirect distribution, 8
Innovation, 146
Innovation audit, 54
Intended strategies, 105

Key (strategic) account, 38
Knowledge, 75
Knowledge assets, 75
Knowledge management, 75

Leadership, 104
Lesser Developed Country (LDC), 183

Market, 3, 61
Market orientation, 61
Market sensing, 25
Market share, 65
Marketing asset, 83
Market-led firm, 61
Mission, 90
Multinational strategy, 175

Net present value (NPV) method, 210

Operational strategies, 130
Organisation culture, 78

Payback, 206
Policy, 99
Political risk, 178
Portfolio, 49
Portfolio analysis, 49
Portfolio planning, 49
Positioning, 12
present value, 208
Product life cycle, 56
Projection, 26
Protectionism, 181

Relationship marketing, 153
Relative market share, 65
Repositioning, 15
Resource audit, 48, 69
Risk, 227

Scenario, 23
Semi-developed country (SDC), 183
Societal marketing concept, 95
strategic alliance, 140
Strategic analysis, 90
Strategic management, 99
Strategic uncertainties, 227
Strategic wear-out, 232
Strategy, 99
Synergistic planning, 99
Synergy, 144

Tactics, 99
Target market, 10

Value activities, 16
Value proposition, 34
Vision, 90

Index

Review form & Free prize draw

All original review forms from the entire BPP range, completed with genuine comments, will be entered into one of two draws on 31 January 2010 and 31 July 2010. The names on the first four forms picked out on each occasion will be sent a cheque for £50.

Name: _____   **Address:** _____

_____

_____

1. How have you used this Text?
(Tick one box only)

☐ Self study (book only)

☐ On a course: college_____

☐ Other _____

3. Why did you decide to purchase this Text?
(Tick one box only)

☐ Have used companion Assessment workbook

☐ Have used BPP Texts in the past

☐ Recommendation by friend/colleague

☐ Recommendation by a lecturer at college

☐ Saw advertising in journals

☐ Saw website

☐ Other _____

2. During the past six months do you recall seeing/receiving any of the following?
(Tick as many boxes as are relevant)

☐ Our advertisement in *The Marketer*

☐ Our brochure with a letter through the post

☐ Saw website

4. Which (if any) aspects of our advertising do you find useful?
(Tick as many boxes as are relevant)

☐ Prices and publication dates of new editions

☐ Information on product content

☐ Facility to order books off-the-page

☐ None of the above

5. Have you used the companion Assessment Workbook?   Yes ☐   No ☐

6. Have you used the companion Passcards?   Yes ☐   No ☐

7. Your ratings, comments and suggestions would be appreciated on the following areas.

	Very useful	Useful	Not useful
Introductory section (How to use this text, study checklist, etc)	☐	☐	☐
Introduction	☐	☐	☐
Syllabus linked learning objectives	☐	☐	☐
Activities and Marketing at Work examples	☐	☐	☐
Learning objective reviews	☐	☐	☐
Magic Formula references	☐	☐	☐
Content of suggested answers	☐	☐	☐
Index	☐	☐	☐
Structure and presentation	☐	☐	☐

	Excellent	Good	Adequate	Poor
Overall opinion of this Text	☐	☐	☐	☐

8. Do you intend to continue using BPP CIM Range Products?   ☐ Yes   ☐ No

9. Have you visited bpp.com/lm/cim?   ☐ Yes   ☐ No

10. If you have visited bpp.com/lm/cim, please give a score out of 10 for its overall usefulness   /10

Please note any further comments and suggestions/errors on the reverse of this page.

Please return to: Dr Kellie Vincent, BPP Learning Media, FREEPOST, London, W12 8BR.

If you have any additional questions, feel free to email cimrange@bpp.com

Please note any further comments and suggestions/errors below.

Free prize draw rules

1 Closing date for 31 January 2010 draw is 31 December 2009. Closing date for 31 July 2010 draw is 30 June 2010.

2 Restricted to entries with UK and Eire addresses only. BPP employees, their families and business associates are excluded.

3 No purchase necessary. Entry forms are available upon request from BPP Learning Media. No more than one entry per title, per person. Draw restricted to persons aged 16 and over.

4 Winners will be notified by post and receive their cheques not later than 6 weeks after the relevant draw date. List of winners will be supplied on request.

5 The decision of the promoter in all matters is final and binding. No correspondence will be entered into.